THE EUROPEAN UNION
IN THE WAKE
OF EASTERN ENLARGEMENT

MANCHESTER
1824

Manchester University Press

EUROPE IN CHANGE

SERIES EDITORS: *Thomas Christiansen and Emil Kirchner*

Amy Verdun
& Osvaldo Croci
EDITORS

THE EUROPEAN UNION IN THE WAKE OF EASTERN ENLARGEMENT

Institutional and policy-making challenges

MANCHESTER UNIVERSITY PRESS
Manchester and New York

distributed exclusively in the USA by Palgrave

Copyright © Manchester University Press 2005

While copyright in the volume as a whole is vested in Manchester University Press, copyright in individual chapters belongs to their respective authors, and no chapter may be reproduced wholly or in part without the express permission in writing of both author and publisher.

Published by Manchester University Press
Oxford Road, Manchester M13 9NR, UK
and Room 400, 175 Fifth Avenue, New York, NY 10010, USA
www.manchesteruniversitypress.co.uk

Distributed exclusively in the USA by
Palgrave, 175 Fifth Avenue, New York,
NY 10010, USA

Distributed exclusively in Canada by
UBC Press, University of British Columbia, 2029 West Mall,
Vancouver, BC, Canada V6T 1Z2

British Library Cataloguing-in-Publication Data
A catalogue record for this book is available from the British Library

Library of Congress Cataloging-in-Publication Data applied for

ISBN 0 7190 6512 7 *hardback*
EAN 978 0 7190 6512 5

ISBN   07190 6513 5 *paperback*
EAN   978 0 7190 65125

First published in paperback 2007

14 13 12 11 10 09 08 07   10 9 8 7 6 5 4 3 2

Typeset in Minion
by Servis Filmsetting Limited, Manchester
Printed in Great Britain
by CPI, Bath

Contents

Figures and tables

Figures

Tables

CONTRIBUTORS

Osvaldo Croci is Associate Professor in the Department of Political Science at Memorial University of Newfoundland, NF

Ben Crum is Assistant Professor in the Political Science Department at the Vrije Universiteit, Amsterdam

Wyn Grant is Professor in the Department of Politics and International Studies at the University of Warwick, UK

Elspeth Guild is Professor of European Immigration Law at the University of Nijmegen, The Netherlands

Beate Kohler-Koch is Professor of Political Science at the University of Mannheim, Germany

Finn Laursen is Professor in the Department of Political Science and Public Management at the University of Southern Denmark, Odense

Sandra Lavenex is Assistant Professor in the Department of Political Science at the University of Bern, Switzerland

Andreas Maurer is a Researcher at the German Institute for International and Security Affairs, Berlin

Melissa Padfield is a Graduate Student at the University of Victoria, BC

Elfriede Regelsberger is Professor and Assistant Director of the Institute for European Politics, Berlin

Jette Steen Knudsen is Assistant Professor in the Department of International Economics and Management at the Copenhagen Business School, Denmark

Amy Verdun holds a Jean Monnet Chair in European Integration Studies and is Associate Professor and Director of the European Studies Program and the University of Victoria, BC

Helen Wallace is Professor at the European University Institute and Director of the Robert Schuman Centre for Advanced Studies

Wolfgang Wessels is Professor at the University of Cologne, Germany and at the College of Europe, Bruges and the Director of TEPSA

Acknowledgements

The enlargement process will have a major impact on the European Union (EU). This effect had already been anticipated back in 1989 when the Berlin Wall came down. However, the process of preparation for the inclusion of many Central and Eastern European Countries (CEECs), and a few Mediterranean ones, took long to prepare. It did not only include the preparation of the EU and the CEECs to one another, but it also required that the institutional structure and the policies of the EU be re-conceptualised and reformed. This book aims at offering insights into how the enlargement process did exactly that: change the process of integration, the way we conceptualise it, its policies and institutional structure.

Many of the chapters of this book were first presented at the European Community Studies Association – Canada (ECSA-C) biennial conference 'European Odyssey: The European Union in the New Millennium'. It was held in Quebec City from 30 July through 1 August 2000. The conference and this publication were generously supported by ECSA-C, the European Commission, a conference grant of the Social Sciences and Humanities Research Council of Canada (SSHRC) and the Department of Foreign Affairs and International Trade (DFAIT), the University of Victoria, and Carleton University. To produce a high quality book that would address the most salient issues and that would be attractive to researchers and graduate students alike meant that we needed to commission a few additional chapters. The final product includes what we think are high quality chapters covering a breadth of topics.

Besides institutional and financial support, this book would not have been possible without the support of many individuals. We wish to thank Lloy Wylie, Melissa Padfield and Stefanie Fishel for their editorial assistance at different stages of this book. (Thanks also to two research SSHRC grants 410-2002-0522 and 410-99-0081 held by Amy Verdun, which provided the funds for this the graduate student assistance.) Our gratitude extends also to Thomas Christiansen, Emil Kirchner and Tony Mason for their continuous support of this project. Though we cannot list here all those who have commented on parts of the book, we do wish to acknowledge Michelle Cini's insightful suggestions on the entire manuscript at a late stage.

Amy Verdun, Victoria
Osvaldo Croci, St John's

Abbreviations

AFSJ	Area of Freedom, Security and Justice
CAP	Common Agricultural Policy
CDU/CSU	Christian Democrats (Germany)
CDU/CSU-FDP	Christian Democrats and Liberal coalition government
CEECs	Central and Eastern European countries
[C]ESDP	(Common) European Security and Defence Policy
CFSP	Common Foreign and Security Policy
COPA	Comité des Organisations Profesionnelles Agricoles
Coreper	Committee of Permanent Representatives
DCT	Draft Treaty Establishing a Constitution for Europe
DG	Directorate General
DPG	Deutsche Postgewerkschaft
EC	European Community
ECB	European Central Bank
ECJ	European Court of Justice
ECSC	European Coal and Steel Community
EDC	European Defence Community
EEA	European Economic Area; European Express Association
EEC	European Economic Community
EFTA	European Free Trade Association
EMU	Economic and Monetary Union
EP	European Parliament
EPC	European political cooperation
ESDP	European Security and Defence Policy
FAO	Food and Agriculture Organisation
GATT	General Agreement on Tariffs and Trade
GDV	Association for German Insurers
HLWG	High Level Working Group on Asylum and Migration
IACS	integrated administration and control system
IFCN	International Farm Comparison Network
IGC	intergovernmental conference
JHA	Justice and Home Affairs
MEP	Member of the European Parliament
NATO	North Atlantic Treaty Organisation
NGO	non-governmental organisation
OECD	Organisation for Economic Coordination and Development
OSCE	Organisation for Security and Cooperation in Europe

PJCCM	police and judicial cooperation in criminal matters
PPEWU	Policy Planning and Early Warning Unit
PSC	Political and Security Committee
PSE	producer support equivalent
QMV	qualified majority voting
SEA	Single European Act
SIS	Schengen Information System
SPD	Social Democratic Party (Germany)
TEU	Treaty on European Union
TRIPS	trade-related aspects of intellectual property rights
UN	United Nations
WEU	Western European Union
WTO	World Trade Organisation

Amy Verdun and Osvaldo Croci

Introduction

The May 2004 enlargement of the European Union (EU) to include a number of formerly Eastern European states is perceived as a milestone in the history of European integration. Not surprisingly, it has been dubbed the 'Eastern enlargement' even if the new members are not exclusively from Eastern Europe but include also two small countries in the Mediterranean. Following this fifth enlargement, the number of EU Member States will increase from fifteen to twenty-five. Though attention has been focused mostly on negotiations and the challenge of policy adjustment for the accession countries, preparations for enlargement within what was then the European Community (EC) began almost as soon as the Berlin Wall came down in 1989.[1] The end of the Communist regimes in Central and Eastern European countries (CEECs) opened a window of opportunity for these countries to re-join those in the liberal-democratic Western part of the continent as well as apply for membership in Western organisations including the EC. Hence, they moved quickly to adopting market principles and installing democratically elected governments.

The EC and its member governments immediately sensed that the political and economic changes taking place in the East would eventually lead to the enlargement of the Community and that such an enlargement would have implications for both EC institutions and policy-making (Avery and Cameron 1998, Friis and Murphy 2000, Preston 1997). Indeed, the prospect of enlargement was used by the Commission to provide a sense of urgency for the launching of discussion on a number of institutional and policy reforms, which some Member States might have been more reluctant to undertake otherwise.

It has often been said that the Maastricht Treaty, which contained far-reaching provisions such as those for an Economic and Monetary Union (EMU), was signed because Germany needed to provide an unmistakable sign of its unswerving support for political integration in Europe to assuage any misgivings its European partners might have about its reunification.[2] German reunification, however, represented also the first accession of a former Communist country into the EC, albeit as part of the Federal Republic of Germany. EU Member States realised of course that the enlargement process would take time, and go through various steps. They first concluded the so-called 'Europe Agreements', which enabled easier trade among the countries of East and West. At the Copenhagen Summit in 1993, the Heads of State and Government of the then twelve Member States set the terms for the enlargement process, which eventually took off with more speed in 1998.

The EU needed time to get its own house in order. First of all it had to begin reflecting on its peculiar institutional structure, which made it more than an international organisation but less than a federal state (Wallace 1983). The question to tackle was: for how much longer could the EU muddle through without making a firm commitment to a definite institutional end goal (or *finalité*)? Institutions and policies had been created in a path dependent fashion. It was a patchwork quilt, which was changed every time new members entered, or whenever the EU needed to deal with new areas of policy-making. The mode of governance had also changed. The EU had increasingly become a professional organisation, which often availed itself of outside experts. Interest groups of all sorts played an important role (Greenwood and Ronit 1994). So did business associations and other lobbyists (Mazey and Richardson 1993, Cowles 2003). The EU was described as being a system of multi-level (Hooghe and Marks 2001) or network governance (Eising and Kohler-Koch 1999). The laws and regulations it produced had also become cumbersome and complicated. The so-called *acquis communautaire* had grown to tens of thousands of pages of legislation that applied to all members and that accession states had to adopt in its entirety before entry. This legislative corpus applied also to international trade, which implied that it had an effect even beyond the borders of the EU.

In the period between the signing of the Single European Act (1987) and the start of the Convention (2003), new elements were added to the ever more complex process of international governance. There were attempts to reach new international trade agreements within the World Trade Organisation (WTO), efforts to create worldwide environmental standards (e.g. the Kyoto agreements) as well as the creation of an International Criminal Court. Nonetheless, conflicts did not stop with the end of the Cold War and many refugees and asylum seekers, both political and economic, have continued to roam the globe. In light of these developments, the EU identified a number of policies in need of reform. Most important among these, were the Common Agricultural Policy (CAP) and asylum and immigration policies. Policy changes, however, are difficult to carry out because they are usually firmly embedded in the practices and experiences of Member States and because for the process to be perceived as legitimate the rationale must be clear to, and accepted by, most politicians and citizens. Hence, another effort that the EU pursued relentlessly throughout the 1990s, even if with different degrees of success, was to make its rules more transparent and bring its governing system closer to citizens (see Lindenberg 2001).

The 'Eastern' enlargement provided an opportunity to reflect on the limits of incremental institutional and ad hoc policy changes made whenever new members joined or as a result of compromises and side-payments during negotiations for new treaties. An example of the limits of incremental change is the (informal) rule concerning the number of commissioners: two commissioners for the large countries and one for all the rest. Besides the fact that such a rule seems in contradiction with the claim that commissioners are neutral and will act in the interest of the EU rather than that of their country of origin, it seems evident that one cannot continue to abide by this rule as EU Member States continue to increase.

This book examines some of the institutional and policy challenges with which the EU has struggled in conjunction with its fifth enlargement. The main question it addresses is: how does the EU need to change in light of the 'Eastern' enlargement? The book is divided in three parts. The first part, 'Enlargement in perspective' examines enlargement from a historical and comparative perspective and reflects on its impact on the current governance structure of the EU. The second part, 'Policies and policy-making' examines the impact of enlargement on some key policy areas. The third part, 'Institutional change' looks at the institutional changes that have been hammered out during the latest intergovernmental conferences (IGC), treaty negotiations and, most recently, the so-called 'Convention'. It should be pointed out that the chapters are not merely descriptive. Each one of them adopts different theoretical frameworks – often more than one and in a comparative fashion – to explain changes.

The first chapter, by Amy Verdun, looks at the issues that the 'Eastern' enlargement raises for the EU with respect to its 'mode of governance' and policy-making. Verdun draws from the historical record of the previous four enlargements to draw conclusions on the likely implications of the current one. In Chapter 2, Helen Wallace presents four different perspectives on, or 'narratives' of, what the EU and the new members need to do in order to enable the 'Eastern' enlargement to be managed. Each 'narrative' yields different conclusions. In Chapter 3, Beate Kohler-Koch conceptualises EU governance as 'network governance' and argues that enlargement is but an extension of this 'mode of governance', which will continue to spread both within and beyond the EU.

The book then moves to discuss developments in various areas of policy-making. The CAP has for a long time been at the top of the list of necessary reforms both because of pressures coming from the World Trade Organisation (WTO) and because of the amount of budgetary resources it consumes. Indeed the prospect of the admission of the CEECs increased the pressure for reform, as it was feared that the accession of Poland, Slovakia, and Hungary in particular (but also of Romania down the road), could lead to a budgetary crisis. In Chapter 4, Wyn Grant provides an analysis of the highly complex bargaining process to reform the CAP both at the macro level of the policy as a whole, and the micro level of the various commodity regimes of which he selects the dairy sector and rice for a more in-depth discussion. Traditionally the service sector has been regulated, as well as protected, by Member States. As the international trade regime has extended to include services, however, the EU has engaged in the liberalisation of this sector as well. In Chapter 5, Jette Steen Knudsen focuses on the service liberalisation process in Germany, a country traditionally reluctant to liberalise in this sector, in order to draw insights that might apply to the new Member States as well as to the future of service sector liberalisation in the EU.

The development of a Common Foreign and Security Policy (CFSP), which might lead, in time, also to a common defence policy, seemed to have taken centre stage in the EU following the completion of EMU. The spring 2003 war in Iraq, however, toned down at least some of the enthusiasm. The strong anti-intervention line taken by Germany, France and Belgium was, in fact, countered by what at any other time would have been perceived as an innocuous statement of transatlantic solidarity released by the UK, Italy, Spain, Portugal, Denmark, the Czech republic, Hungary and Poland. Under the circumstances, however, the statement was seen as a strong endorsement of the American position. Much to the dismay of France and Germany, the countries belonging to the so-called Vilnius Group - all candidates for accession to NATO and the EU – also released a similar statement. These events not only led French President Jacques Chirac to issue a rather un-diplomatic warning to the 'Eastern' members but also rekindled doubts about ways to reconcile NATO with the EU's attempts to develop its own defence capability.[3] The chapter by Elfriede Regelsberger and Wolfgang Wessels focus on the evolution of the CFSP. Their optimistic prognosis is that its steady, although not constant, process of Brusselisation is unlikely to be slowed down, let alone reversed, by enlargement.

Chapter 7, by Sandra Lavenex, and Chapter 8, by Elspeth Guild, examine a policy area in which the prospect of 'Eastern' enlargement has led to some substantial changes, namely that of the Third Pillar of the EU. Lavenex focuses on the origins and evolution of the Third Pillar, which used to be called Justice and Home Affairs but was renamed 'Police and Judicial Cooperation in Criminal Matters' after the Treaty of Amsterdam moved immigration and asylum policies to Pillar I of the EU. Guild instead, concentrates more precisely and in depth on the evolution of these two policies.

Perhaps the most commonly held view in the period leading to enlargement was that the institutions that had been designed for a community of six, had served rather well for a community of twelve and had made do for fifteen could not possibly continue to provide a minimum of efficiency in a community of twenty-five or more members. The book concludes, therefore, with three chapters devoted to institutional reform. In Chapter 9, Finn Laursen examines the work on institutional reform done during the IGCs that led to the Amsterdam and Nice Treaties focusing in particular on three issues: the re-weighing of votes in the Council, the composition of the Commission and the increased use of qualified majority voting (QMV) in the Council. Andreas Maurer's chapter does the same beginning with the pre-Nice IGC and finishing with the IGC that convened in Rome in October 2003 to discuss the work submitted by the 'Convention.' Finally, Ben Crum assesses in the detail the achievement of the Convention and the prospect that the EU might be moving towards its institutional end goal (or *finalité*).

Helen Wallace (2000) noted not long ago that the 'Eastern enlargement' was largely a 'neglected subject' at least by academics. This book has been conceived in part to remedy this lacuna. As is usually the case, in an edited work not all angles can be covered while, at the same time, some degree of overlapping is inevitable unless one is willing – and able – to act as a stern general with the contributors. We hope that our effort will not only provide a convenient reference tool for the 'Eastern enlargement' but will also make a worthy contribution to the debate on the future of the EU.

Notes

1 A clarification on terminology is in order here. Legally speaking, the European Community (EC) came into existence on 1 July 1967, following the ratification of the so-called 'Merger Treaty' (signed on 8 April 1965). This treaty established a single Council of Ministers and European Commission for the three existing communities – namely the European Coal and Steel Community (ECSC) founded in 1951 and the European Economic Community (EEC also known as 'the Common Market') and Euratom (European Atomic Energy Community) founded in 1957. The three communities already shared the European Parliament and the Court of Justice. Although, technically, the Merger Treaty created the European Communit*ies*, the singular form 'European Community' was more commonly used probably because, by the end of the 1960s, the EEC had emerged as the most significant of the three and could be said to have all but legally incorporated the other two. The Maastricht Treaty, which came into force 1 November 1993, legalised this usage, as it were, by revising Article 1 of the EEC Treaty, which now states that 'the High Contracting Parties establish among themselves a European Community'. The Maastricht Treaty brought together, in a structure commonly represented as a Greek temple with the Three Pillars, all the institutions as well as cooperative procedures that the process of European integration had created since the early 1950s. The EC forms the First Pillar of the EU. Its main task continues to be the advancement and management of the single European market. What distinguishes the EC from the other Two Pillars is that decisions in its areas of competence are taken through institutions having, at least partly, a supranational character. All the intergovernmental cooperative procedures known until then as European Political Cooperation and pursued outside the treaties' framework were grouped in the Second Pillar and renamed Common Foreign and Security Policy. In time, this Pillar is expected to include also a Common Defence Policy. The third Pillar brought together a series of cooperative procedures in the area of domestic security. Originally called 'Justice and Home Affairs', this Pillar was later renamed 'Police and Judicial Cooperation in Criminal matters' after some of its areas of competence were transferred to the first or EC Pillar.

2 This view can be disputed as the EMU process was well underway in 1988 and 1989. However, one could argue that the political momentum was high for leaders to close historic deals.

3 The statement can be found at http://news.bbc.co.uk/1/hi/world/europe/2708877.stm, while that of the Group of Vilnius (Albania, Bulgaria, Croatia, Estonia, Latvia, Lithuania,

Macedonia, Romania, Slovakia, and Slovenia) is at www.setimes.com/html_text_only2/
english/030206-SVETLA-001.htm. Chirac is reported to have commented about the
initiative of the Group of Vilnius: 'They missed a good opportunity to keep quiet. When
you are in the family, you have more rights than when you are asking to join and knock-
ing on the door' www.guardian.co.uk/france/story/0,11882,897891,00.html.

PART I

Enlargement in perspective

Amy Verdun

1

The challenges of European Union: where are we today, how did we get here and what lies ahead?[1]

Introduction

The European Union stands at a historical crossroads. It is confronted with two simultaneous processes: widening and deepening. In order to accommodate the enlargement with ten new countries in May 2004, to become a Union of twenty-five, the institutions and policies of the EU are in need of reform. Attention is once again on what changes will be made and how these changes might impact on the development of the EU.

Eastern enlargement has recently been at the top of the European agenda. At the same time, however, the deepening of policy-making has also continued. More and more policies find their origins at the European level. Some scholars estimate that as much as two-thirds of all policies are influenced by European rules and regulations (Richardson 1996). Furthermore, the nature of policy-making is gradually changing. It is increasingly becoming a multi-level process (Hooghe and Marks 2001). Many different actors are involved. They range from committees, policy experts, lobby groups, non-governmental organisations, consumer groups and citizens, to the more traditional political actors, such as national governments and the European institutions (Green Cowles, Caporaso and Risse 2001, Kohler-Koch and Eising 1999, Maurer and Wessels 2001). Finally the question is whether the EU is now becoming a multi-speed Europe with some countries involved in more deeply integrated policies (such as Economic and Monetary Union (EMU), or Schengen) and others staying outside those policies.

This chapter aims at providing a general overview in simple terms of the issues at stake regarding governance and policy-making in the European Union in light of the Eastern enlargement. Its core questions are, what mechanisms of governance and what policy-making issues need change in order to have successful enlargement? What lessons can be drawn from earlier waves of enlargement? The chapter examines these questions in the following way. The first section gives a historical background of enlargement. It examines the earlier waves of enlargement and what changes were made to policies and governance. The second section discusses the lessons from enlargement. The third examines the reforms of the EU. It discusses how the 'constitution' of the EU needs to be changed to deal with the success of deepened integration and the potential resulting from enlargement. The fourth section draws conclusions and reflects on the challenges that lie ahead.

Four waves of enlargement

Ever since the European Communities (EC) came into existence it was understood that membership of the then EC would be open to all European countries. In fact, the Treaty of Rome stipulates that it is 'Determined to lay the foundations of an ever closer Union among the peoples of Europe' (*Consolidated Treaties*, p. 43). Thus, any *European* country can apply for membership. The concept *European* is interesting in itself. It is worth noting that the geographical boundaries of Europe are unambiguous to the West, South and North, but much less so to the East and the Southeast (Krenzler 1998, Loewenhart, Hill and Light 2001). Moreover, one can wonder whether it makes all that much sense to emphasise the geographical linkages among the countries rather than the economic, cultural or historical ties that bind the various nations (Schimmelfennig 2001). For example, in 1984 Morocco applied for membership to the European Community, which was rejected allegedly because it was ineligible, lying outside Europe. At the same time, the European Union accepted Turkey as a candidate country in (1999) even though formal negotiations have not yet started. Likewise, it is conceivable that the EU might consider Russia and the Ukraine as candidates for EU membership. Wherever exactly the geographical borders of the European continent might lie, it is without question that parts of Russia and Turkey are located on the Asian continent.

When the three European Communities[2] were founded in 1957 the original six Member States represented countries that were in many ways similar. France, Italy and West Germany were larger Member States, whereas the Benelux countries were small or medium-sized countries. They had all recently experienced an era of devastation following two world wars and numerous wars before that. Furthermore, they were on the 'same' side in the political area (i.e. to the 'West' in the East-West divide). They were liberal democracies and were fairly similar in how they fared economically. Even culturally, these countries had a lot in common.

The first enlargement happened in 1973 when Denmark, Ireland and the United Kingdom joined.[3] This enlargement occurred at a time when the EC was considering its next steps in the economic integration process. The customs Union had been completed ahead of schedule and the Member States were planning to start the process which would create an EMU (Verdun 2000). The addition of the United Kingdom, in particular, implied that some policies had to be changed, e.g. the EC regional policy. As the UK was capable of paying for its own agriculture, it bargained to have some of the policies work in its advantage – regional policy would be further developed to support regional areas that had a lower level of economic development (Swann 1999).

The second and third enlargements took place in 1981 and 1986 respectively. The 1981 enlargement led to the incorporation of Greece into the EC. When Greece was finally admitted negotiations were also already underway for Portugal and Spain, which eventually joined in 1986. These three countries were in two important ways different from the nine Member States which constituted the EC before the second enlargement took place. These three countries moved from totalitarian regimes (military dictatorships) to democratic regimes. They were only able to apply for membership of the EC after that process was completed. In Portugal and Spain this occurred in 1975 and 1977 respectively. Thus, these countries had a significantly different political past. A second important difference was that these countries were weaker economically, in part because of their past totalitarian regime and the difficulties of moving from a command to a market economy. As a result, when they joined, the EC committed itself to developing policies that would specifically benefit these countries, so that they could 'catch up'. In the 1980s, they gained significantly from the regional funds and structural funds. These countries had an average gross domestic product (GDP) per capita that was considerably lower than the GDP per capita in the existing Member States. Note in this regard that Ireland was also a country that was weaker economically and that benefited from these policies. As is well-known it caught up beautifully in the 1990s up to the point that it now has one of the highest GDP per capita in the EU (*Financial Times*, February 2002).

The fourth enlargement came in 1995 when Austria, Finland and Sweden joined. These countries had a higher per capita income than the EU average, and little was needed to accommodate them. They had been outside the EC and later the EU because they had not been willing to join the advanced regional integration of the EC when they instead could be member of the European Free Trade Association (EFTA), an economic arrangement that was less ambitious.[4] However, over the years they realised that the trade relations between the EU and the EFTA countries were becoming dominated by decisions made by the EU. This dominance of the EU became increasingly apparent when these countries negotiated the European Economic Area (EEA), and the EU insisted on EEA countries adopting EU standards. Thus for them to have more say in the integration process they needed to become members. The fourth enlargement was not as far-reaching an event for the EU as the previous three enlargements had been. It must be noted however that the integration process had moved on considerably since the 1980s. Thus the so-called *acquis communautaire* that new Member States had to adopt in order to become members was much more extensive than at any earlier enlargement. Moreover, this enlargement implied accepting the Northern countries with their history and tradition of egalitarianism, a major role for the welfare state, and a strong commitment to democratic principles and in some cases a policy of neutrality. It did require that the EU change a little in order to accommodate the needs of these new countries. There was no clear immediate effect, but it did have an implicit and gradual effect on policies such as the general principle of transparency and accountability in governance etc. (see Ingebritsen 1998).

Besides changes to policies, governance rules and stipulations were changed in each of these cases because of enlargement. Regarding governance, enlargement implied changes to the number of votes in the Council, the number of Commissioners, European Parliamentarians as well as the composition of all kinds of institutions. In bureaucracy, it meant hiring civil servants from the new Member States. In the day-to-day policy-making and politics, it meant adding one or more official languages to the already high number of official languages first in the EC and later in the EU.

In March 1998, the EU formally launched the fifth enlargement process. It initially embraced the following thirteen applicant countries: Bulgaria, Cyprus, the Czech Republic, Estonia, Hungary, Latvia, Lithuania, Malta, Poland, Romania, the Slovak Republic, Slovenia and Turkey. The enlargement to the East and the inclusion of several microstates implies that this enlargement process looks to be considerably different from the previous ones (see also Friis and Murphy 2000, Lavigne 1998).

The countries joining in May 2004 are in many ways different from the Members of the EU-fifteen. First, these countries have a different political past. Most of them experienced a communist government until 1989 and have had a political culture and modes of governance that were based on a planned economy which stands in stark contrast with the governance of the fifteen EU Member States. Since 1989, and even today, the former communist countries are working towards becoming full, liberal democracies and catching up to their Western neighbours. Second, the process of changing from a command economy to a liberal democracy took a high toll in terms of unemployment, abandonment of former production processes that were not replaced by new ones, and a general malaise among some of the citizens who are unable to make rapid changes. Thus, these countries need additional support to deal with the societal effects of the painful route to developing a market economy. Third, because of the first two factors, these countries have a significantly lower per capita income. Fourth, their economies are more rurally oriented; a larger portion of the working population is in the agricultural sector. Fifth, the fifth enlargement will imply the entrance of ten new Member States. Furthermore, many of these countries are small or even very small (e.g. Cyprus, Malta, Slovenia) and thus they do not fit nicely into the overall framework of the EU institutions and modes of governance. It is difficult – if not impossible – for these very small countries to perform the duties related to, for example, holding the presidency. Likewise, would it still make sense to grant these countries the same status as a larger country, including veto power and the right to have its national language fully recognised as an EU official language (when for example some minority languages in other Member States are not recognised in the same way)? At the moment, each new entrant receives the right to have its national language considered an official EU language.

The impact of the fifth enlargement is thus considerable. The EU has moved on so much more than it had during the first and second enlargements. In order to adopt the full *acquis communautaire*, these countries were required to adopt much more legislation than had been the case in earlier waves of enlargement. Given the differences between the accession countries and the EU-fifteen Member States the implications of the fifth enlargement on EU policies are considerable. The EU has had a backlog in modernising and restructuring certain policies and modes of governance. The sheer number of countries joining and the fact that they are different in a number of ways has put pressure on the EU to propose those changes. The entry of the new Member States also poses all kinds of challenges for institutions and voting. We shall turn to some of those issues in the subsequent sections.

When applicant countries submit their application to the EU, they do so hoping to get something out of being a member. Likewise, the EU hopes to have new Member States join that can in turn contribute to the EU. Both can do so in a number of ways (see *inter alia* Sedelmeier 2000, van Brabant 1998). They can merely be part of a larger set of countries that broadly speaking share a similar set of norms, beliefs and practices. They may also seek to be part of the EU to have access to a larger market (although that can also be obtained by having the so-called 'Europe' agreements or the earlier mentioned EEA). Another reason may be to be part of the system of governance that now de facto makes the rules (this was, as mentioned, a motivation of the applicant countries of the fourth enlargement which joined in 1995). In the case of the Central and Eastern European countries (CEECs), it became clear that the EU felt a moral obligation to have these countries join, after the end of the communist regimes (see also W. Wallace 2000). Moreover, because the EU has significantly more power than the applicant countries, it is in a position to set the rules (see also H. Wallace 1999). Thus, it need not worry too much about what it gets out of it. By contrast, the applicant countries, negotiating bilaterally have been in a much weaker position to bargain over their conditions for entry.

Let us list some of the pros and cons of the fifth enlargement. There is of course not one exclusive list of pros and cons. The list below states the advantages given by the European Union on their webpage (note that they do not have a list of the 'disadvantages' of enlargement). The European Union lists as the pros of enlargement[5] mainly the following political reasons:

- The extension of the zone of *peace, stability and prosperity* in Europe will enhance the security of all its peoples.

- The addition of more than 100 million people, in rapidly growing economies, to the EU's market of 370 million will *boost economic growth and create jobs* in both old and new Member States.
- There will be a *better quality of life for citizens* throughout Europe as the new members adopt EU policies for protection of the environment and the fight against crime, drugs and illegal immigration.
- The arrival of new members will enrich the EU through increased cultural *diversity,* interchange of *ideas* and better *understanding* of other peoples.
- Enlargement will *strengthen the Union's role in world affairs:* in foreign and security policy, trade policy, and the other fields of global governance.

The possible reasons for the EU to object to enlargement are many. They include:

- enlargement might *jeopardise the process of 'deepening';*
- having to *share budgetary means* with the applicant states;
- being sceptical about the applicant states to be able to *implement the EU acquis communautaire;*
- fear of *mass migration* from the accession countries to the old Member States;
- concern that the *EU will no longer be governable* with so many Member States and without clear institutional and policy-making reforms.

It should be clear that these general pros and cons all depend on how the 'old' and 'new' Member States interact with one another once they are part of the new enlarged EU. Also, the fifth enlargement has forced the issue of institutional and policy-making reform. After this brief historical overview of the earlier four waves of enlargement, let us now turn to reflect on the lessons from these previous enlargements.

Lessons from enlargement

What lessons can we draw from the previous enlargements in light of enlargement to the East? What were the Member States' fears when new countries joined? Did the events they feared happen?

Looking at previous enlargements one can see that a number of issues that were present in the past are resurfacing again with the fifth enlargement and its immediate aftermath. The first concern frequently heard when discussing Eastern enlargement is *fear of migration.* When Greece, Portugal and Spain joined there were serious concerns that the citizens of those countries would move to the Northern European countries in search of prosperity. The way the EC dealt with these fears was to introduce transition periods for the free movement of people. However, migration to the North did not turn out to be a problem. After the rules that disallowed the nationals of these countries to move to other countries expired, Europe did not witness massive migration to other EU countries. In fact, the opposite was true. To take the case of Portugal, a higher number of Portuguese citizens returned to their homeland from Belgium, West Germany and the Netherlands than those who left the country.

A second concern that is often heard is that new countries will use up a considerable amount of the *budget to improve their economic status*. In part that fear has been grounded, but only insofar that one can speak of net contributors and net benefactors of the EU budget. The budget itself has remained frozen at 1.27 per cent of EU GDP, so it does not refer to a very large budget. Those countries (in particular Ireland) with the lowest per capita income have benefited from net contributions to their economy.[6] With the accession of CEECs it will be likely that the fifteen Member States will be contributing more to the EU budget than they will be getting out of it. This concern is particularly salient in the current 'poorer' Member States such as Greece, Portugal and Spain. As is often the case in the EC, compromise solutions are sought, often in the form of transition periods to let countries adjust to the diminishing and eventual disappearance of the funds. Note that all countries will have to submit applications for structural and cohesion funds. Existing Member States have the benefit of having the experience and perhaps the resources for putting in applications.

A third concern regards *governability*. The fear is that the EU will not be as governable as before. Many of the rules, regulations as well as general policies and modes of governance assume a relatively small EU. For example the voting procedure and allocation of Members of the European Parliament (MEPs) and Commissioners assume that there is a finite set of Member States, and that this number is not too large. It had already been decided to agree on a maximum number of MEPs and Commissioners, even though the Treaty of Nice overruled those decisions. Clearly, a small country, such as Malta, cannot have the same representation as the average EU Member State. Indeed the Constitution envisages that these microstates have a representation as nations; when the Heads of States and Governments have to vote by unanimity the Maltese Prime Minister would have a veto power just like all other leaders. However, the result is that Maltese citizens are overrepresented in comparison to for example Germans. The proportion of Maltese citizens to Members of the European Parliament is much lower than that of the German citizens (and to the weighted voting in the Council when voting is by qualified majority voting[7]) (see also Laursen, chapter 9 and Crum, chapter 11, this volume).

Another example that illustrates the types of problems that occur when an institutional structure thought out for a small group of countries becomes larger is the language issue. In the past, every piece of legislation would be translated into the nine official languages of the EU. With the expansion of the number of EU Member States, this number will go up considerably. Yet, it is not said that the EU will be less governable. It has often been identified that the EU governance structure has been in need of reform for many years. For example, the Nice Summit was one of those summits overshadowed by bargaining, deal-making and self-interest rather than focusing on joint government (see also Lindenberg 2001, Verheugen 2001, Wessels 2001). More so than at most other summits, at Nice the Heads of State and Government were driven by self-interest and unable to solve all the salient issues for the upcoming enlargement. Many spoke about the Nice Treaty being a failure before it was even ratified. (It is of course ironic that the Heads of State were unable to complete the December 2003 Brussels Summit with a new Constitution, which means that the Nice Treaty is the base Treaty at the start of the enlargement.) The Laeken summit indicated that the EU is in need of a change in its constitution and that the European Convention would have to study some possible paths to successful reform. Convention President Valéry Giscard d'Estaing came with his draft Constitution in June of 2003 (see for details on the Convention, Crum Chapter 11, this volume), which was eventually revised and accepted by Heads of State and Government in June 2004.

A fourth important concern is that *any single country will have less power* when more countries join. Related to this concern is another one namely that it may be more *difficult to approve policies* if there are many countries having either a veto power, or able to mount a *blocking minority*. Let us look at these related fears one by one. The first fear is that a country in a group of six has more power over the whole than a country in a group of twenty-five. One could argue that this fear was there when earlier enlargements occurred, though with a jump from fifteen to twenty-five this fact is more salient. Let us now examine the second statement. It is often used as an argument that EU policy-making will lose in efficiency if members use their veto power. Clearly if a country keeps its veto power over some issues it would not make a difference whether the EU has six or twenty-five Member States. However, because it would not be productive for each country to use the veto continuously, it is imaginable that veto powers will be used less in a Community of twenty-five than in a Community of six. In this regard, the same reasoning would apply for one country using its veto power or a set of countries continuously blocking the policy-making process through a coalition. However, to date this fear does not seem to be well founded. Scholars such as Jon Golub (1999) have argued that the EC Member States have not used voting very often. Instead, they have tried to reach consensus building, that is, have adopted the strategy of finding a solution that would be acceptable to all. Thus, the impact of the introduction of qualified majority voting (QMV) may be much less influential than has been thought by those who examine the underlying principles. Similarly, one need not necessarily worry too much about adding more Member States in terms of losing influence.

The lessons from the fears and the experience with previous waves of enlargements suggest that more than ever before, the EU would need to change to accommodate enlargement. It would need to make alterations regarding its policies (notably structural funds and agricultural policies) as well as institutional structure and mode of governance (language, voting, number of Commissioners and MEPs). Certain special privileges may also have to go. If the habit of policy-making by consensus changes, the veto powers may have to be restricted in favour of more QMV so as not to block completely the process of policy-making by one country. At the same time, it is clear that the EU is in a strong position. It places the obligation on the applicant states to change their policies and modes of governance so that they fit into the *acquis communautaire* of the EU. Changes referred to here are in the area of governance (or constitution) and in the area of policy-making (most notorious are agriculture and structural funds). Let us turn to what changes would be necessary.

Reforming the EU

The institutional design of the EU was the result of incremental policy-making. It did not necessarily follow a grand design in which the 'constitution' of the EU was thought through. The EU emerged out of the EC with only few changes as time went by. Its institutional structure was based on what was necessary in the 1950s for the small European Communities dealing with Coal and Steel, Atomic Energy and an Economic Community.

It was a compromise between Monnet's functionalist-supranationalist ideas and Member States' reluctance to embrace that model fully (hence the institution of the Council of Ministers that Monnet thought or hoped to be temporary).

Important changes were made with the reform of the voting principles that were passed with the Single European Act. The Maastricht Treaty aimed at redesigning the Communities further and introduced the EU. It created the three-pillar structure because it was the best possible compromise. However, many issues were left unresolved. The Intergovernmental Conference that opened in Turin on 29 March 1996, which ultimately culminated in the Treaty of Amsterdam, tried to make further changes, but was not able to reform the structure of governance in order for policy-making to become more efficient.[8] The Nice (June 2001) and Laeken summits (December 2001) aimed at offering those changes so that enlargement could occur within the framework of a more efficient system of policy-making. Some examples of inefficiencies are the continuous moving back and forth of the European Parliament between Brussels and Strasbourg. The other issue that uses many resources and slows down the process is that all legislation is translated into all languages of the Member States and simultaneous translations occur into these languages during EU meetings. These are issues that are born historically but may not be feasible to maintain in the future as it might not be efficient and effective. Yet, it is understood, that it is politically a very sensitive issue to tackle. Policies that are in need of reform are agriculture (see Coleman and Tangermann 1999, Daugbjerg 1999 and Grant, this volume). For the applicant countries, the cohesion and structural funds are of immense importance as well. Increasingly, policies were added on and the government structure was adjusted but only to deal with the most salient issues.

Many difficult issues have been left for future generations because EU leaders at the time did not see how it would be possible to deal with them. The idea has typically been to deal with matters when the time is right. The founding fathers as well as more recent leaders have been unclear about the end goal of European integration. As a result, there have been certain governance issues that have been dealt with in a 'patchwork' type fashion. There are a number of *governance* issues that have to be dealt with.

Voting in the EU institutions

In order to have an equitable division of votes among the old and new Member States each Member State should have an equitable number of votes in the European Parliament (EP), the Council, and one or a shared Commissioner. These issues need to be dealt with satisfactorily, trying to balance the need to be fair and equitable and at the same time strike a balance between fairness and forceful governance. It would, for example, not be good for effective governance to have too many Commissioners or MEPs. The voting issue also always raises the question of representation by territory and by population. Germans are per capita the least well represented. At the same time, due to its size that country does carry the strongest weight in voting in absolute terms (even if not in relative terms; note however that in the Council it has as many votes as the other three large Member States – France, Italy and the United Kingdom). As is discussed in chapter 11 (Crum, this volume), the Convention proposed a scheme that aims at both being equitable and workable. The 2003 IGC discussed it further. The Constitutional Treaty may or may not obtain support from all Member States, as giving up accepted rights is always difficult for Member States (for example losing the right to have a 'national' Commissioner).

Languages

So far, each Member State has had the right to have all the legislation and discussions in the EU meetings (the EP, the Council etc.) available in its respective national language(s). That arrangement was still feasible when the EC only had up to twelve or even fifteen Member States. But it is questionable whether it would be equally sensible to have all the languages represented in an EU of twenty-five, or more, in the years to come. As stated above, for now this arrangement has been maintained, but it is unclear whether it will be an effective and fair way to govern in the longer run (note that there are a number of minority languages in the EU that are not considered an official language). It is of great symbolic importance to the new Member States that they start off having their national language recognised, which is why it was decided to accept them as official languages. But as was stated above, it is unclear whether it might make governing in Europe too expensive or too slow.

Governance structure

The governance structure of the EU is the still subject of debate. It currently stands as a process that is leaning towards a federal Europe, yet is still stuck at a stage where it is a messy half-way house between an international organisation and a federation (although some claim it is already a federal state, see Börzel and Risse 2002). On the one hand the EU is pursuing policies that are supranational; on the other hand there are many policies for which the Member States still hold almost all responsibility. Eastern enlargement might imply that EU governance will become characterised by multi-speed integration as well as different degrees of integration – more so than had been the case in the run-up to May 2004 (see also Chapter 2, by Helen Wallace, this volume).

Particular policy-making issues

In the negotiations with the accession countries, the strategy has been to discuss accession by referring to various so-called 'chapters'. They refer to policy-making issues on which the EU and that particular accession country need to find an agreement before moving to full membership. There are thirty-one chapters.[9] The most salient ones have been:

- agriculture;
- structural funds;
- budgetary issues more generally.

In other words, the integration process has been moving along gradually. It has implied making changes to governance structures and the contents of policies. The enlargement process has added a new dimension to this process. The applicant countries in a sense 'threaten' the existing Member States in a number of ways and hence it is felt that the applicant countries can only join in if they accept the whole *acquis communautaire*. In addition, the resources these countries would need imply a redistribution of the funds from the financially weaker existing Member States to the new applicant states. As for the process of governing, there are some processes and procedures that have been put in place as the Community and later the Union was developing. The current process is not done with more vision or insight, but merely with another attempt at patchwork corrections. Enlargement in the past implied the acceptance of gradual changes to the policy-making process. The same thing is happening regarding the enlargement process to the East.

What will the EU look like when it is enlarged? What kinds of challenges is one likely to see?

The overall mandate of the EU will not change significantly just because of the enlargement process. Its policies and government structures will more or less remain the same. However, what the EU means for the applicant countries will change. What will the new countries contribute, and how does that contribution blend in with existing EU of fifteen? New countries will bring to Europe some sense of historical connection, but at the same time they will bring to the EU a different type of political and economic culture as well as a different history and different economic and cultural opportunities. Realising the extent of the difference is important as it makes the citizens of those countries feel a different (possibly less) solidarity to one another. In addition, these countries are considerably poorer than the average Member States. Hence, it is only natural that those countries are eager to get a larger share of the EU pie.

The EU will find that its overall role will probably change. It will first be more focused on the economic and political capacity to 'deliver'. It should be able to deal with market issues, regulations, but also the capacity to stand up against the United States when its views are out of line with those in Europe.

With enlargement, it is almost more important that citizens accept the EU. Eurobarometer data in both the EU and in applicant states indicates that the political acceptance of the EU is very high (Eurobarometer 2003a, 2003b). In the summer of 2003 the percentage of supporters of enlargement in the accession countries topped 79 per cent (up 4 per cent from the previous reporting period, six months earlier).

Finally, geopolitical issues are at the forefront of the EU leaders. They see that with the fall of the wall, and the need for CEECs to find a new 'home', it is important to signal the value of the EU being composed of all these former totalitarian and communist countries. It is very good for the overall study of the EU, but still needs further elaboration and clarification.

Conclusion

The fifth enlargement signalled more clearly than before that the mechanisms of governance need to be adjusted in order to facilitate the expansion of the EU from fifteen to twenty-five Member States. The institutional structures need adjustment and its gradual changes need to be reflected upon and formalised. It is this process that the Convention and the 2003 IGC worked on. Other matters have been neglected as they are politically too sensitive to deal with in the early days of an EU of twenty-five. For example, the language issue has not been reformed but adjusted in line with what occurred during earlier enlargements. The fifth enlargement also made more salient the importance of reform in some areas of policy-making. In particular, agriculture, structural funds and budgetary matters are in need of a major overhaul.

The chapter examined the earlier waves of enlargement to see what lessons can be drawn from those experiences. It is remarkable that a number of issues about which there were concerns at an earlier enlargement resurface again: fear of mass migration, concerns over redistribution of EC/EU funds from the rich areas to the poorer areas, implications of enlargement on the feasibility of governance structures and policies. Although similar concerns in the past often turned out to have been unfounded, they are voiced again. At the same time the EU did go through a process that tried to deal with a few necessary reforms before the accession of ten new Member States in May 2004. Whether it will succeed in completing these reforms (get approval through the ratification of the draft Constitution in national parliaments) remains to be seen.

The challenges that lie ahead are many. The new Member States want to join an EU that is fair and equitable to all. Clearly they want to profit in a way in which new Member States profited in the past. Yet, they are joining at a time in which the Member States are less inclined to subsidise poorer Member States indefinitely or with large sums of money. In order to keep the EU project fair, balanced compromises need to be struck between what is fair and just for newcomers and what is politically feasible in the Member States that are net contributors.

Notes

1 Earlier versions of this chapter were presented at an International Symposium, 'Re-imagining the European Union: Dynamics of Enlargement in the 21st Century', University of Alberta, Edmonton, 1–2 March 2002, at the Politicologenetmaal (Dutch Annual Political Science Conference), 23–24 May 2002, and as the inaugural Lecture of the Jean Monnet Chair in European Integration Studies, at the University of Victoria on 17 October 2002. The author wishes to thank participants at these conferences as well as Osvaldo Croci for helpful comments and suggestions. The usual disclaimer applies.

2 Three European Communities were founded. They are often referred to as 'The European Community' or 'EC'. This usage changed after the Treaty on European Union entered into force on 1 November 1993, after which time it was referred to as the 'European Union'. There are legal subtleties regarding the usage, but suffice to say that for the purpose of this chapter we will refer to the pre-November 1993 as EC, and the post November 1993 as EU.

3 For literature on earlier waves of enlargements see Avery and Cameron (1998); Preston (1997). See also H. Wallace (2000).

4 The European Free Trade Agreement (EFTA) aimed at creating and maintaining a free trade area rather than a customs Union. Thus the EFTA did not have a common external trade tariff. Moreover, it did not have common standards which were developed in the EC and later the EU to complete the so-called Internal Market. It soon became clear, however, that EFTA countries needed to adopt EC/EU standards in order to trade with the EU.

5 http://europa.eu.int/comm/enlargement/arguments/index.htm.

6 However, until recently the same was the case for some countries – such as the Netherlands and Denmark – who were net beneficiaries because they benefited largely from agricultural funds.

7 Under the Treaty of Nice, a German MEP represents 829,000 citizens, whereas a Maltese MEP represents only 76,000 citizens. Likewise, a German minister has 29 votes in the Council of Ministers when its votes with qualified majority (meaning that the artificial single vote would represent 2.8 million people). The Maltese counterpart, by contrast, has 3 votes, which makes the artificial 'single' Maltese vote in the Council represent 126,000 people. (It is artificial because each minister only has 1 vote; it is just weighted in this case 29 and 3 respectively). Of course the Treaty of Nice tried to rectify this imbalance in the Council voting's lack of equal citizen representation by creating a triple majority, which includes a population component. Triple majority includes: (1) qualified majority of the weighted votes; (2) a majority of the Member States, which in fact is implicit in the system qualified majority voting; and (3) a demographic majority of at least 62 per cent of the

total population of the EU. The Constitutional Treaty, if ratified, will change these voting rules (see Chapter 11, this volume).

8 The Treaty of Amsterdam was signed on 2 October 1997 and entered into force on 1 May 1999. This treaty renumbered the EC and the EU Treaties. The subsequent Treaty of Nice signed on 26 February 2001 came into force on 1 February 2003. The Treaty of Nice, the former Treaty on the European Union and the EC Treaties have been consolidated into one version. Further changes will be made as a result of the Treaty on the Accession of ten Member States which was signed on 16 April 2003 which entered into force on 1 May 2004.

9 For more details on the 'chapters' see http://europa.eu.int/comm/enlargement/negotiations/chapters/.

Helen Wallace[1]

2

Can a reformed European Union bear the weight of enlargement?

Introduction

There is a conventional narrative about how the EU needs to be reformed in order to enable Eastern enlargement to be managed. This conventional narrative links the intergovernmental conference (IGC) 2000, policy reform and adjustments on the part of the candidate countries. All these elements are linked to a particular linear view of the EU model of integration and all elements conflate Europeanisation with 'EU-isation'. There are, however, at least three alternative narratives. The 'insights from history' narrative draws on – mostly positive – experiences from earlier enlargements. Here the issue is whether or not Eastern enlargement represents a category difference from earlier – Western and Southern – enlargements. The 'changing model' narrative suggests that the EU model of integration may itself be changing in fundamental ways. If this is so, then the implications for enlargement need to be reappraised. The 'Europeanisation is not EU-isation' narrative holds that Europeanisation is a process which has its own dynamics, which are not solely – and maybe not primarily – induced by association with the mechanics of the EU. If this is so, then the issue about what would make for 'successful' EU enlargement may have more to do with Europeanisation than with EU-isation. All of these narratives take the EU and its responses to enlargement as the focal points. In addition we need to consider the way the story sounds from the perspectives of the candidates.

This chapter reviews each of these narratives as a means of shedding further light both on the way in which we might assess these issues by academic analysis and on how the practitioner process is being conducted. The debate has now to be understood in a context in which the results of the IGC 2000 and its consequential Treaty of Nice have been jeopardised by the negative referendum about its ratification in Ireland in June 2001, as well as the parallel discussions taking place in the 2004 IGC which opened in Rome on 4 October 2003. The discussions for this further IGC are grandly referred to as about 'the future of Europe', the phrase inserted into the conclusions of the Nice European Council. This was given more content at the Laeken European Council in December 2001, which also agreed to set up a 'convention' to prepare the next IGC. The Convention which was headed by Valéry Giscard d'Estaing eventually published a draft Treaty which is used as the basis for discussion in the IGC (see Chapter 11 by Crum, this volume).

The conventional practitioners' narrative

The conventional account of how EU reform and Eastern enlargement are related has three main elements: institutional reform, policy reform and accession adjustments.

Institutional reform

The conventional institutional reform agenda was laid out in the IGC 2000 process and the various proposals that were drawn into the Treaty of Nice. The argument was that dealing with the 'Amsterdam leftovers' was a necessary and perhaps sufficient step to modify the EU institutions for a larger membership (see the chapter by Laursen, this volume). The leftovers involved adjusting for a larger number of Member States and adjusting for the relative power of Member States by altering some of the methods of representation and altering some of the decision rules. The main concerns here were with the Council of Ministers and the European Commission, as the two institutions apparently most affected. There was, of course, an associated issue about the size of the membership of the European Parliament. In addition there was an increasing concern about the impact of enlargement on a European Court of Justice (ECJ) which was already suffering from an 'overload' of cases from the EU of fifteen. We should note here that reforms to the ECJ are really very important indeed to the extent that the vitality of the 'Community of law' is a key ingredient of the EU model of integration, both for the system as a whole and for the way the process impacts at the in-country level.

These arguments were repeated in practically every official document relating to the IGC 2000, both from within the EU institutions and from the governments of the current Member States. What was, however, not made clear was how the specific reforms being debated would actually make a difference to the workings of the EU institutions. There was a gulf between these reform issues and the more focused accounts of deficiencies in the performance of the EU institutions, some of which were beginning to be addressed in the non-treaty reform discussions about, in particular, the Council and the Commission.

These 'practical' questions were being pursued within each of the two institutions. In the case of the Council there was, and continues to be, an iteration of internal efforts to improve its performance, although as yet with inconclusive results. In the case of the Commission Neil Kinnock, a Vice-President of the Commission, has been steering forward a complex and controversial package of management reforms.

The inadequacy and/or inappropriateness of the debate on the Amsterdam leftovers were reflected in the subsequent emergence of two other institutional issues to be addressed. One was the debate on 'flexibility' or 'closer cooperation' (there is much confusion of semantics and of meanings in this discussion). A series of speeches started by Joschka Fischer in May 2000 breathed life into this discussion by breeding a new conventional wisdom to the effect that what must be safeguarded is the capacity of the really committed 'vanguard' or 'pioneer group' to forge ahead with the deepening of integration, whatever the size and heterogeneity of the membership (see the chapters by Crum (11) and Kohler-Koch (3) this volume). This view was accompanied by calls for a more constitutional formula for reform.

The other source of concern was the evidence of quite widespread public dissatisfaction at the drift of policy powers to 'Brussels' and the EU institutions, either because this move to Brussels caused overload or because it drained too much power away from central or local/regional levels of government in the Member States. The latter is another version of the subsidiarity debate, fuelled most explicitly by concerns among the German *Länder* governments. Hence we should expect to observe some pressures not only to stabilise the allocation of powers between EU and Member States, but also some pressures to 'repatriate' powers back to the Member States.

Incremental policy reform

It has long been widely argued that the EU needs to make a number of policy reforms in order to accommodate new members. Here the conventional wisdom remains that reforms are most needed in the EU budgetary system and in the Common Agricultural Policy (CAP) (see also chapter 4 by Grant, this volume). It is interesting to note that other policy areas are not so much discussed in this context. Hence the main points had apparently been addressed in the Agenda 2000 debate, more or less resolved at the Berlin European Council of March 1999. However, that debate made only limited progress with CAP reform, where many points were deferred until later, some would argue until the next financial perspective that would need to be agreed for 2006 onwards. Overall it has been hard to see a sense of urgency on the EU side in pushing forward policy reforms to the CAP. It may well be that the crucial dynamics have more to do with the World Trade Organisation (WTO) negotiations than with EU enlargement, or perhaps the increasing concerns about the animal health and food safety issues that have latterly gained prominence.

One further observation that is relevant to the EU's 'European' policy – the Agenda 2000 debate failed significantly (Laffan and Shackleton 2000) to address the issue of likely levels of spending as a result of the EU's European responsibilities to the not-yet (or maybe never) candidates in South-Eastern

Europe. This has emerged as a major burden on EU expenditure which is poorly addressed by the current ad hoc programmes. Given that the borderline between candidates and non-candidates is hard to draw in practice, there is an under-appreciated set of 'challenges' here, as Chris Patten, the Commissioner for External Relations, now – rightly – repeatedly points out (see http://europa.eu.int/commcommissioners/patten/index_en.htm).

Accession adjustments

Beyond the two points above conventional wisdom holds that everything depends on unilateral adjustments by the candidates towards the adoption of the *acquis communautaire*. This argument is similar to those made during pre-vious enlargements, where the EU side (then formally still the EC) argued that it is up to the candidates to adjust to the rules and practices of the EU that they wish to join. There is, however, a difference from previous enlargements in the extent to which this time the EU side has insisted so much on 'pre-accession' adjustments by the candidates, in contrast with the emphasis in previous enlargements on 'post-accession' adjustments. Hence we should note that in the case of the candidates from Central and Eastern Europe the EU insists on *very tough conditionality*.

We should note that the management of this process was for a long time mainly in the hands of the Commission, as it prepared the process of accession negotiations. Issues were dealt with in a fragmented way according to their sectoral logics, with only weak linkage to the strategic issues. In addition the process for a long time moved at a gentle, i.e. rather slow, pace, not only because the Helsinki European Council of December 1999 added to the number of candidate countries involved, but also because there was no urgency imposed by target dates.

As the IGC 2000 drew to a close the momentum of accession negotiations started to alter and the member governments began to take more active interest in the process. The Swedish Council Presidency set about speeding up the process and a much more sharply focused discussion began on some of the more tricky issues. By the time of the Gothenburg European Council in June 2001 a roadmap was laid out which began to envisage target dates for the more ready candidates. These envisaged that new Member States were able to take part in the 2004 IGC.

Some general observations on the conventional practitioners' narrative

The conventional practitioners' narrative is widely repeated in much of the out-sider commentary. Several elements recur.

- It rests on a 'hub-and-spoke' model of EU extension. Enlargement proceeds through the bilateral negotiations between the EU and each individual can-didate. Power is asymmetrically distributed between incumbents and can-didates. Candidates are estranged from the multilateralism that is so important to the EU model.

- It is predicated on a linear model of EU integration, with defined stages of achievement to be reached in an order predefined by the prior experience of the current Member States. The issue is thought to be which and how many stages particular candidates can reach – and by when.
- It presumes a dominant institutional paradigm around an orthodox picture of the EU institutional architecture, hence the emphasis on the Council and the Commission, and their roles in combination as providing the policy escalator.
- It discards a great deal of the experience of previous enlargements as irrelevant to the new candidates. Furthermore, it derives little from previous accession processes about what are realistic and what are unrealistic constraints on the adjustments by candidates to the *acquis communautaire.*

Thus the model of integration implied is very much a *West* European model, which presumes: viable states; mixed market economies; pluralist democracies; and so forth. EU-isation is what counts. The issue is about whether and when each of the candidates will be sufficiently 'EU-ised'. Quite what the timeline for the process will be remains hard to predict. Developments in years before the closing of the various chapters on which negotiations were being held suggested that at least some of the candidates were optimistic about the 'end game' being in sight. What also was striking was a kind of competition among the candidates to be in the leading group.

The 'insights from history' narrative

The conventional practitioners' narrative is informed by the belief in an inevitable tension between widening and deepening. Thus, so the argument goes, enlargement always puts at risk the trajectory along the linear path towards deepening of policy and institutions. Newcomers are risky recruits and hence need either to be resisted until they are really ready or need to be pinned down by obligations that will prevent them from backsliding – and from pulling the prior incumbents backwards.

But what does the record reveal?

1 It is correct to observe that several earlier recruits have resisted forms of deepening – but essentially for political reasons (driven by their domestic politics of autonomy) rather than for economic reasons or because of economic underdevelopment. Thus the opponents of deepening have mainly been from countries such as Denmark, the UK and latterly Sweden.

2 The conditionality of accession negotiations has in the past been as often to protect the incumbent Member States' interests that are vulnerable to competition from recruits as the result of demands from candidates. Thus typically in agriculture and in some industrial sectors the EU-led conditions have delayed the moment at which a recruit's industry might be able to

become competitive. Take the example of pharmaceuticals. Here the Spanish industry did not achieve full market access until 1995 because it was too effective in terms of price competition, not because it was not up to scratch. Note the replay of this in the accession negotiations between the EU and Hungary, which inherited a strong pharmaceutical industry from its place in the old Comecon division of industrial production. Note also the insistence on delayed application of free movement of labour (now persons) for applicants because of (misplaced) fears by incumbents.

3   Yet each round of enlargement has in practice been accompanied by deepening (Michalski and Wallace 1992):

   • 1972/73 new goals set and new policies adopted (see conclusions of Paris Summit of December 1972), as well as new funding envelopes.
   • 1985/86 the single market, environmental policy, cohesion arrangements, institutional reforms.
   • 1991/92 enlargement to include Eastern Germany – agreement on Economic and Monetary Union (EMU) and institutional reforms.
   • 1996/97 incorporation of Schengen, and the move towards a common security and defence policy.

But an examination of the historical record also needs to include the 'in-country' trajectories of change and modernisation within acceding countries. After all, it is what happens within individual countries that seems to have a powerful impact in determining whether or not there is a synergy between domestic change and adjustment to EU disciplines. Note this point carefully in relation to the discussion in the 'Europeanisation' literature about whether or not there is a 'good fit' between domestic and European processes. In this context four late-joiners stand out as having achieved remarkable trajectories of change alongside their accession to the EU: Ireland, Spain, Portugal and Finland. Note that in all four cases there has been rather strong 'domestic political ownership' of changes and that all four have confounded the expectations of many other European partners. Against this background the Irish referendum defeat of the ratification of the Treaty of Nice (albeit on a very low turn out of voters) is particularly disturbing.

The 'changing EU model' narrative

It was argued earlier that the conventional practitioners' narrative rested on a particular given version of the EU model of integration, with the dynamics linked to linear progression. But what if the character of the EU model is changing? What if the reform issues have to be addressed to a different kind of EU? What then might be the EU templates that the candidates have to import?

Here I argue that the EU model is undergoing secular change for a variety of reasons. There is no longer – if there ever was – one EU model, but a cluster with several variants.[2]

1   The Monnet model for the 'Community method' – as it has developed for the CAP and the development of the customs Union and so on – is thought to be particularly vulnerable to enlargement.

2   The EU regulatory model – as it has developed around the single market – is thought to be vulnerable to enlargement and accounts for an enormous proportion of the *acquis* to which the candidates are being required to adjust. The greatest difficulties lie with process regulation rather than product regulation.

3   The EU distributional model – as it has developed around the cohesion policies in particular – is also thought to be vulnerable to enlargement, although not so much perhaps because of the recruits as claimants as because of the limits to the generosity of the net budget payers. The EU distributional model may be more at risk from changes to the EU economic paradigm than from enlargement, given both the fiscal disciplines of EMU and the 'new European economy' debate.

4   The new 'benchmarking' and 'soft' policy cooperation (Hodson and Maher 2001) model is evident especially clearly in the 'Luxembourg to Lisbon' development of economic and employment measures via policy coordination and comparison using 'OECD techniques'. Benchmarking and soft policy coordination are seemingly becoming a process in its own right rather than a staging post towards traditional hard policy cooperation. There seems little reason to suppose that this model of governance is particularly vulnerable to enlargement.

5   'Intensive transgovernmentalism' embraces the methods being adopted for EMU, Common Foreign, Security and Policy and defence, and Justice and Home Affairs. In these areas we should note the emergence of new and experimental institutional methodologies (different in each of the three areas) with intensive engagement by relevant national policy communities, with much less involvement as yet by traditional EU institutions and with the development of new *sui generis* agencies (European Central Bank, Europol etc.) and in the defence field perhaps the importation of 'NATO[3] techniques'. The conventional presumption in these areas is that they are difficult areas for the vanguard EU countries and hence by definition must be vulnerable to enlargement. This presumption is open to question.

Most of the discussion about policy reforms and institutional changes to accommodate Eastern enlargement refer to the first three variants of the EU model outlined above. Moreover, they are the three variants which are directly and in most detail discussed in the accession negotiations and have generated specific prescriptions about pre-accession adjustments to the *acquis communautaire*. Very little of variants (4) and (5) has yet been drawn into the negotiations or into the conventional narrative, although the development of justice and home affairs is becoming increasingly recognised as critically salient in the context of enlargement.

Variant (4), soft policy cooperation and benchmarking, seems to be elastic enough, because of its intentionally permissive character, to accommodate the candidates rather easily. In this context we might note the 'good fit' between Irish domestic practices of social partnership – which have changed significantly over the years of Ireland's EU membership – as a positive example for the candidate countries (See Irish Election study:(www.tcd.ie/Political_Science/ ElectionStudy/ frame989064.html). In the Irish case a distinctive domestic modernisation trajectory has been combined with adaptation to broad EU templates and specific EU rules with over many years apparently a 'good fit' between the two. However, we should note the contestation during early 2001 of this room for domestic manoeuvre claimed by the Irish both as regards tax competition and as regards the high budget surplus, the former criticised by some other member governments as 'disloyal' competition and the latter argued to be outside the disciplines of EMU. Here lies a crucial set of issues for the accession countries, which may want to follow the Irish precedent in the sense of keeping the space for their own domestic policy choices.

Variant (5) at first sight looks more difficult, precisely because on the conventional linear model of EU policy deepening of the relevant policy areas look as if it would be achieved later not earlier by new members. However, maybe this linear model is deceptive.

- Economic and Monetary Union in the full sense looks as if it would be achievable only late in the process of integration, but 'Euro-isation' might well come earlier for some of the accession countries, indeed ahead of formal EU membership to the extent that transactions in the economies of Central and Eastern Europe in practice start to be conducted in euros (formally or informally), as some had already been in deutschmarks.

- Cooperation in Justice and Home Affairs (both the Schengen obligations drawn into the First Pillar and the Third Pillar policies) has increasingly been drawn into the formal accession process, with high hurdles beginning to be set for the accession countries to reach in terms of the allegedly relevant 'standards'. Also the debate on closer cooperation has included suggestions that this is an area where the vanguard group of EU Member States should run ahead of the rest. Yet here functional logic and common sense suggest that this line of argument does not make sense. The physical geography of Europe suggests that the more countries that can be drawn into intensive cooperation and the sooner this can be done the better the chances of exercising a modicum of public policy control over transnational crime, unauthorised migration and so forth. In other words the more cooperation with candidate countries the better, and why wait for EU accession? Indeed much the same could be said of the need to engage in as substantive cooperation as possible with the 'next neighbours', irrespective of whether and when they become candidates for EU accession.

- Foreign, security and defence policies – it has in the past been suggested (there was a British-Italian initiative on this several years ago (see www.esteri.it/eng/archives/arch_press/miscpapers/do200799ea.htm) that the candidate countries should be involved in this area of cooperation sooner rather than later. To be very concrete, the Helsinki European Council of December 1999 set a headline goal for a number of troops to be mobilised collectively as a European rapid reaction force. The Czech Republic, Hungary and Poland are NATO members already and could surely contribute troops, an increment which might even increase the chances of meeting the headline goal. Moreover, EU non-NATO countries will also be contributing troops, as could some of the other East European countries that are members of NATO's Euro-Atlantic Partnership Council. We should also note here the particular complication of Turkey, a longstanding NATO member, but as yet only a paper candidate for EU membership.[4]

In other words, if one starts to look at the newer and more experimental areas of dynamic EU policy cooperation the hurdles for the candidates do not look quite so high. Moreover, their less mechanical rules of decision and implementation allow some scope for elastic arrangements for the involvement of candidate countries.

The Europeanisation not EU-isation narrative

As we saw above, the 'conventional practitioners' narrative pins its arguments to a process of EU-isation as the core of what is required for Eastern enlargement of the EU to be manageable. This emphasis on EU-isation is argued to be necessary because the EU is vulnerable to dilution or distortion if new members are admitted before they are subject to thorough EU-isation. That is, before accession the candidates need to prove a propensity to EU-ise by adopting, importing and embedding EU policy and institutional templates. The only countries, on this argument, that were able to handle accession quickly were the most recent new members, i.e. Austria, Finland and Sweden, which had – partly unilaterally and partly through the European Economic Area – previously imported a very great deal of the *acquis communautaire*.

But what if EU-isation is different from Europeanisation and what if it is Europeanisation that the candidates need to achieve in order to practise EU-isation? What might this distinction mean? I have argued elsewhere (Wallace 1999) that Europeanisation is a process independent of the EU; rather, a condition of enabling the EU to succeed than directly the consequence of the EU. This is not to deny the catalytic or embedding character of EU involvement in terms of institutions, legal infrastructure or policy regimes, but rather to argue that the EU has succeeded on all of these dimensions because it has been superimposed on an underlying process of Europeanisation.

What then does this underlying process consist of? In my argument it consists of two key factors: on the one hand, a willingness and a capacity to practise 'constructive multilateralism' with European neighbours; and, on the other hand, a set of sustained domestic policies and practices that achieve a kind of synergy between domestic preferences and managed transnational interdependence.

Thus other international regimes in Europe are relevant to this process as well as the EU, for example the Council of Europe, or NATO, or the functional regimes for dealing with specific forms of interdependence, e.g. the Rhine and the Danube, or the Baltic and Black Seas and so forth. The engagement of countries in these various other arrangements provides learning experiences of constructive multilateral management, with disciplines that feed into domestic policy and institutional choices. Part of the success of the EU is that it feeds off these other forms of transnational cooperation.

Synergy between the domestic arena and the European is the other key ingredient. Thus trajectories of change at the domestic level – but with variation between countries to meet individual country contexts and circumstances – are part of what enables countries to manage the interconnections. Again my four country examples from the existing EU membership all seem to bear this out: Ireland, Portugal, Spain and Finland. Each had very different starting points and legacies, none of them straightforward indicators of successful adaptation to the wider European framework of cooperation. Yet their records suggest that – by significantly different routes – their trajectories of adaptation have 'Europeanised' these four countries. Here, it might be suggested, is a soft version of Alan Milward's argument (Milward 2000) that the EU (or rather for him the earlier forms of the European Community) provided a vehicle for the individual countries to 'rescue' a kind of state autonomy. This is a lesson that should not be carelessly cast aside by EU practitioners who are rather too quick to urge the imposition of presumably uniform EU templates on candidate countries.

Conclusion

The conventional practitioners' narrative is locked into path dependencies associated with an old model of West European integration. It has powerful influence over the way that the EU reform and enlargement processes are being handled. It reinforces the asymmetries between incumbents and candidates. It is strengthened by the various neuroses about the risks of change. It is, however, an extraordinarily powerful narrative.

The insights from the *history narrative* provide in essence a more variegated picture. It is less path-dependent. It contains 'path-opportunities', that have been exploited such that enlargement in the past at least has generated dynamics of change that have not weakened or diluted the EU model of integration.

The changing *EU model narrative* depends on judgement and interpretation. If these new variants of policy and institutional cooperation are both emerging and delivering substantive results, then they may be at least as relevant to the potential for enlargement to be accommodated, as are the older variants.

They also allow scope for the waters to be tested by involving some or others of the candidates to see what forms of new variant cooperation can bear fruit.

The *Europeanisation not EU-isation narrative* leaves more of the ownership of the process at the country level and the more informal channels of transnational cooperation. Here societal and economic factors and vectors of interdependence and communication are probably critical, as are the habits of multilateralism that are encouraged by other European multilateral frameworks.

So can a reformed European Union bear the weight of enlargement? The first narrative suggests not so easily, but, in my view, is narrowly construed. The second narrative provides less certainty, but positive examples of unexpected dynamics. In this sense it is a more optimistic narrative. The third narrative acknowledges powerful factors of change to the EU model, with productive dynamics that could be elastic enough to accommodate some of the candidates at least to some extent in the short to medium term. The fourth narrative suggest that much depends on what happens in particular countries and in particular European neighbourhoods, and that much depends on how substantive and functional requirements are addressed in practice. Rather less, according to this narrative, depends on the mechanical processes of EU institutional and policy reforms or on the technical arrangements for accession.

A missing element in all of these narratives is what are the perspectives evident in the candidate countries? Which of these narratives informs their thinking? Or are there yet further narratives that have to be made explicit? My own short answer is that those in the candidate countries familiar with previous enlargements believe that the insights from the history narrative offers opportunities for them as well: Poland like Spain, Estonia like Finland and so forth. The conventional practitioners' narrative is a necessary part of the reality with which the candidate countries have to engage – but a very irritating narrative, precisely because of its asymmetric character. Moreover the conventional practitioner's narrative systematically disregards the potential impact of changes to the EU model. It also seems rather evident that association with NATO and other European security organisations is a critical component of the policies of Central and East European countries. Moreover, the 'return to Europe' component of post-communist reform seems to be about becoming engaged in the wider European multilateral process. The EU is a hugely important part of this process, but not the only part. Thus for the candidate countries a version of Europeanisation that goes beyond EU-isation is perhaps the crucial perspective.

Notes

1 This chapter is based on a lecture delivered at the Third Biennial European Community Studies Association – Canada (ECSA-C) Conference in Quebec City, 31 July 2000. The themes of the chapter draw on the work of the British Economic and Social Research Council's *One Europe or Several?* Programme, directed by the author from January 1998 to August 2001 from a base in Sussex European Institute.

2 These are set out in Wallace and Wallace (2000), especially chapter 1, and further
   addressed in a special issue of *Journal of Common Market Studies* (2001).
3 North Atlantic Treaty Organisation (NATO).
4 For a long time the Turkish government put enormous obstacles in the way of efforts to
   develop managed cooperation between the EU and NATO. In November 2001 the
   Turkish government relaxed its objections, although resolution of the issues was then
   impeded by the Greek government, on the argument that Turkey was being accorded
   over-privileged treatment for a non-EU member.

BEATE KOHLER-KOCH[1]

3

Network governance within and beyond an enlarged European Union

Conceptualising the European future

The EU is moving ahead, not to an uncertain future but to a European federation. This message was given by the German Minister of Foreign Affairs (Fischer 2000) and was subsequently supported by the German Chancellor.[2] I shall argue here that this interpretation of the ongoing constitutional debate in Europe is off track. The future of Europe will not resemble the state-building which took place in the past. First, it is highly unlikely that the EU will be transformed into a state. Second, even if a core community might unite and form a federation, it will be a political system that resembles the present status quo much more than it will resemble the model of the Westphalian State. In my view, a continent-wide system of governance has to be different from that of the traditional nation state. With a low level of social integration and powerful political players with credible exit options, responsiveness is the key issue in organising efficient and legitimate governance. Therefore, the system of governing in the EU in the future will not be a hierarchy but a network.

This chapter will develop this argument in the following way. I will support my argument by theorising about the particularities of the European system of governance both within and beyond the EU. The underlying hypothesis is that though both levels have distinct features, the patterns of governance are functionally related, they are supported by the same constitutive logic, and are mutually reinforcing. I will first take a look inside the EU, characterising the particularities of what I have called 'network governance'(Kohler-Koch 1999: 25–26) and make the argument that this system will not be transformed easily. The reason is that governance inside the EU is firmly enshrined in constitutional conceptions, which have been translated into institutional settings. These settings in turn orient behaviour and support vested interests. Network governance goes together with the omnipresence of EU regulation and the spread of transnationalism. The EU has turned into an undivided space of interest intermediation. It has altered governing strategies and the role of authoritative actors.

This phenomenon is not unique to the European Union. The differentiation of our societies and globalisation are trends which support this process also in other parts of the world. At the same time, constraining factors are at work. Europeanisation[3] which includes the spread of network governance, usually falls short of altering the core structures of national systems and does not cause the withering away of the nation state. On the contrary, my argument will be that network governance is highly conducive for the enduring coexistence of national and transnational rule. National actors are ready to increase even further their mutual interdependence and to commit themselves to transnational functional regulations. They agree to be tightly linked together but they want to have a say in this process because they want to integrate on their own terms.[4]

Second, I will explore the larger framework of the European consociation. My hypothesis is that within and beyond the EU a system of multiple networks is evolving which has put national governments in a central position for managing interdependence. European integration has always been pushed by some small core coalitions. 'Multiple bilateralism' is a well-established strategy both to promote the European case and to secure partial interests. Transgovernmental cooperation is supplementing the 'Community method' in the EU system. Already now we have a differentiated system of European cooperation which looks like a Russian doll. When they are well designed those dolls fit smoothly one into the other but it would take witch-craft to make them walk. In other words, the metaphor does not give us any idea of how the units relate to each other in a dynamic system of joint policy-making. Managing such an interdependent system is further complicated because it is embedded in wider networks of regional and global cooperation and subject to international regimes covering a broad range of sector policies.

At both the national and the European levels of analysis I come to the conclusion that for good functional and normative reasons network governance is the preferred mode of governing these systems. The lesson to be learned is of general interest. The EU is not a unique case. Quite the opposite, I would argue that we are facing a more general phenomenon. We are witnessing a rescaling of government and we have to adapt our constitutional thinking to a changing reality. Both territoriality and functional scope will be the organising principles of political rule in the future. They are the ground where European studies and international relations studies should meet. Due to limited space, however, I shall not be able to cover this wider topic.

Looking inside: the EU – a system of network governance

Constitutional conceptions matter

In order to assess the present and the future political architecture of the European enterprise, I suggest exploring the factors that give the living constitution of the EU direction and stability.[5] First of all, institution building is not just a matter of writing and implementing a constitution. Institutions develop and change through interaction in daily routines which put institutional provisions into practice. Actors pursue interests, but their preferences are imprinted by ideas. Therefore, the second argument is that constitutional conceptions make a difference. They incorporate different normative and factual beliefs about the essence of politics and about the best way to arrive at collectively binding decisions. The majority view with respect to the European Union is that its main reason for being is to enable efficient problem solving. It is considered to be an expedient institution that contributes to the common good because by virtue of superior size it is better equipped to meet the challenges that reach beyond national boundaries. Problem-solving is, however, not just a matter of coordination and knowledge-based technocratic strategies. Usually decisions have to be taken that demand political choice. Therefore, EU policy-making is a conflict ridden process. In order not to antagonise the participants procedural mechanisms have to be installed that will balance competing interests. In view of the plurality of interests, and the long lasting historic cleavages that have separated the European nations, majoritarian institutions would be ill equipped to smooth over contradictory preferences. What is needed is a highly inclusive system of consensus formation safeguarding the autonomy of its constituent parts as far as possible.

Apart from these causal beliefs about the functional prerequisites of good governance, constitutional conceptions are based on strong normative assumptions. The EU is not – and for most people it should not become – *l'état nation*, a community of its own that confers identity to its citizens. The persistent vitality of the nation state is more than a representation of a factual account. Citizens still view the nation state as the legitimate framework for value allocation. It is a normative preference in favour of a community that is based on the equal opportunity to communicate and has roots of practised solidarity. Calling for 'consociation',[6] i.e. a consent requirement that respects both the vital interests of the individual parties involved and the 'common advantage' of the community, goes beyond institutionalising a functionally expedient system of decision making. It is a tribute to preserving national and other group autonomy and to minimising exclusion.[7] These constitutional conceptions are embodied in the institutions of the European Union and have been translated into the distribution of competence and are present in a shared understanding of 'appropriate' political behaviour. Within this framework a distinct mode of governance has developed.

Network governance at work

I choose the term 'network governance' both because it is a metaphor that visualises best the particular ways of governing in the EU and because it is a well known concept in other fields like business. It is not saying that 'government' will be substituted by a network. Networks do not have actor quality. Instead, a network links corporate bodies together which still exert authority but share it with others in a wider system. Interdependence is the main feature of the system, no single unit can ignore what others are doing. A network mostly involves a multitude of actors without imposing a central hierarchy. It is 'governing without government' (Kohler-Koch 1996) based on its units and nodal points of interaction (Vibert 2001:136). Different categories of units take part, both public and private corporate actors join in an ongoing process of consultation and negotiation. Policy-making is epitomised by openness and inclusiveness and many times monitoring and programme implementation also includes stake-holders and share-holders alike.

The European Union, in particular the First Pillar of the EC has developed such a network system. By law policy initiatives are still the privilege of the Commission. However, there is an increasing demand for EU-wide regulations originating from different segments of society, pushed and channelled through the system by transnational advocacy coalitions which include national and European policy-makers. The EU is a penetrated system of governance both with respect to the process of policy formulation and policy effect. Different levels of governments and different types of actors are involved in each stage of the policy process. National, sub- and supranational governments take part in it but their delegates fall short of representing a unitary actor. The sector approach to European policy-making has the effect that representation has become fragmented according to functional domains. The authority of territorial entities is split up in functionally segregated units at the domestic level which interact regularly and incessantly with their counterparts from other Member States and the Commission. Non-governmental interests make every effort to get inside the policy network. Interest groups have established a multi-level presence and EU institutions, above all the Commission, have encouraged non-state actors to get involved in the process of political deliberation.[8]

The quest of organised interests to be heard meets benevolent acceptance. The reason given is that by taking in those who have a claim, acceptance and consequently compliance will be enhanced. In view of limited administrative resources, external advice is valued for improving the problem-solving capacity of the system. Many neo-corporatist arrangements have started as informal practice, became a well-tried routine, and like the idea of 'partnership', finally gained a footing as a general principle in the Treaty, thereby adding legitimacy to the EU intervention at the sub-national level. In the meantime 'network governance' has become part of the official philosophy. When presenting the new Commission's working programme in Parliament, Romano Prodi suggested that 'we have to stop thinking in terms of hierarchical layers of competence separated by the subsidiarity principle and start thinking, instead, of a networking arrangement, with all levels of governance shaping, proposing, implementing and monitoring policy together' (Prodi 2000). In addition, the White Paper on European governance 'proposes opening up the policy-making process to get more people and organisations involved in shaping and delivering EU policy' (Commission 2001a).

Because EU policy-making is highly issue specific, it allows for splitting up differences. Differentiation and – when necessary – delineating policy areas in a new way are well tried strategies to mitigate conflicts and soften opposition. Therefore, despite the multiplication of actors and the heterogeneity of interests decisions are taken well above the lowest common denominator. The flipside of the coin is that policy-making is deficient in terms of coherence and transparency, that it is biased in favour of resourceful actors and is lacking democratic accountability.

Negotiations with resourceful actors are a common feature in any kind of polity. In order to classify it as something new, network governance should have some specific features that qualify it in comparison to other modes of governance.[9] A major novelty of this concept of 'network governance' has to do with its notion of the state. It is no longer seen as constituting the supreme authority but rather as an 'enabling structure'. The second way in which the concept of 'network governance' moves away from traditional views of governance relates to the patterns of interaction between the public and the private. It is no longer organised according to authoritative allocation decided at the top of a hierarchy but aims at coordinating related interests in multilateral negotiations to approximate positions. Such patterns are based on the belief that appropriate behaviour and innovative activities, concurrent with public objectives, cannot be induced by command and control but only by treating target groups like partners.

In regional development, environmental protection and social relations, the European Union has in the last few years committed itself to a more decentralised approach and now deliberately aims at 'a more systematic and pro-active approach to working with key networks to enable them to contribute to decision shaping and policy execution' (Commission 2001a). Apart from widening the involvement of interest groups in policy formulation and testing new strategies to improve implementation by target-based contracts with sub-national actors, the Commission and Member States are advocating new modes of governance. 'Open coordination' should support and complement the Community legislation and strengthen Member State compliance. Whenever EU policy-making is making inroads into highly sensitive policy fields, as in immigration policy, there is a preference for soft governing strategies. Open procedures of coordination are considered to be best suited in view of the multi-dimensional aspect of the issues at stake. They can better take into account quite dissimilar national situations, respond to the large number of actors involved and are more compatible with the continuing responsibility of the Member States for policy implementation.[10] In order to ensure coherence and respect for Community-wide standards, a set of procedures and instruments have been introduced. The key element is the approval of multi-annual guidelines accompanied by specific timetables and translated into national policy targets which have to be met by national action plans. A wide range of actors is invited to take part in monitoring national performance and in evaluating the achievements in view of developing a common European policy.[11] The basic assumption is that mobilising a wide range of actors, promoting cooperation, reducing transaction costs for the exchange of best practice and institutionalising evaluation and monitoring will develop a common approach living up to best standards and encourage a convergence of practice and procedures.[12]

Supporting trends

This transformation of governance is not just a phenomenon which occurs at the EU level but can also be observed at the nation state level. It may be attributed to the growing differentiation of national societies, the increasing autonomy of social actors and to the ambition of the welfare state to produce optimum conditions for production and consumption. Although in the 1990s, deregulation and downsizing the welfare systems was at the top of the agenda in Europe, state interference in economic and social life is not in decline. Public activities still range high in strengthening international competitiveness and adapting domestic systems to a changing environment. What has changed, however, is the mode of intervention; the readiness of the central state to leave it to sub-national actors and to accept common European rules.

Another supporting trend is the rise of the 'information age' (Castells 2000) and with it the spread of globalisation. It is considered to be a main factor for the changing modes of governance. 'Deterritorialisation', connoting that globalisation has rendered state sovereignty in critical policy areas devoid of meaning[13] is a buzzword in the current literature signalling that the Westphalian system has come to an end (Krasner 1993, Ruggie 1993, Walker 1993). There is a growing common understanding that what we aim for can no longer be achieved within national borders. Efficient self-government has to pursue transnational problem-solving strategies and has to adjust to claims of universality and the competing demands of democratic self-rule in other parts of the world. We are told that these competing claims can neither be resolved on the spatial terrain of the territorial state nor in the traditional way of inter-state regimes.

This discourse about the transformation of statehood and governance in response to the increasing permeability of borders in a world of global interdependence is not the popular view on the European Union. The popular version of the Union's role in a changing global context is to project it in terms of a powerful unitary actor. This 'the bigger, the better' concept adheres to the idea of territoriality and state sovereignty. On the expert level, however, discourse and political practice is adjusting to the challenges that accompany a differentiated expansion of functional systems that cut across not only national but also across EU borders. There is widespread agreement that EU regulations have to pay tribute to 'globalisation' (Robertson 1995), i.e. the interconnected-ness between the local and the global. To meet these patterns of cross-border relations, both within and beyond the EU the rescaling of governance has to follow different lines than the transfer of competence from the national to the EU level. It will be organised along the functional and transnational, rather than the territorial and supranational dimension.

Constraining factors

Functional necessities never translate as such into political practice. Even when there is widespread agreement that cooperation might be the most efficient response to global interdependence, real actors have to translate insight into action. Concurrent strategies have to be pushed by influential actors who believe that it is in their interest to promote a different kind of political process and get it institutionalised. The multitude of actors and the density of interaction in the European Union suggest that there is a wide range of public and private actors that find it rewarding to mobilise resources in order to play a part in European policy-making networks. There is no other region in the world with such an overflow of trans-border activities and which is subject to such a high level of common regulation. Does this imply the rolling back of the state?

All available evidence supports the conclusion that, in spite of a high level of transnational interaction, European policy-making has not distracted atten-tion away from the national theatre of action. Public and private interest groups, trade associations as well as big business have close contacts with both levels of decision making. The frequency of interaction of those actors is still significantly higher with the national administration and – to a lesser degree – with the national parliaments than it is with European levels of government, such as the Commission and the European Parliament. Even the European federations of interest groups do not concentrate their contacts exclusively on the EU institu-tions, but are in frequent contact with national governments (Eising and Kohler-Koch 2004). Comparisons over time tell us that interest groups address national targets not less, but even more often than before (Sidenius 1999).

Nevertheless, the frequency of contact does not give us a clear indication about the substance of politics. Does the multi-level, multi-actor production of EU regulations which is crowding out national regulations, bring about a system change? The answer we find in the literature is ambivalent. Our conclusions differ from conventional wisdom:[14]

1   Distinct national and regional policy styles affect participation in the EU network system and the implementation of EU regulations at home.
2   Ideas travel easily and paradigms propagated by the EU have become acknowledged terms of reference. But the structures of policy networks, administrative routines and institutions are reluctant to change.
3   Policy instruments are easily adopted on grounds of efficiency, but adap-tation stops whenever competing party interests are at stake or whenever

the new procedures threaten to disturb the delicate mechanisms of balancing out distributive interests. In essence, German regional policy did not change because nobody wanted to take the risk of dismantling a well established package deal.

One should not disregard the constraining effects of national politics. The Member States still constitute the political arena where the struggle about power and legitimacy is decided. Political life is still geared towards government. Parties fight for electoral victory because being a member of the national parliament and participating in the national government is the key to power. In other words, there are strong forces in domestic politics that are keen on not being disturbed in their own realm of politics by outside interference.

A puzzle to be explained

Political action is not at all consistent. European integration is pushed ahead by exactly those actors who are objecting to a definite loss of their political autonomy. National politicians aim at Europeanisation in national colours, i.e. they accept interference that conforms to fundamental structures or is in line with the kind of modernisation they are looking for. They warmly welcome EU regulations when these help them to thrust aside the opposition of vested interest groups which do not support their views. They invite interference when EU provisions enable them to streamline established routines and provide them with a superior problem-solving capacity. What political actors are looking for, primarily, is *flexibility*, that is, a sharing of responsibilities and an improved capacity to act. It is like wishing to have your cake and eat it. In order to accomplish this aim, political actors pursue policy strategies that have loose strings attached.

The EU offers its members a differentiated array of policy strategies, ranging from common policies to providing legal frameworks for mutual recognition, delegating standard-setting powers to regulatory agencies, supporting private self-regulation. Within the EU framework but not based on the Treaties, member governments are progressively interested in 'policy making without legislating' (Héritier 2002). Whenever a common effort may look rewarding, but ways and means of achieving the ends are highly contested, 'policy coordination' is a perfect solution. What in the past used to be 'a mechanism of transition from nationally rooted policy-making to a collective regime' (Wallace 2000a: 32) is nowadays a mode of governance in its own right.[15] It heavily relies on 'benchmarking' which is considered to be the key to success: Problem-solving strategies are evaluated and rated by experts. In a process of 'deliberation' experts and politicians define 'best practice' and agree on targets to be met. Norm-oriented behaviour is stimulated through the back door. Common objectives will have to be met by individual efforts. National policies are based on mutual obligations but though they have chosen the institutional framework of the Community, there is no legal commitment. Compliance can only be achieved through public accountability. Governments have to live up to the expectations that they themselves have raised by intention. With their public announcement they have legitimised demands on corresponding performance. Governments that fail will risk losing public support.

It is an indirect way of becoming dedicated to a common cause and to encouraging transnational policy transfer. It gives governments a free hand to choose policy strategies. Above all, they keep their re-distributive powers untouched. Nevertheless, even though they have not entered legal commitments, they have agreed to mutual obligations and are tied together because each is pulled forward by the motion of the others.

It appears that we are confronted with two realities. On the one hand, the EU is affecting our daily life by the prevalence of European regulatory policies. Network governance has integrated the individual states into a single political space. On the other, national governments have developed new strategies of cooperation that give them leeway to pursue their own interests. Apart from regulatory competence, the redistributive function of the nation state is still fully operational. National taxation and public spending is up to now only marginally constrained by the existence of the EU. All complaints about the waning influence of the nation state tend to underrate the distributive and redistributive powers of the welfare state. It is still the nation state that is investing in the well-being of its citizens and enforcing solidarity in terms of financial transfers. Distributive and redistributive policies are highly relevant for mass politics and national (and sub-national) governments have kept it under their control.

How this delicate balance may evolve over time is not just a matter of the internal evolution of the EU. Europe is a system of multiple networks that stretches beyond domestic relations within the EU.

Europe: a system of multiple networks

Networks of cooperation
Member state governments are promoting and constraining the evolution of the European system. New policy initiatives and constitutional politics, in particular, demand unanimity. Most of the time, however, new moves are initiated and promoted by a small number of countries. Particularly prominent is the close cooperation between France and Germany. This Franco-German collaboration is routinely celebrated. Indeed, it is more than a successful public relations exercise. It has substance which is founded on a strong belief system that the cooperation of former 'arch-enemies' is beneficial not just to themselves but to the European Union community more broadly, giving the EU strength and stability. The Franco-German collaboration is supported by a well-established organisation which has diminished transaction costs and is based on a solid agreement on principles and rules of behaviour. It has a driving force just because these two countries, which work together so closely, have different opinions on

many issue of substantive policy. Whenever they pursue parallel interests, their European partners become fearful of hegemonic ambitions.

Bilateralism is, however, not an exclusively Franco-German privilege. It is a firmly established pattern of relations, handled in a smooth and flexible way with alternating partners. It is a daily routine that hardly receives any media coverage except for spectacular mutual agreements that signal a change in policy such as the British-French St Malo summit on security affairs (Howorth 2000). Important initiatives covering new ground in European cooperation have been prepared and pushed by core coalitions. This holds true for the cooperation in Research and Technology, in Social Affairs, the Single European Act, the Barcelona process or the stability pact for Central and for South-Eastern Europe. Governments realise that they are well advised to look for partners to pursue their interests and make an initiative a success. Helen Wallace has identified 'multiple bilateralisation' as a guiding element in the approach of the UK Labour government, deliberately chosen to advance British interest in the EU.[16] It is an opportunity for countries marginal to the EU core to strengthen their position by linking to like-minded countries. Smaller countries follow the same strategy, but they have to rally a broader coalition to have an impact.

The interaction between multilateral and bilateral relations is still a heavily under-researched field of inquiry. Empirical evidence gathered so far[17] prove correct the assumption that most bilateral activities relate to coalition building concerning EU policies. It is part of conventional wisdom among EU diplomats that the key to success is 'winning friends and making allies among their European partners' (Grant 1998: 4). Depending on tradition, dominant policy paradigms and administrative capacity individual countries assume specific roles. Germany is more multilateral minded than the other large Member States addressing policy initiatives directly to EU institutions, be it the Commission or, particularly in affairs of high politics, to the presidency.[18] Though it is said that 'Germany has exploited the use of the smaller states in the coalition-building process in the European Union much better than France or the United Kingdom' (Pijpers 2000: 187) a detailed network analysis revealed that with regard to contacts and the attribution of reputation, it is, rather, a recipient than an active contributor to bilateral relations (Thurner, Stoiber and Pappi 2002). Nevertheless, Germany has been heavily engaged in the applicant countries in Central and Eastern Europe, both on the level of intergovernmental and societal transnational relations.

Sub-regional cooperations like the association of the Benelux or the Nordic countries stimulate not just multilateral but also close bilateral relations. Because these are deeply rooted in 'like-mindedness' they can easily extend to neighbouring countries. This logic pertains to the relation of the Nordic countries with the Baltic states. From the very beginning, i.e. the time of political independence, the Nordic states established close cooperation with their neighbours across the Baltic Sea. They have – in different bilateral constellations and in varying degrees[19] – recollected historical ties and cultural affinities and became an active advocate for their early accession to the EU (Kadunce 1995:8). Economic support like the 'Baltic Investment Programme' and numerous initiatives of cultural exchange, administrative assistance and social activities aimed at speeding up the transition to market economies and democratic societies. Relations are predominantly bilateral and focused on civil society (Herolf 2000: 141).

Without more systematic research it is difficult to assess how bilateral relations and sub-regional cooperation fit into the overall policy process of enlargement. In the case of Baltic cooperation it is quite obvious that the importance of the European Union and the difficulties of the applicant countries to meet the *acquis communautaire* has enhanced the willingness of all partners involved to deepen their engagement. The EU on its part has encouraged bilateralism by initiating and financing 'twinning' programmes that encourage a direct transfer of administrative expertise from a Member State to an applicant country (Grabbe 2001: 1024). This programme has initiated the most wide-ranging transfer of personnel and because of the de-central organisation it strengthened the variety of administrative cultures within the EU. In addition, the Commission has sponsored the formation of transnational associations of sub-national actors like the Union of Baltic Cities and the Baltic Sea States Sub-regional Cooperation. This latter initiative provides a good example of the overwhelming influence of the EU in channelling the enlargement process (Lippert 2000). The EU provides the institutional framework, the resources and the legitimacy for public action. But still, the opportunity to get organised and to associate with like partners in other Member States is an asset. It increases the power of 'voice' and it changes the relations from 'between us and them' to relations 'between the future us' (Graham Avery, quoted in Lippert 2000: 152).

The 2004 enlargement has, like no other enlargement before, activated bilateral and sub-regional activities of both private and public actors.[20] It has stimulated an open debate on flexibility and 'enforced cooperation' that now gives legitimacy to think about new institutional models of cooperation.

Self-binding strategies

Helen Wallace has coined the term 'transgovernmentalism' for a new kind of intergovernmental cooperation. Economic and Monetary Union, the Schengen Agreement, and the Common Foreign and Security Policy (CFSP) were developed outside the common institutions and in groupings not necessarily including all Member States. Instead of talking about intergovernmentalism, she prefers the term 'transgovernmental', 'to connote the greater intensity of some of (the) examples, where EU member governments have been prepared cumulatively to commit themselves to rather extensive engagement and disciplines, but have judged the full EU institutional framework to be inappropriate or unacceptable' (Wallace 2000a: 33).

This kind of cooperation has distinct characteristics. The idea of the initiative, the formulation of the objectives and the operation of the new enterprise is developed with little interference from Community institutions. It is a matter of 'core executives' (Dyson and Featherstone 1999) that control the process and take the decisive decisions. It is an executive's heaven with hardly any involvement of societal actors or parliamentary representation in the process of policy formulation. Member states of the EU become involved in regime building. They start outside EU institutions, engage in legal commitments which later may or may not become translated into Treaty amendments and subsequently design new institutions for their operation. What does this process of transgovernmental regime building imply for the future of European cooperation?

Working outside the EU institutions provides for greater flexibility both in terms of membership and substance. Regimes leave greater autonomy to their members than is allowed for within the EU framework. The process in which to come to an agreement is less formalised and the level and form of obligations may be more varied than within the EU framework. Regimes are considered to be soft, but not necessarily weak, international institutions. On the contrary, although judicial review and sanctions are lacking, the material contents of the commitment may be far reaching and compliance may be assured.

The transgovernmental model of cooperation conforms to the so-called model of consociation. As the transgovernmental model has been tried with great success in recent years it is not unequivocal that the institutional development of the EU would lead us towards creating a European federation. A federation implies organising a polity which concentrates authority and which once and for all delineates the realm of political responsibility. Its legitimacy is based on the principle of territorial representation and the spatial congruence of power and accountability.

Rather than moving towards a European federation it seems to me that we are moving into the opposite direction, i.e. from supranationality to transgovernmentalism. This development may be interpreted in two different ways: either as departing from past patterns of cooperation which rejects the principle of institutionalised supranationalism, or as building an additional layer of cooperation on the foundations laid by a highly organised and firmly established system of joint policy-making. In my reading, Member State governments engage in ever closer transgovernmental cooperation not in order to substitute, but to profit from an institutional framework that knits them together.

Russian dolls in politics

The most crucial issue for the constitutional future of the European enterprise is how this new type of transgovernmental regime relates to the existing EU. Already the first enlargement triggered a discussion in academic circles about a differentiated system of European integration. The overriding concern was to find a modus operandi that would allow deepening of European integration despite the opposition of some Member States. The prospect of widening the Community to the East from at that time twelve to up to more than twenty members put the issue on the political agenda again. Before Member State governments convened to amend and revise the Maastricht Treaty to accommodate new Member States, influential members of the German Bundestag launched a discussion paper advocating a 'core' Community of 'the willing and the able'.[21] In view of the accession of the Central and Eastern European Countries it was evident that enlargement could not follow previous practice of a 'mere arithmetical projection of current arrangements' (Sedelmeier 2000: 221). At stake was a recasting of the integration model that would pay tribute to large numbers, stronger differences of structural characteristics and political preferences, new global constellations of power and the attraction to cooperate outside the Treaties (Wallace 2000c). Before and during the Amsterdam treaty negotiations (1996/97) a wide range of propositions were tabled ranging from a 'multi-speed Europe' within a single institutional framework to different opting-out schemes and strong preferences for a 'Europe à la carte'. Finally, the principle of 'flexibility' was accepted and institutionalised (Stubb 2000). But conditions and qualifications were added that make it difficult for any vanguard group to speed up integration. The main reason was opposition to a differentiation of status between Member States and insecurity about institutional implications. Even today there is no master plan about how to manage overlapping regimes and organise members with different rights and obligations in one institutional set-up. Nevertheless, when negotiations on the Constitutional Treaty arrived at a deadlock at the end of 2003, the debate about building an avant-garde came up again.

The envisaged shape of the enlarged system looks like a Russian doll. At the core there is a small but solid element, maybe a European federation of a small group of committed Member States, encapsulated by a supranational institution, which in turn is placed in a larger case of institutionalised intergovernmental cooperation, which, last, but not the least, is put in a casting that is formed by a wider regime of economic and political cooperation. The metaphor helps us to imagine what a flexible system may look like. Unfortunately, it does not give any guidance as to how this differentiated 'portmanteau' system may be operated. It is a compound structure and therefore it makes sense to organise it according to the principle of loosely coupled systems. The components are highly interdependent, but each of them is eager to preserve its political autonomy. Hierarchy will not work. Instead, coordination and cooperation will follow the logic of organising a network. Again, this abstract idea has to be made operational and the operationalisation, most likely, will require institutional innovations.

It seems quite obvious that nation states will not disappear and that Member State governments will continue to play a decisive role. Since the components of the system have a different constitutional quality – only the agency of the core European federation would be undisputed – governmental actors will provide the most influential links. It will be network governance, though not within the European Union but between the components of the enlarged and differentiated system.

Matching specialisation

Networking will be prominent between EU Member States and with external actors in order to join forces. Let us take the case of security. To make crisis intervention a success, the envisaged build-up of joint rapid reaction forces will have to be backed up by a high-tech command, control and communication infrastructure and a larger military force for support. In order to become operational without exhausting limited resources, European states will have to agree to specialise. The task ahead is to match high mutual dependence with the persistent aspiration to take final decisions autonomously. Thus, the efficient management of interdependence is on the agenda.

Security cooperation does not stop at the European borders. Collective defence is still organised within NATO. Even with respect to crisis intervention, assured access to NATO capabilities is necessary to back up European military action. The interface with NATO has to be organised in a smooth and efficient way. Therefore, institutional links have been built to NATO.[22] These bridges, however, further complicate the institutional structure of European security arrangements. Because of power discrepancies, overlapping memberships, diverging organisational structures and different regime philosophies, the institutional fit is not easy.

Security is not the only example, but offers the most visible and plausible case to illustrate the complexity of this interwoven system. It also proves that the juxtaposition of different types of political institutions is not just a transitional phenomenon. Policy coordination is needed and it has to pay tribute to both organisational complexity as well as competing claims.

Networking beyond the scope of Europe

Unilateralism has lost legitimacy. The US have received support for its 'war on terrorism' by their European allies. But subscribing to the same aims does not entail accepting the same strategy. As was seen prominently in the spring of 2003 when the war on Iraq took place, many continental European governments have been quite outspoken that they do not support any unilateral military move against those countries that the Bush administration has called the 'axis of evil'. They insist that without international backing, i.e. without a mandate from the United Nations, no military action is legitimate and likely to endure. The continental European categorical insistence on multilateralism is not without a certain degree of self-interest. But the main message is that in a world of global interdependence unilateralism will be counterproductive in the long run. Communication and concerted actions are needed to accommodate competing interests and to find common grounds concerning the appropriateness of common actions. Democratic governments have to legitimise their action at home and abroad. They will find it less difficult to persuade a critical and mixed audience when they manage to relate their political objectives and strategies to universal principles.

Apart from communicating with the public, decision makers have to coordinate their action. Crisis management in former Yugoslavia made it quite obvious that conflict resolution may not be controlled successfully by the responsible institution or a coalition of neighbouring countries. The Organisation for Security and Cooperation in Europe (OSCE), the UN, the EU and NATO were all involved and individual states, in particular the United States and Russia made it quite clear that they wanted to have an individual say in the negotiations. An organisational mechanism had to be devised to institutionalise an ongoing process of communication and consensus formation between international organisations and powerful state actors. The 'contact groups' for Bosnia and Kosovo established an informal but efficient policy-making core (Boidevaix 1997). When the institution failed to bridge opposing positions, another intergovernmental forum, the G-8 provided a platform for the peace agreement (Schwegmann 2003).

The West European members of the contact groups (France, Germany, the United Kingdom and as a late-comer Italy) made sure to inform and consult with their EU partners. The EU, especially the forum of the Common Foreign and Security Policy (CFSP), was an important arena for consultation, but so has NATO been. Smaller Member States, in particular those in charge of the rotating presidency, had at least an indirect influence on crisis management. Consultation, however, is not the same as a common EU foreign policy. Members of the contact group did not want to be restricted by consensus formation within CFSP. They participated in the contact groups in their own right and though they took into consideration the position of other EU partners, they were not representing a common EU position. What happened in former Yugoslavia does not correspond to the unitary actor paradigm that some people evoke when talking about the future of the EU.

Instead, international conflict management will be about concerting positions within and between international organisations. This conflict management will be done mainly by individual governments supported by the 'good services' of international organisations. It is an exercise in network governance that takes place at a different level of aggregation but has similar characteristics. It is a non-hierarchical negotiating system with changing participation according to issues at stake. Which actors will be included is not just a matter of capabilities and interest but also of role ascription. They have to be identified as legitimate participants both in terms of international law and international political practice. The choice has to be justified in public discourse and will be influenced both by international and domestic public opinion. The latter is assigning an increasing value to non-state actors. Not least because of the upgrading of non-governmental organisations' (NGOs) patterns of international negotiations change. Bargaining will have to give way to arguing in order to convince public interest groups, i.e. political objectives and strategies have to be legitimised by referring to universally accepted principles.

Managing networks: the task ahead

Moving towards differentiated systems

Irrespective of how enlargement will affect the constitutional development of the European Union, Europeans will go on living in two worlds:

1   Citizens will live in the political environment of national political systems. These systems are responsive and responsible to distinct political societies and they will, above all, pay tribute to the demands of social equality. Besides, national systems will qualify as actors in the wider political arena.
2   Citizens will also be part of a transnational political space that is highly important for functional regulation across national boundaries. They can participate directly and those who can raise a voice will be heard. Transnational policy-making has a real, but rather diffuse, constituency and weak mechanisms of accountability.

Political actors have to pay tribute to the permeability of both worlds. To be effective they will engage in an exercise in networking, in coordinating related interests and in promoting multilateral negotiations to approximate positions. Agreements will be functionally specific, cutting across different levels of public responsibilities and involving numerous stake-holders. In the context of the EU, in particular, they have learned that arguing is an art to pursue generalised interests. My projection is that 'network governance' will become the most prevalent mode of governing to manage these two interconnected worlds.

Network governance, however, is no neutral exercise. Opening the space for political action is, first of all, offering new opportunities of influence for those who have an immediate, partial interest and the resources to participate in the new game. This assessment is true inside the EU where elitist circles mainly influence policy regulations and, above all, strategic economic decisions. It is also true in relation to the management of interdependence in the wider European context.

The situation described is a far cry from the normative criteria of democracy. Those who act or at least believe they act in the generalised interest of the people escape direct accountability. 'Voice' is distributed unevenly. It is given to those who also have an 'exit' option (Hirschmann 1970). Irrespective of diverse Community initiatives to improve the communication with the broader public, citizens have no equal rights of participation. Equality, however, has never been the driving force nor has been the natural companion of dynamic change. Friendly corrections from above, anticipating or responding to public demands, will not turn the tide. Up to now the European Union is still a neglected arena for political participation, be it in terms of electoral turnout, the organisation of social movements or contentious action (Imig and Tarrow 2001). Some argue that all the efforts 'to bring the Union closer to the people' and the Commission's firm position that '[p]articipation is not about institutionalising protest' (Commission 2001a) may have mitigated potential protest. The record of transnational civic activities challenging EU policies is still mixed but recent EU summit meetings have prompted spectacular protest.[23]

Challenges ahead for the research agenda

In order to grasp the dynamics of future developments we should check our research agenda. We have accumulated insight by a huge amount of case studies which provide us with a fair knowledge about the functioning of the European system, what it has in common with other political systems and how it differs, and how Europeanisation affects national regulations. A comparative political system approach and policy analysis do not, however, tell the essence of the story. The political dynamics of the EU can only be grasped when the analytical conceptualisation pays tribute to the ongoing struggle about the adequate form of governance in a system that is still in the making. The approach of 'network governance' may help to broaden the view to see the interdependent development of regional integration and nation state transformation. In addition, it provides a perspective that gives account of the deficiencies of the system. We have no difficulty in imagining in which direction a European network system may move and how it should be organised in order to function efficiently. Efficient problem-solving and peaceful conflict resolution endow the European system with legitimacy. But the de-territorialisation of politics affects the democratic legitimacy of political rule. Network governance does not meet the terms of representative democracy and alternative concepts are not yet convincing. Therefore, we have good reasons to give more thought to the kind of system we might live in tomorrow.

Notes

1 This chapter is a revised version of a keynote address delivered at the Third Biennial European Community Studies Association – Canada (ECSA-C) Conference in Quebec City, 31 July 2000.

2 See the motion to the SPD party convention, proposal dated from 30 April 2001.

3 Europeanisation, the new buzzword in European studies, is mainly used in a narrow sense, indicating that Member States are increasingly subject to the adaptive pressure of EU regulations. I suggest a more extensive concept which pays tribute not just to the supranational but also to the transnational dimension of European interaction and interdependence and which does not focus exclusively on a top-down process, i.e. the local effects of external impacts but also devotes attention to the bottom-up process, i.e. local actors taking advantage of new windows of opportunities. Therefore, in my reading, 'Europeanisation' is synonymous with 'enlarging the scope of the relevant unit of policy making' (Kohler-Koch 2000a: 22): national politics is drawn into a wider process of interest intermediation and decision making that is organised predominantly but not exclusively by the European Union.

4 Therefore, it is not surprising that the breakdown of negotiations in the Intergovernmental Conference on the Constitutional Treaty in December 2003 was provoked by disagreements about the voting power of Member States.

5 For a more systematic treatment how divergent constitutional conceptions relate and give rise to distinct ideal type systems of governance see Kohler-Koch (1999).

6 The concept of 'consociation' has been developed by Althusius (1603/1914, see Hueglin 1999). For Althusius, the essence of politics was 'a permanent process of community building' (Hueglin 1999: 86) and his main concern was to elaborate a general principle of politics that would balance the aspirations of self-governance with 'universal unity of action' (Hueglin 1999: 108). Hueglin has linked up the writings of Althusius with present day discussions about the political organisation of a post-statist world. He argues persuasively that Althusius 'provides a coherent set of premodern concepts for fragmented postmodern times' (Hueglin 1999: 199).

7 A careful reading of Fischer's speech (Fischer 2000: 6) reveals that his concept advocates a strong role for the nation state: 'even for the finalized Federation the nation state, with its cultural and democratic traditions, will be irreplaceable in ensuring the legitimation of a Union of citizens and states that is wholly accepted by the people'.

8 For more details, see the Discussion Paper on 'The Commission and Non-Governmental Organisations: Building a Stronger Partnership' (Commission 2000) and the White Paper on European Governance (Commission 2001a).

9 For an ideal-type differentiation of characteristic elements of different types of governance see Kohler-Koch (1998a) and Eising and Kohler-Koch (1999: 6).

10 For more detail see the Commission's communication on immigration policy (Commission 2001b).

11 EU policy proposals advocate an active involvement of civil society and the reviews of the national action plans include comments on the cooperation achieved between authorities from different levels of government and non-governmental organisations.

12 The communication on immigration policy presents the new approach in a nutshell (Commission 2001a). For a more systematic analysis across different policy fields see Héritier 2002.

13 Lankowski 1999:V; other authors call the same phenomenon 'denationalisation' (Albrow 1996) or focus on the process of 'debordering' and put 'boundaries in question' (Albert and Brock 2000, Linklater and Macmillan 1995).

14 The conclusions are based on a number of comparative research projects launched at Mannheim in recent years and the national research programme on 'European governance'. For more details see Kohler-Koch 2002.

15 This was most pronounced at the European Council meeting of Lisbon; see European Council (2000): Presidency Conclusions of the Lisbon European Summit, 23–24 March 2000.

16 'The underlying analysis was that it would not be possible to replace the Franco-German tandem with a single key coalition, and similarly that there was little chance of replacing the bilateral coalition with a triangle of the three 'leading' member governments . . . The British policy involved a search for partners and joint initiators issue-by-issue and policy domain by policy domain' (Wallace 2000c: 231–232).

17 Some conclusions are drawn from an on-going research project at Mannheim University on 'Multiple Bilateralism' comparing larger and smaller EU Member States.

18 It was the German government that – in vain – immediately after the terror attack of September 11, 2001 asked the Belgian presidency to convene a special summit.

19 Sweden established close relations to each of the Baltic states; Denmark was active in a trilateral cooperation with Germany and Poland to support Polish accession to NATO; Finland concentrated its efforts to secure that Estonia would be in the first round of accession (Antola 1999).

20 In the case of the Southern enlargement, i.e. the admission of Greece, Portugal and Spain after the breakdown of dictatorship, bilateral governmental interventions were less

frequent and apart from the German political foundations non-state actors were hardly involved (Kohler 1982).

21 'Überlegungen zur Europäischen Politik' ('Reflections on European Politics'), Deutscher Bundestag, Bonn 1 September 1994. The authors, Lamers and Schäuble, though deputies of the governing coalition did not speak on behalf of the German government. For a detailed account see Maurer and Grunert (1998).

22 See in particular the 'EU-NATO Declaration on ESDP' from 16 December 2002, NATO online library:www.nato.int.

23 The meeting of Heads of States and Governments in Nice in December 2000 which marked the end of the Intergovernmental Conference on institutional reforms and the meeting in Gothenborg in June 2001 which was dedicated to employment, enlargement, and environment came with violent demonstrations.

PART II

Policies and policy-making

WYN GRANT

4

The Common Agricultural Policy: challenges in the wake of Eastern enlargement

A central theme of this chapter is an exploration of the impact of Eastern enlargement on Common Agricultural Policy (CAP), placed within the context of a broader discussion of CAP reform. After the disappointment of the limited outcome of the Agenda 2000 discussions which were supposed to prepare the EU for enlargement, the Copenhagen agreement in 2002 allowed for the phasing in of CAP in the ten new Member States joining the EU in May 2004. It thus managed to defuse what many had feared would be a budgetary crisis once enlargement took place. However, the budgetary problems may still arise in the longer run. It also became increasingly evident that the accession states were ill prepared for accession in the area of agriculture. Administrative systems were not ready and processing plants often fell well short of EU standards.

The issue of enlargement

The precise budgetary costs of enlargement have always been difficult to calculate, but when it was first mooted some rather alarmist figures were circulated about the possible impact on the budgetary situation. Such a reaction was perhaps not surprising when it is realized that the accession of Poland alone will increase the existing total of farmers in the EU by one-third, many of them operating on a semi-subsistence basis. The Commission initially tried the ploy of attempting to deny arable aid payments to the new Member States from Central and Eastern Europe. The Commission tried to argue that as these payments were introduced to compensate for the 1992 MacSharry reforms in cereals, they need not be applied in Central and Eastern European countries (CEECs) as they had never benefited from the cereals support regime in the first place. Not allowing CEECs the same compensations would have meant that on one side of the Austro-Hungarian border, farmers would have been receiving arable aid payments, whereas similar farms a few miles away would receive nothing. This inequity was clearly neither justifiable nor politically sustainable. From 2001 onwards, the Commission switched to the more politically viable option of phasing in arable aid payments and other subsidies. One of the factors that convinced the Commission seems to have been the realisation that it would be difficult to apply supply control measures without compensatory payments.

The Commission took the view that productivity in the agricultural sectors of the CEECs was likely to be the deciding factor in terms of the impact of enlargement on the CAP (European Commission 2001). It is argued that a number of obstacles will prevent any rapid increase in agricultural production in the accession countries. Indeed, the agricultural balance of trade has moved substantially in favour of the EU-15. In part this reflects the role of export subsidies but also the fact that higher value processed foods are not being produced in sufficient quantity and quality to meet increasingly discerning consumer demand. Lower quality and food health and animal welfare standards are likely to continue to be important barriers to increases in agricultural and food exports from the accession countries to the EU-15.

Adapting to EU regulations is likely to considerably increase the costs of processing and handling in the new Member States. It is possible to draw the policy conclusion that there will not be a marked increase in output in response to the application of CAP prices and other support mechanisms. Indeed, the failure in many countries to set up adequate administrative systems may mean that the immediate budgetary impact will be more limited than anticipated as claim rates may be lower than expected and rejection rates higher.

It was evident throughout the negotiations that the Commission's strategy was to leave difficult farm support issues until the end of the negotiation process. This meant that enlargement issues increasingly became entangled with the mid-term review scheduled for 2002, which had been seen as an opportunity to reinvigorate the reform process. The deal that was reached at the Copenhagen summit in 2002 appeased the accession states, especially Poland (which got €1bn paid into its national treasury as what was described as a 'cash flow facility') but at the cost of only €400 million in 'new' money in the budget. CAP arable aids in the accession states will be phased in at 25 per cent of the EU-15 level in 2004, 30 per cent in 2005 and 35 per cent in 2006 until they reach the EU-15 level in 2013. However, the accession states will be able to decide whether to 'top up' these payments so that they reach 55 per cent of the EU-15 level in the first year of membership. Some of this money can be diverted from the €9.8m set aside to deal with poor rural infrastructure, effectively a form of dynamic modulation in reverse. However, there is a 20 per cent limit on the amount of the rural development allocation that can be diverted in this way and all payments will have to be co-funded by the accession state. By the third year of membership farmers in the accession countries would be able to receive almost two-thirds of the full amount.

As accession approached it became increasingly apparent that a number of countries were not fully prepared for accession in the agricultural sphere, particularly Poland, Slovakia and Malta. The problems were particularly serious in Poland where they were underpinned by a more general Commission concern about what was seen as the rising level of corruption in the country that undermined almost all public administration. The Commission monitoring report issued in November 2003 found that Poland was experiencing severe problems in establishing the necessary bureaucracy for CAP aid to flow. The integrated administration and control system (IACS) was far from complete and the Paying Agencies that hand out subsidies were not ready either. Sufficient staff had yet to be recruited and there were particular problems with IT and the lack of an adequate land registry. The Commission was also very worried by the fact that Poland had yet to establish proper procedures for the disposal of animal by-products and control of BSE and related diseases. Numerous meat and dairy plants would be barred from selling to the rest of the EU if they do not show drastic improvements. Border controls were not yet adequate in the seven sites selected for inspection posts. On rural development much remained to be done if Poland was to benefit from the measures available. Animal welfare requirements had yet to be met, including provisions on live animal transport. The EU has the sanction at its disposal of withholding or delaying CAP payments if Poland or any other country was thought not to have met the required standards at the time of accession.

The entry of the ten new Member States will have a profound effect on the balance of decision-making within the EU. The new Member States are likely to be preoccupied with obtaining their share of existing funds, rather than supporting further CAP reform, although they may see the benefits of a further emphasis on rural development measures. There have been particular concerns about the possibility of an alliance between France and Poland that would block further reform. That was why it was important to complete the 2003 reforms before accession occurred so as to create a momentum for further reform.

Reforming the CAP

The reform of the CAP is a highly complex political bargaining process. Leaving aside the various institutions involved, the CAP has to be reformed at two levels: the macro level of the policy as a whole and the micro level of the various commodity regimes. Each commodity regime generates its own particular pattern of politics. The major regimes, such as cereals and dairy, concern each of the Member States. In other cases, only one or two Member States may be interested in the particular regime. They may be able to push for particular solutions that are in their interest, but then these have to be integrated into the CAP as a whole.

There is thus a two-level system of bargaining. Agreements have to be reached in relation to the particular commodity regime that take into account such factors as structural surpluses, international trade agreements, and the concerns of particular Member States. These then have to be the subject of overall packages that may involve trade-offs between different national interests. They also have to take account of budgetary constraints and international trade considerations. These processes will be illustrated in relation to the example of rice later in the chapter.

As a stylised fact, it can be argued that the cereals reform was largely complete by the time of Agenda 2000. The 1992 MacSharry reforms were essentially a cereals reform and this process was continued under Agenda 2000 with minor commodities such as rye being dealt with in the 2003 reform. Forecasts of likely outcomes are susceptible to the world supply and demand balance in grain, to the 'world price' and to currency movements. In particular, 'The Euro/US dollar exchange rate is critical in determining the value of EU farm goods and therefore when and to what extent cereals, particularly wheat, can be exported without restitution' (OECD 2000: 35–36). Nevertheless, the EU is rapidly approaching a situation where its prices will be around world market levels, unsubsidized exporting can take place and intervention stocks can be eliminated (OECD 2000: 34). This is a not insignificant achievement in a major commodity sector, but it will have taken over ten years to achieve. Moreover, arable crops will still be indirectly subsidized through the area payments system. Meanwhile, many other commodity regimes, notably wine, olive oil and sugar, remain largely unreformed, although plans for the reform of olive oil and sugar were announced in 2003.

Commodity regimes

The next section of the chapter will consider the political economy of some largely unreformed commodity regimes. One major commodity regime (dairy) and one minor one (rice) have been selected. The dairy regime poses some of the most difficult unresolved problems for the EU in relation to the CAP. In a liberalised world market, most of the dairy farmers in Europe would be uncompetitive. Equally, some of them would be highly competitive. The solution might appear to be allowing the less competitive farmers to go out of business, leaving the rest to compete on world markets. However, the marginal dairy farmers are numerous; they are spread across most Member States, and they are well organized and militant. 'The widespread bankruptcy of European uncompetitive dairy farmers would result in large parts of European rural areas becoming very "empty"' (Baas, Potten, Wazir and Zwanenberg 1998: 43). Continuing to subsidise them may be the political line of least resistance.

The minor regimes are worth considering if only to illustrate the complexity of EU agricultural politics. This complexity is not entirely accidental. It erects high entry barriers to any outsider attempting to understand what is going on. Sectoral policy communities are able to arrive at their own mutually satisfactory deals with little public scrutiny or consideration of whether the wider public interest is being served.

The dairy sector

The newsletter, *Agra Europe*, a supporter of reform of the CAP, has declared that 'The dairy sector is a lost cause in terms of reform' (4 February 2000: A/2). A review of the main conclusions of Agenda 2000 in relation to the dairy sector shows why such a conclusion could easily be reached. The quota regime was renewed until 2006. A 15 per cent cut in intervention prices was adopted, but this would not start until 2005 and would be phased in through three annual 5 per cent steps. In the meantime, against a background of structural surplus, quota had been increased by 1.5 per cent in most Member States from the year 2000.

High levels of support for the dairy sector are not a phenomenon confined to the EU. Organisation for Economic Coordination and Development (OECD) data shows that around one-fifth of the total support to agricultural producers goes to the dairy sector. The measure of the total value of government support policies to the producer as a proportion of the value of output (the producer support equivalents, PSEs) for dairy were 58 per cent in 1998 compared to 37 per cent for all commodities. Although only about 7 per cent of dairy production is traded, dairy products account for around 29 per cent of all export subsidies (*Agra Europe* 24 September 1999: p. A/2).

Why should the dairy sector in particular attract such high levels of support? Because milk is a highly perishable product, it attracted early attention from governments seeking to stabilise supply and demand and protect farmers from a power imbalance with dairy companies. This propensity to intervene was reinforced by the perception that the dairy sector was a principal bastion of the 'family farmer' who was seen as the essence of a particular construction of the rural way of life. Once quotas and other forms of intervention had been put in place, it was difficult to remove them. A number of actors were able to extract rent from them, not just the dairy farmers themselves, but also quota traders and the bureaucrats whose purpose was to administer the quota schemes and other forms of intervention.

Although the dairy sector is extensively supported in North America as well as in Europe, there is a particular pressure for sustaining high levels of support in the EU. The EU is the major player in world dairy trade, but a high proportion of its dairy farms would be uncompetitive on a liberalised world market. Indeed, research by the International Farm Comparison Network (IFCN) suggests that even the best European Union dairy farms would have difficulty competing against the low-cost, grass-based systems of Oceania or even the largest and most efficient dairy units of the Western United States (*Agra Europe* 7 August 1998: A/1). The extent of the gap is shown by the IFCN's figures for production costs:

- approximately $50 per 100kg of milk for EU farms with around thirty cows;
- around $38 for EU farms with 60 to 75 cows;
- USA, Central Europe, Brazil and South Africa with costs of $25 to $30; and
- costs around $20 in Argentina, Uruguay, Australia and New Zealand.

Within the EU, variations in efficiency have a clear relationship with the politics of dairy policy. The 'London club' or 'gang of four' of Britain, Denmark, Italy and Sweden formed an informal alliance within the Council of Ministers to press for more effective reform of the dairy sector. For example, they advocated a 30 per cent cut in intervention prices, which is the level of reduction that would be required if the EU was to compete on world markets without export subsidies. Such a position is clearly in the interests of Britain as 'Dairy farms in the UK have a significant total cost advantage relative to the other EU countries, approximating to the cost level of the average of US farms ($32 to $38) (*Agra Europe* 7 August 1998: A/2). Denmark and Sweden also have highly commercial sectors. Italy has large-scale dairy farming in the Po Valley, although its support of dairy reform was partly due to the advocacy of the agriculture minister at the time and was also related to difficulties it had experienced in administering the quota regime. Italy's policy stance changed after the Berlusconi government came into office.

One would expect countries with large numbers of farmers producing milk at a greater cost than in Britain to be less enthusiastic about reform, and France, Germany and Ireland sought to maintain the status quo. 'Only 40–50% of German dairy farmers would be able to bear a 30% support price reduction, as proposed by the "Gang of Four" countries' (*Agra Europe* 27 November 1998: EP/11). Many of the less competitive dairy farmers are found in Bavaria, which has often been able to 'punch above its weight' in German domestic farm politics. Southern countries apart from Italy also tend to have fragmented farm sectors. For example, 'half the dairy farms in Spain are too small to be able to meet the requirements of the EU milk hygiene regulations' (*Agra Europe* 30 October 1998: N/1).

One might expect the dairy processing industry to be supportive of reform, given that it would not want the cost of its raw material to be forced up by inefficient producers or its ability to export constrained by trade agreements which place limits on the permissible level of subsidised exports. Indeed, its general stance is reformist. However, it has not been as great an influence in favour of reform as might have been hoped. Indeed, this has been a general problem with the food processing sector, in part a consequence of its product heterogeneity leading to very distinctive sets of interests in particular subsectors (Grant 1987). Indeed, Franz Fischler felt obliged to appeal directly to an audience largely made up of food company executives to exert more influence on CAP reform: 'I am somewhat surprised by the conspicuous absence of public comment by the EU's food industry and traders on the implications of Agenda 2000 or indeed on the implications of doing nothing' (Fischler 1998: 8).

From its side, the industry has questioned the purpose of Fischler's 'Round Table' discussions for food industry stake-holders. Some food industry members 'have claimed that the "stakeholder dialogue" is just little more than a public relations exercise, and that the Commission will take little account of it when it comes to table its reform proposals' (*Agra Europe*, 23 November 2001: EP/5).

The process of consolidation and rationalisation, which is in progress in the dairy sector, may enable it to exert greater political influence than in the past, less restrained by an identification with the dairy farmer, which was certainly a factor in the significant portion of the industry based on agricultural cooperatives. As they have gone through a process of merger and expansion, the large dairy cooperatives are now indistinguishable from any other commercial enterprise. In Britain, deregulation and reorganisation of the dairy processing sector has produced significant tensions between farmers and processors as prices have been driven down, reflected in a series of 'direct actions' that have blockaded processing plants.

The prospect of the admission of CEECs to the EU provided an imperative for renewed attempts to reform the dairy sector. The dairy farming sector in these countries has experienced a decrease in cow numbers, but a significant increase in yields. Milk production is expected to increase in the period up to 2006 with half of this increase occurring in Poland as household farming gives way to more commercial forms of agriculture. 'The price received for milk by Polish farmers is currently about half the EU average; application of the EU pricing system would be a major stimulus to increased production' (*Agra Europe* 19 November 1999: A/1). The real problem is thus Poland. Hungary produces milk on large-scale farms, has yields not far below the EU average and has traditionally been a dairy exporter. In Poland, however, a network of peasant smallholdings survived through the Communist era. 'At least a quarter of Poland's milk is produced by about 1 million individual farms, holding only 1 to 3 cows, while 50% of the milk is produced by farms in the 3 to 9 cow category' (*Agra Europe* 19 November 1999: A/1) The large numbers of very small dairy farmers may prove more difficult to deal with than Warsaw currently envisages and there is little doubt that the larger and enlarging producers will undoubtedly be producing more (*Agra Europe* 25 February 2000: A/2).

The way out of these problems might appear to be through the imposition of milk quotas very close to current production levels. In other words, accession countries and farms within them are not to be permitted to produce much more milk than they were in the early years of the first decade of the twenty-first century. The application and administration of the quota system may, however, be difficult given the large numbers of very small dairy farmers and inadequacies in the administrative infrastructure. The real solution is to bring about an effective reform of the dairy regime.

Franz Fischler indicated that he saw the mid-term review as a window of opportunity for re-opening the debate on dairy reform. It became increasingly apparent that the dairy sector took the biggest hit from the 2003 reforms, even though taxpayers can expect to be paying more than €3 billion in dairy aid payments by 2007, a figure that will increase as enlargement kicks in. The dairy payments will be paid to farmers in accession states in accordance with the Copenhagen phasing-in formula. The dairy quota regime, which has contributed to the ossification of the sector, will be maintained until 2015. However, butter intervention prices are to be reduced from 2004 by 25 per cent over five years (10 per cent more than agreed under Agenda 2000) and there will be new butter intervention purchase ceilings. Although the impact on farmers will be highly variable, a median forecast would be that returns to dairy producers will have fallen by 20 per cent by 2007 and that only 60 per cent of this price cut will be compensated for by direct aid payments. Throughout Europe one can expect an accelerated rate of exit from the dairy sector which is an important activity in some remote and less prosperous rural regions.

Minor commodity regimes: the case of rice

Systematic scrutiny of what is happening in a CAP commodity regime decreases in proportion to its size. Some of the smaller commodity regimes are of interest principally to one or two Member States. Nevertheless, the policy networks defending them are highly protective. As Daugbjerg notes (1999: 414): 'Members of cohesive networks are powerful because they control the expertise within their policy field and when outsiders threaten their control over the field, the consensus on policy principles enables them to meet reformers with forceful counter arguments. These are often of a highly technical nature.'

The Luxembourg Compromise has not been abandoned in the Agriculture Council.'The existence of the veto opportunity is a major obstacle to fundamental policy reform' (Daugbjerg 1999: 421). Of course, no one would be allowed to exercise a veto in relation to a minor commodity regime which could hardly be claimed to be a matter of vital national interest. However, the preference within the Agriculture Council is to reach a consensus by bargaining without overriding the strongly expressed preferences of a particular national state. This is reinforced in the case of minor regimes by a desire not to allow disagreements on such matters to block the resolution of more important issues. Hence, the tendency is for the Member State(s) concerned with the issue to make some concessions that lead to incremental and moderate policy changes (Daugbjerg 1999: 414).

The politics of some of the minor commodity regimes is complicated by the fact that they embody North-South conflicts with Northern states wanting market oriented reforms and the Southern states wanting to maintain existing supports as far as possible, particularly in advance of Eastern enlargement. The 'club Mediterranean' countries, which include France, consider that the balance of support is weighted too far in favour of the 'Northern' products which formed part of the original CAP when it was first established. Rice is a classic example, as some 60 per cent of EU output comes from Italy, followed by Spain with 17 per cent, the other principal producers being France, Greece and Portugal.

Intervention stockpiles have been run down and largely eliminated in the major commodity regimes, but in April 2000 there were half a million tonnes of rice in EU intervention stores, much of it in danger of rotting. This amount represents 20 per cent of EU annual production. Too many producers are growing simply to sell into intervention (at the price paid by the EU for rice which then is put into store), with 140,000 tonnes of rice being offered on the first day of the intervention season (*Agra Europe* 7 April 2000: EP/7). Because of trade reforms, imports from India and Pakistan are increasing.

A reform package was supposed to have been produced in the autumn of 1999, but has been repeatedly delayed. There were internal divisions within the Commission over the issue which in turn reflected anticipated difficulties when it was brought to the Council. The reform package eventually put forward by the Commission in June 2000 effectively proposed to integrate rice into the general arable model by replacing intervention buying by a partially decoupled area payments system. There would also be set aside requirements. The proposed changes would have brought savings of €38 million a year on spending of €200–250 million.

The proposals led to demonstrations by rice farmers in Italy. The then Italian minister of agriculture claimed that the proposed cuts in the surface area of paddy fields would place 100,000 birds at risk. Divisions opened up in the Council between producer and non-producer countries. Pro-reform countries like Britain were unwilling to press Italy on the rice issue because of concerns that it might risk Italian support on more vital issues such as dairy reform. Because of the low profile of the sector, there was little public or media pressure for reform. By the summer of 2001 the Commission was forced to admit that the abolition of intervention in rice was so controversial that it might not be able to proceed with the proposals. The best way forward appeared to be to 'bundle' rice reform with a series of other issues as part of the 2002 mid-term review. This might make it easier to negotiate a reform as part of an overall package. Where one country has a strong interest in a particular sector, reform becomes difficult to achieve.

A complex compromise had to be arrived at in the 2003 reforms to placate Italy which nevertheless brings rice into a model similar to that for other arable crops. There will be annual ceiling on intervention purchases of rice and the intervention price is to be cut. In compensation, direct aid is more than doubled, but half of it will be decoupled from production.

The European 'model of agriculture' and multifunctionality

While what happens in particular commodity regimes is important, the CAP also has to be seen as a whole. The way in which paradigms of a policy are constructed and presented to the outside world can both reflect the preferences inherent in the policy community and also shape those preferences. A so-called 'European Model of Agriculture' which provided the basis for the subsequent discussion about multifunctionality emerged in the context of the Agenda 2000 discussions in the autumn of 1997. This suggested that agriculture provided a number of public goods apart from the provision of food. 'However, the concept of multifunctionality remains vague, which can be helpful, especially in negotiations. Very few contest that agriculture is not only about producing food, and that it has other functions, including non-trade objectives' (Landau 2001: 916).

Indeed, the concept was adopted by the so-called 'Friends of Multifunctionality', which included Japan and European countries outside the EU with high subsidy levels. The European model of agriculture seems to have been first mentioned in the context of the Council discussions on Agenda 2000 in October 1997. It may well have been devised by the European farmers' organization Comité des Organisations Professionnelles Agricoles (COPA). The secretary general of COPA, Risto Volannen, criticised the Agenda 2000 package 'because it failed to defend the "European model of agriculture"'. It is interesting that at this early stage Volanen linked the model with the concept of multifunctionality. He stated that the model meant ensuring 'that farmers' incomes kept pace with the rest of society and emphasizing the "multifunctional" role of farming by recognising how agriculture preserved the rural landscape and maintained employment in the countryside' (*Agra Europe* 10 October 1997: E/5).

Certainly COPA missed no opportunities to push the advantages of the model. After a head to head debate at a conference in Brussels in April 1998 with New Zealand's then international trade and agriculture minister, Dr Lockwood Smith, Volanen returned to his office and brought back two slides which he showed at the end of the day's proceedings. One was of an industrial style feedlot enterprise for cattle on semi-arid land with a cluster of tall concrete silos in the middle (it was supposedly located in Colorado). The other slide, which was stated to display the European Model of Agriculture, showed a small group of contented cows grazing on verdant grass in front of a lake beyond which could be seen clustered the traditional farm buildings of the 'family farmer'.

Whatever the origins of the model, it was rapidly taken up by the agriculture Directorate-General. It became 'a mainstay of DG-AGRI [Directorate General for Agriculture] thinking on the philosophy of agriculture policy, a prominent feature of several keynote speeches by Fischler in 1998, and revered totem of the traditionalist majority in the Council of Ministers' (*Agra Europe* 8 January 1999: A/1). Elsewhere in the Commission, not least by the then trade commissioner Sir Leon Brittan, the European Model was treated with dismissive scorn. He told the Oxford Farming Conference: 'Some people still advocate a type of "European agricultural model" which would involve a retreat behind high tariff walls, closing our farming industry off from growing world markets and leaving only an internal market. This is not the "European model" I would want to defend or create' (*Agra Europe* 8 January 1999: A/1).

Nevertheless, as far as the Agenda 2000 proposals published in March 1998 were concerned, the model had 'become a totem and a policy concept in its own right, to be respected whenever the policy is under internal or external attack'. The Agenda 2000 proposals were described as being 'designed to ensure that the European Model of Agriculture [by then referred to in capitals and without inverted commas] can be sustained for the long term' (*Agra Europe* 20 March 1998: A/1).

The definition offered of the European Model by Franz Fischler reflected the contradictory mix of objectives at the heart of the Agenda 2000 process:

> [A] competitive agriculture able to compete on world markets; an agriculture whose methods of production are safe, respectful of the environment and able to supply products with a quality that matches the expectations of our consumers; an agriculture whose richness lies in its diversity and whose mission is not only to produce but also to maintain the diversity of our countryside and an active living rural community. (*Agra Europe* 13 March 1998: A/3)

Such a definition could encompass a wide range of policy possibilities and it may be that a search for more precision was one of the motives for a shift towards an emphasis on multifunctionality. 'Multifunctionality' was also not geographically limited in the way that the European Model of Agriculture was. It was also a way of answering the objection made by the UK Agricultural Advisory Group that 'there is not, nor can there be, a single model of agriculture in Europe' (*Agra Europe* 29 January 1999: E/10). Multifunctionality could encompass a range of different models, providing that each of them served a purpose other than producing food. It has been presented by Fischler as a means of tackling 'new age' issues such as the effect of globalisation on the environment, health, social standards and cultural diversity.

In practice, however, 'multifunctionality' has proved no easier to define or defend than the European model. As the Seattle WTO talks on trade approached, the Finnish presidency of the EU issued a paper pointing to the need for a definition in order to provide a clearer idea of what was being defended. 'We are faced with the need to transform the concept of multifunctionality into operational demands and offers that can be handled in the negotiations' (*Agra Europe* 20 August 1999: EP/4). By March 2000 the EU was still struggling with a definition of the concept. It stated that 'it looked forward to "elaborating the precise nature of the [multifunctional] role, covering as it does in particular the environment, rural development, food safety, food security and animal welfare and the instruments necessary for safeguarding it"' (*Agra Europe* 24 March 2000: EP/4).

One hope was that it might in some way be possible to link the concept of multifunctionality with that of sustainable agriculture and in that way win support from the Food and Agriculture Organisation (FAO). However, this idea received short shrift at a conference on the multifunctional character of agriculture and land organised by the Dutch Government and the FAO in September 1999. Leading participants were anxious to separate discussions on sustainable agriculture from trade related discussions. The view was taken that the multifunctional character of agriculture and land was concerned with the substance of agriculture and related land use with multifunctionality being concerned specifically with the effects of policies on trade.

The EU was not able to get the concept of multifunctionality inserted into the draft text on agriculture at the Seattle WTO talks. It had to accept that 'so loose a justification for protection would prevent any progress being made in the further reduction of import barriers, export subsidies and domestic support' (*Agra Europe* 3 December 1999: A/2). The EU was satisfied with an acceptance that Article 20 of the 1994 Uruguay Round Agreement should form a basis for negotiation. This was seen as a means of achieving multifunctionality without the label. The draft text stated, 'the negotiations shall take into account non-trade concerns. These include, in particular, the need to protect the environment, food safety, the economic viability and development of rural areas and the safety of agricultural products' (*Agra Europe* 3 December 1999: A/2). The unadopted draft text has no legal status, but it does suggest that the EU may be able to achieve some progress with the notion of multifunctionality.

By March 2000, as a new round of discussions on agriculture got under way at the WTO, the EU was still searching for a definition of multifunctionality. Of course, in many ways, a certain vagueness is helpful as it makes it easier to move the goalposts. At some point, however, just as was the case with the precautionary principle, the EU is going to have to spell out what it is talking about. The central claim that has been advanced by Franz Fischler is that 'Agriculture is different. European agriculture provides public goods such as preservation of environment and biodiversity' (*Agra Europe* 13 October 2000: A/1). The underlying issue is the need to preserve the 'blue box', which protects key subsidies from challenge under international trade rules. The EU is 'seriously vulnerable to substantial support reduction in the area where it has the greatest political problems: in the dairy and beef sectors where the "small farm" problem is concentrated. It is for this reason that it is putting so much of its negotiating effort into the multifunctionality issue' (*Agra Europe* 17 August 2001: A/2). The 'small farm' problem is of considerable importance for a number of the accession countries, such as Poland.

New Zealand has argued that many of the objectives of multifunctionality can be achieved without subsidy. The country's agricultural trade envoy Malcolm Bailey argued: 'Proponents of this concept argue that farm subsidies have to be paid to keep the countryside looking good, to keep people in rural areas . . . But without any production subsidies in New Zealand, we are achieving very positive results with regard to this list of desirable outcomes' (*Farmers Weekly* 17 March 2000).

There is, however, a considerable difference between agriculture in New Zealand and Europe. In European countries, farming over the centuries has built up a landscape that is valued by urban dwellers. Hill farming landscapes, for example, would change dramatically if farming ceased. Payments to preserve landscape value need not have a distorting effect on international trade.

Agricultural economists are inclined to be sceptical about the significance of the debate about the European model and multifunctionality, seeing it as a piece of defensive ideology which, at most, may not serve farmers well by distracting them from the need to adjust to changing economic and political realities. A political scientist would argue that such paradigms, however ill thought out they might appear to be, can help to construct issues in a way that has a significant effect on which policy options are considered acceptable. For example, the European Model helped to perpetuate the COPA myth that it is only the Commission and a few academics who are in favour of reform. Moreover, as Josling and Tangermann warn (1999: 383), 'the Commission is in danger of raising European farmers' expectations that the multifunctionality card can be played to gain more border protection'.

Progress on reform?

Defenders of the Commission would argue that the CAP was put on a new path by the MacSharry reforms in 1992 which reached its latest stage in the reforms agreed in 2003. It is the case that with farmers now to be to funded through a single farm payment, which is likely to be fully decoupled in many Member States, there is no longer any incentive to over produce in order to claim subsidies. Rural development spending has also been increased. However, the so-called 'Second Pillar' of the CAP remains weak and we are a long way from a comprehensive rural development policy. This would pay particular attention to the needs of remote rural areas, including those in Eastern Europe, that often suffer from a series of problems including less competitive agriculture and deficient services. A comprehensive rural package would still include some support for agriculture, but it would emphasise environmental and landscape considerations. In particular, it would ensure that the rich biodiversity of flora and fauna present in many accession states would be maintained for future generations.

If reforming the CAP was simply a matter of winning the debate, significant change would have been achieved long ago. It should be remembered that nearly half of the EU budget is still spent on agriculture which is not how most people would want to see the budget constructed. European agriculture still operates behind high tariff walls, and benefits from substantial export subsidies (although the EU has now made an offer to phase these out in the Doha Round), both of which harm third world countries reliant on agricultural exports. The political realities are well known. The benefits of the CAP are concentrated on a relatively small group (farmers, particularly large-scale ones) and the costs are more diffuse (taxpayers, consumers). It is in the interest of farmers, or at least their organisations, to keep a constant watching brief on the CAP. Public interest is more sporadic and focused on issues such as genetic modification. It certainly does not reach the less well-known commodity regimes. The policy networks are well insulated from external criticism and are adept at making enough adjustments to buy off criticism without significantly reducing the opportunities for their participants to extract rent. Even when exogenous shocks occur, 'the cohesiveness of the agricultural policy network [can help] the EC to resist the most radical changes in policy' (Coleman and Tangermann 1999: 402).

The current situation does not mean that we can anticipate nothing more than incremental reform at a speed determined by the Member State most resistant to a particular change. Pressures from the need to adjust to Eastern enlargement are likely to increase as subsidies are increased to their full level. At the end of 2003 the 'peace clause' (Article 13) in the Uruguay Round agreement which protects CAP policies (or, more strictly speaking, those in conformity with the provisions of the Agreement on Agriculture) from challenge through the WTO dispute settlement mechanism expires.

Europe may gradually evolve towards a two-tier agriculture. Its most competitive agriculture will compete on world markets with residual support payments set at world prices and with export subsidies effectively eliminated. More marginal agriculture whose maintenance is seen as essential to pursue social objectives such as preventing rural depopulation and maintaining cherished landscapes will receive decoupled support linked to environmental objectives among others. Accession countries such as Poland could benefit from such an approach, although deficiencies in administrative infrastructure may frustrate the effective implementation of a rural policy.

The effects of enlargement

Estimating the effects of enlargement both on the EU-15 and accession countries is complicated by uncertainties such as trends in world market price, the dollar–euro exchange rate and productivity trends in the CEECs after accession. Leaving aside Slovenia 'where average productivity is close to 68% of the EU average, gross agricultural production per hectare is in value terms only between 8.5% and 35% of the EU-15 level' (*Agra Europe* 9 November 2001: A/1). Given under-capitalisation and a surplus of largely unskilled labour, the much feared spurt in production may not occur. There was no major productivity acceleration in Mediterranean countries after Southern enlargement. The countries with the greatest production potential have the most serious structural problems (European Commission 2001). 'Lower quality and food health and animal welfare standards are likely to remain important barriers to increases in agricultural and food exports from the CEEC countries to the EU-15' (*Agra Europe* 6 July 2001: A/1).

Enlargement may have a greater impact on agriculture in the accession countries than in the EU-15. Small subsistence farms remain important in Poland and Romania and the achievement of only half of current productivity levels of the EU-15 would drive four million people off the land (Pouliquen 2001). These threats are of increasing importance in Polish domestic politics, with one farm party becoming a coalition partner after the general election of autumn 2001 and a more radical rural party attacking government policy from the sidelines. Given transition arrangements, the impact of enlargement on the CAP in the EU-15 may be much less than has often been claimed. More important drivers for reform are likely to be the Doha trade round, despite the failure at Cancún and the 'green agenda' of less intensive, more environmentally friendly farming which may offer opportunites for accession countries. In general, however, membership may lead to difficult social problems in many rural areas in the accession countries.

Jette Steen Knudsen

5

Breaking with tradition: liberalisation of services trade in Europe[1]

> Whereas the Customs Union was achieved by mid-1968 and regulatory barriers were at least addressed subsequently, little to nothing was accomplished in services until the early or mid-1980s. From an economic point of view this was a curious form of neglect. (Pelkmans 2001: 118)

Introduction

Traditionally domestic service sector regulations have been exempted from international oversight. There are numerous reasons why services have not been part of international trade regimes: most traditional services had to be produced in the country where they were consumed; many service sectors are large-scale employers and hence employees have substantial political clout; services trade often requires establishment in the 'importing' country which is costly; barriers to services trade are frequently part of domestic institutions which are difficult to change; and, finally, many services have provided an employment shield against economic fluctuations.

What has now changed is that many services – telecoms for example – are increasingly perceived as exportable, and thus they are becoming important in international trade negotiations. Although services make up less than 25 per cent of the volume of international trade, their growth rate is twice that of trade in manufactured goods (Paemen and Bensch 1995). In Europe the economic significance of the Single European Act is to be found especially in services (Pelkmans 2001). Services have changed in at least five ways. First, a German businessman who wishes to send mail for advertising purposes within Germany now has more options than just using the incumbent provider. Private postal operators pick up the mail in Germany and drive it to the Netherlands in order to take advantage of the cheaper Dutch postal rates. The mail is then returned to Germany and distributed there by the incumbent postal administration. Thus, postal services no longer have to be produced in Germany even though they are consumed there.

Second, although many service sectors continue to be large employers, their traditional political clout has been reduced. Telecoms services have become increasingly diversified, branching into multimedia services, mobile services, internet services, and so on. As a result, the political interests of employees in telecoms have also diversified. In Deutsche Telekom many employees still see the traditional union for post and telecoms workers Deutsche Postgewerkschaft (DPG) as representing their interests. By contrast employees in new multimedia and internet firms frequently see themselves as having more in common with media people or designers and hence prefer to join other unions such as IG Medien. Furthermore, many employees in these new services are not interested in trade Union membership because they see unions as having an inflexible view of working time, salary, job protection, etc.

Third, with the adoption of the principle of the single licence and home country rule, establishment abroad has become easier and less costly. For example, in insurance services, the principle of a single licence has been adopted throughout the EU in both business and personal insurance services. This means that non-German insurers who have already obtained a licence to sell insurance in another EU Member State are also allowed to sell personal insurance in Germany.[2] Fourth, although many service sectors traditionally have been part of an intricate domestic institutional set-up, these institutional structures have now been changed. Today foreign telecoms providers – German as well as non-German – are allowed to offer services in Germany. Finally, the German telecoms monopoly was previously used as an employment shield against economic fluctuations. During economic recessions, investment in telecoms infrastructure was typically increased and directed to German regions, which were particularly hard hit (Noam 1992). Today in contrast Deutsche Telekom is a private enterprise and operates on regular market terms and therefore is neither required to nor interested in safeguarding employment as a social goal.

Germany's support for liberalisation of services is especially surprising because traditionally that country has been a 'service desert' (Dienstleistungswüste) where high quality services were as rare as water in the desert. Services constitute a lower share of employment in Germany compared to most EU countries and in particular the United Kingdom (UK). In the 1985–89 period service employment (excluding public administration, education, health and social and personal services) was 29 per cent in Germany and 41 per cent in the UK (Iversen and Wren 1998: table 2). Germany's trade balance in services has been consistently negative. From 1976 to 2001 every single year Germany's trade balance in services was negative while during the same period the UK consistently enjoyed a positive trade balance (International Monetary Fund 1995: 388–389 and 774–775; International Monetary Fund 2002: 372–373 and 870–871). Today, however, Germany welcomes competition in previously closed sectors such as telecoms, insurance and to some extent the postal services.

This chapter asks the question why and how services that were not previously thought of as tradable have increasingly been opened up to international competition in EU Member States including in Germany? Next, this chapter addresses the question how lessons from Germany and the EU may apply to services reform in an enlarged European Union? The focus in this chapter is largely on Germany. Germany is particularly interesting because Germany traditionally has been very reluctant to liberalise its services. A focus on national level policy-making processes such as in Germany adds important insights into understanding the difficult processes of reform as service sector liberalisation has for so long concerned national governments and not the EU. The chapter is divided into three sections. The first briefly presents two theoretical perspectives on services trade liberalisation: an interest-based perspective and an EU-based perspective. Section two traces the adoption of reforms of the German telecoms, insurance and postal sectors and presents arguments about how and why reforms came about. Finally, section three explores how lessons from Germany and the EU concerning service sector liberalisation might apply to the new Member States.

Theoretical perspectives on services trade liberalisation

In order to explore potential implications of enlargement for services trade reform in Europe this chapter first explores how and why services trade liberalisation has taken place in a reluctant EU Member State such as Germany. The section starts out by contrasting two theoretical perspectives. The purpose is not to prove one theory entirely correct or entirely dismiss it but to assess the relative importance of economic interests and EU membership.[3]

Interest-based explanations

Interest-based explanations stress primarily the political pressure through legislatures from domestic social groups such as producer and labour groups (Alt and Gilligan 1994; Olson 1965; McKeown 1984). These explanations mainly view economic policies as a response to coalitions, which represent distinctive economic sectors and which form and reform in response to changes in the international economy that shift the underlying interests of their members (Hall and Soskice 2001).

Frieden for example assesses distributional effects of increased capital mobility and determines the impact of these distributional effects on lobbying for policy (Frieden 1991). Factors such as geographical location, human resources and skills, and so on are important characteristics that determine the ease with which factors of production can be re-deployed. The effects of trade liberalisation depend on the specificity of the relevant actors' characteristics and their degree of international competitiveness (Frieden and Rogowski 1996). If a sector tends to be internationally competitive, producers and labour will favour free trade. Likewise, they will prefer protection if it is not. The interests of export and import sectors are therefore diametrically opposed. The focus of the chapter is on specifying the economic preferences of societal actors, in particular the preferences of economic sectors. In addition, this chapter hypothesises that since trade – according to standard liberal economic theory – is expected to reduce the costs of traded products, consumers will favour liberalisation of services that might be internationally traded. The following hypothesis follows from an interest-based model: sectoral liberalisation reflects pressure for reform from a sector that is likely to be internationally competitive as well as pressure from users of such services.

Strengths and weaknesses of interest-based theories
The strength of interest-based theories is their ability to specify how policies change. These theories can account for how changes in the constellation of preferences shape changes in public policy. Interest-based theories also recognise the importance of political processes for the adoption of economic policies (Frieden and Rogowski 1996: 42). The case studies presented below illustrate that liberalisation has taken place even in services where both users and providers were opposed to reform. One example is liberalisation of trade in personal insurance services. Another example is liberalisation of basic telecoms services.

In order to explain liberalisation it is therefore necessary to account for how opposition to reform was overcome. A more fine-grained analysis of the impact of public institutions and political processes on policy outcomes is required. Legislation to liberalise services trade is not just adopted in Member States such as Germany but also in the EU more generally and lately also within the context of the World Trade Organisation (WTO). Therefore the relative impact of domestic political factors as well as the impact of the EU first needs to be clarified. The next section addresses the impact of EU level pressure relative to Member State pressure for reform.

The impact of EU membership
How has Germany's liberalisation of telecoms, insurance and postal services been shaped by EU membership? Was liberalisation mainly a result of the Commission's promotion of services reform as guardian of the Treaty of Rome? Or was reform largely due to pressure from the European Court of Justice (ECJ) to push open borders in services by issuing rulings to this effect? Such questions feature in the debate between state-centric theorists (liberal intergovernmentalists) and those who focus on political actors other than the state, such as EU institutions or even regional actors (multi-level governance theorists). This debate is well known and therefore only briefly presented below.[4]

Moravcsik proposes that European integration can best be explained with a 'liberal intergovernmentalist' framework. At the core of liberal intergovernmentalism are an assumption of rational state behaviour, a liberal theory of national preference formation and an intergovernmentalist analysis of inter-state negotiation. Moravcsik's central claim is that 'the broad lines of European integration since 1955 reflect three broad factors: patterns of commercial advantage, the relative bargaining power of important governments, and the incentives to enhance the credibility of interstate commitments' (Moravcsik 1998: 3).[5] The following hypothesis follows from the state-centric perspective: decisions to liberalise services in the EU reflect the relative bargaining power of important governments in pursuit of commercial interests. It is unlikely that services would be liberalised against the wishes of the German government unless the German government is able to secure other desirable bargaining outcomes in return.

THE MULTI-LEVEL GOVERNANCE PERSPECTIVE

According to the multi-level governance perspective, the state no longer monopolises European-level policy-making. According to Marks, Hooghe and Blank (1996) decision-making is shared by actors at different levels rather than monopolised by state executives. In addition, collective decision-making involves a significant loss of control for individual state executives. Finally, political arenas are inter-connected rather than nested. The following hypothesis follows from the multi-level governance perspective: EU institutions play a key role in defining the nature and scope of EU governance. If EU-level actors and rules shape EU legislation and subsequently legislation in EU Member States, then legislation should reflect pressure from the European Commission and the ECJ.

Evidence

Telecoms

Referring to telecoms, Morgan and Webber (1986: 56) argued that 'with the exception of defence and agriculture, no other sector has been so politicised and so protected'. In their view the telecoms regime in Germany (the legal and institutional framework within which telecoms policy is formulated and implemented) was 'an island of stability' (Morgan and Webber 1986: 56).

However, since 1986 Germany's telecoms sector has undergone a major transformation (Schmidt 1991; Werle 1999). In 1988 terminal equipment was liberalised and in 1990 value-added services were opened up to international competition. In particular, the 1996 Telecoms Act created the framework for today's open borders, introducing competition in all telecoms services including basic services and removing the public monopoly of the cable-based telecoms network.

AN INTEREST-BASED EXPLANATION

Can telecom reforms best be explained as a result of pressure exerted by an internationally competitive sector as well as by users in favour of liberalisation? In the 1980s German producers of telecoms equipment and the monopoly service provider as well as some users voiced strong opposition to telecoms reform.[6] Producers of computer equipment favoured reform but they were not well organised within the industry associations and did not constitute a strong voice in favour of reform. Furthermore, telecoms equipment producers and computer equipment producers were members of the same industry associations. Given the divergent interests of computer equipment producers and telecoms equipment producers concerning trade liberalisation, the industry associations could not organise strong support for reform.

In addition to opposition from telecoms equipment producers, users of postal services – including newspaper deliveries, publishing houses and mail order firms – also opposed reform. The reason was that these firms traditionally benefited from cross-subsidisation of letter services by telephony (Morgan and Webber 1986; Grande 1989). The financial sector was interested in faster data transfer and favoured reform but the opposition from newspaper deliveries, publishing houses, and so on muted their support.

The union for post and telecoms workers DPG feared that a separation of the postal and telecoms branches of the post office would lead to a massive rationalisation of the loss-making postal division and result in a decline in employment and working conditions (Morgan and Webber 1986). The incumbent operator enjoyed monopoly rents and did not want to give up this special status (Vogel 1996). Furthermore, in 1989, firms such as Mannesmann, which later successfully diversified into telecoms, did not lobby for reform.

In sum, opposition to reform was so significant that pressure from users and providers in favour of liberalisation was not strong enough to bring about reform in Germany. Thus, an interest-based explanation cannot account very well for telecoms liberalisation.

THE IMPACT OF EU MEMBERSHIP

The European Commission released directives to open up the terminal equipment market in 1988 and the value-added services market in 1990 based on Article 86.3 (ex Article 90.3) of the Treaty of Rome. This article allows the Commission to issue directives without the cooperation of other bodies such as the Council of Ministers or the European Parliament. Specifically, the Commission can establish competition in areas where it is found that monopolies are not operating in the public interest.

Concerning value-added services, the Commission struck a compromise with the Council of Ministers and issued its services directive (Commission Directive 90/388/EEC) with a Council directive on open network provision (Council Directive 90/387/EEC). This way a compromise was reached between the Council and the Commission. However, the Commission's use of

Article 86.3 (ex Article 90.3) is rare. Domestic political sensitivity is a chief constraint on the Commission's ability to pursue reform (Schmidt 1998).

Turning to the impact of the ECJ on telecoms reform we find that the founding treaties of the EU do not contain an explicit mandate for undertaking common policies in telecoms. However, the ECJ in a March 1985 ruling confirmed that the European Community competition rules applied also to telecoms. Furthermore, the ECJ in March 1991 upheld the Commission's right to liberalise equipment based on Article 86.3 (ex Article 90.3) vis-à-vis the Member States and in 1992 upheld the 1990 Commission service directive. In general, the ECJ refrains from adopting rulings that would be politically unpopular (Scharpf 1997). Key political actors in favour of reform in Germany including the government and the Economics Ministry (Baggehufvudt 1993) welcomed the ECJ decision to apply competition rules to the telecoms sector. Political pressure from the EU did not force reform down the throat of a reluctant Germany.

The multi-level governance perspective emphasises the sharing of power between Member States and other actors such as EU institutions and also stresses loss of Member State autonomy. While EU institutions were not unimportant for the adoption of services liberalisation, reform depended very much on government support as predicted by liberal intergovernmentalism.

A BREAK IN GOVERNMENT OPPOSITION TO REFORM

Traditionally, the Christian Democrats (CDU/CSU) had been cautious of liberalisation measures that could result in further unemployment in the post office and the equipment manufacturing industry. In addition the CDU/CSU feared that a more cost-oriented structure of changes could lead to increased rates for local calls, whose price covered only about 50 per cent of the costs. These price increases would be unpopular with voters. Party strongholds also included the countryside and sparsely populated regions in Germany. The CDU/CSU therefore worried that liberalisation could end the principle of uniform services at affordable cost, possibly resulting in higher charges and a deterioration of services in rural areas. Finally, the CDU/CSU has traditionally been the party for civil servants. Since traditionally postal employees were civil servants who enjoyed good working conditions these employees did not favour reform.

Reform discussions had begun in the late 1970s (Grande 1989). These discussions gained momentum with the coming to power of the conservative coalition government in 1982. The government favoured telecoms reform and appointed a dedicated supporter of telecoms reform, Dr Schwarz-Schilling of the CDU/CSU, as the minister for post and telecoms. The belief was that deregulation was required in order to fully utilise the growth potential in information and communications technologies.

The election of 6 March 1983 was a victory for the coalition government between the Christian Democrats and the Liberals (CDU/CSU-FDP). According to the government statement of 4 May 1983, the government intended to present an extensive program to strengthen the development of microelectronics and information and communications services (Grande 1989: 207). The goal was to improve the framework conditions for production of German information technology.

Schwarz-Schilling set up a government commission for telecoms in 1985, chaired by Dr Witte. The report's recommendations were closely in line with the recommendations in the European Commission's 1987 Green Paper on telecoms. The European Commission and the Witte Committee in fact worked closely together (Government Commission for Telecoms 1988; interview, Dr Witte, 27 March 1998). The Witte Committee's recommendations were somewhat modest, suggesting only liberalisation of value-added services and telecoms equipment while arguing that a monopoly for basic services and the network should be maintained. Nonetheless, the Social Democratic Party (SPD) and DPG members of the Witte Committee issued separate statements denouncing the Witte report as too liberal.

Only a few years after the government had promised that only value-added services would be opened up to competition while basic services and the network would remain a public monopoly, the government promoted privatisation of the incumbent telecoms operator and complete liberalisation of basic services and the network. The government's proposal was supported by Social Democrats, who adamantly opposed such reforms in the past. How was domestic opposition to reform broken?

The government came to support privatisation of Bundespost Telekom because with unification the government needed to finance costly infrastructure developments in the former East Germany. Privatisation would enable Deutsche Telekom to raise much needed capital. The government also came to support liberalisation of basic telephone services and the network. Liberalisation of value-added services had resulted in the development of a range of new services and the government expected liberalisation of basic services to result in a massive growth of new and improved services. Deutsche Telekom gradually came to support this position. The organisational separation of telecoms services from postal services had begun to result in a more market-oriented outlook. The sheer size of Deutsche Telekom in combination with its fairly high-level technical skills and services meant that Deutsche Telekom gradually came to favour an international strategy and hence to support international liberalisation.

In order to win the support of consumers, the government argued that international trade in telecoms services could be combined with sheltering of German consumers. In particular, the government argued that universal service provisioning at affordable cost could be guaranteed by adopting domestic regulation to protect consumers (*Süddeutsche Zeitung*, 23 March 1992).

In the end the Social Democrats agreed to fully liberalise the telecoms sector. The Social Democrats felt 'morally' justified in agreeing to liberalise telecoms because of the adoption of early retirement plans for postal and telecoms employees, the promise not to lay-off employees, the creation of generous pension schemes, and other provisions (interview, Mr Börnsen, 7 April 1998; interview, Mr Cloes, 20 November 1997; interview, Dr Witte, 27 March 1998).

Insurance reform

Since the 1980s Germany's regulatory framework for insurance has changed substantially. Previously, insurance prices and conditions were extensively controlled, but today the German government favours liberalisation of insurance services and has implemented a new legal framework based on the principle of home state rule in non-life business insurance. Surprisingly, the German government has even liberalised personal insurance, which has traditionally been extensively regulated in Germany. Why has the German government agreed to open up its traditionally protected insurance sector, including even personal insurance, to competition within the EU and how has liberalisation of insurance services come about?

AN INTEREST-BASED EXPLANATION

While liberalisation of business insurance can be partly accounted for by an interest-based explanation, this is not the case for liberalisation of the personal insurance market. Concerning providers, in the 1980s the Association of German Insurers (Gesamtverband der Deutschen Versicherungswirtschaft, or GDV) argued in favour of liberalisation of business insurance (GDV, Annual Report 1983; interview GDV, 20 May 1998). A main reason for the GDV's support was that demand for business insurance was changing. Large international manufacturing firms increasingly demanded that insurance firms provide for all their risks abroad (Boissier 1986). Large insurance firms expected that the implementation of the single European market would lead to an increase in the international operations of large firms and hence increase demand for large-scale insurance services.

By contrast German insurance providers strongly opposed opening up Germany's personal insurance market to foreign competition. They argued that liberalisation would end transparency and hence erode consumer protection (*Lloyds List*, 27 August 1988: 8; Biagosch 1984; Monopoly Commission 1988). A reason why insurance providers opposed liberalisation of personal insurance was that personal insurance traditionally has been more profitable than business insurance (Finance Committee hearing, 25 April 1990: 74/12 and 74/6–74/32). Personal insurance providers were known to extract rents by over-calculating premiums for personal insurance in relation to risk.

Most consumers opposed liberalisation of personal insurance such as motor vehicle insurance (Finance Committee hearing, 25 April 1990: 130). While consumer organisations favoured the possibility of lower prices, they feared even more that liberalisation would reduce transparency thereby making it impossible for customers to compare prices and insurance conditions (interview with the German Federal Insurance Supervisory Office, 26 June 1998). Personal insurance customers were satisfied with the available insurance products (Lambsdorff 1991).

In conclusion, interest-based explanations can account for reform of business insurance but not personal insurance as both providers and users opposed personal insurance reform.

THE IMPACT OF EU MEMBERSHIP

European Commission initiatives in insurance services were severely constrained by Member State opposition. In 1975 the European Commission proposed the Second Non-Life Insurance Directive to create an internal market based on the principle of a single licence and home state rule for large business risks. The directive was not adopted until thirteen years later in 1988. Furthermore, the Commission did not propose the Third Non-Life Insurance Directive until the Council of Ministers had adopted the Single European Act and set the deadline of 1 January 1993 for liberalisation of services including insurance services. This directive was adopted in 1992 and established the principle of a single licence and home country rule for all insurance risks. Concerning business insurance, the ECJ in 1986 allowed for a greater utilisation of the concept of free provision of services (Dehousse 1998: 89–90).[7] In personal insurance on the other hand, the ECJ noted that in the absence of Community rules regarding the conditions of operations of insurance companies, Member States had the right to require and to control respect for their own rules concerning services offered in their country (Dehousse 1998). Given the need to ensure consumer protection the ECJ also conceded the legitimacy of authorisation procedures according to which national authorities can make sure that in personal insurance an insurance firm fulfils the regulatory conditions. Thus, the ECJ established as a principle the freedom to provide services in business insurance but allowed room for national exceptions in order to provide consumer protection in personal insurance (Finance Committee hearing, 25 April 1990: 74/11). The ECJ was careful not to push liberalisation substantially beyond what Member States wanted. In sum, EU proposals relied extensively on Member State support.

Multi-level governance approaches emphasise the sharing of power between Member States and other actors as well as the erosion of Member State influence. However, insurance sector reform did not move forward until Member State support had been secured. It is therefore crucial to examine how government preferences changed.

CHANGES IN GERMAN GOVERNMENT PREFERENCES

The German government initially only supported liberalisation of commercial insurance and transport insurance and argued that the consumer market should be left alone (*Financial Times* 1984: 2). The government believed that the large size of some of Germany's major insurance firms such as Allianz constituted an advantage in a liberalised market because financing of operations abroad would be relatively easy.

Economics Minister Lambsdorff in 1982 had proposed liberalising personal auto insurance but failed to win support for his proposal. However, Lambsdorff's ideas gained support after the Monopoly Commission and the Deregulation Commission[8] in the late 1980s and early 1990s had argued that liberalisation of personal insurance would lead to cheaper and better products for the consumer (Monopoly Commission 1988; Deregulation Commission 1991). They also argued that the consumer could be guaranteed protection (Finance Committee in the German Bundestag, hearings concerning the third EU non-life insurance directive).

As Farny points out, the report from the Deregulation Commission shows that pressure for reform was strong within the German government and supplemented pressure for reform in the EU (Farny 1991: 287). The report pointed out that the insurance sector was growing but was suffering from market inefficiencies due to restrictive national regulations and both reports argued that liberalisation would be a useful tool for making the sector more efficient.

Both the Monopoly Commission and the Deregulation Commission suggested an end to the setting of uniform insurance conditions as well as price regulation. In order to protect insurance customers against bankruptcies both reports proposed the undertaking of regular solvency checks. Professor Ernst Starke in his (critical) evaluation of the proposals made by the Monopoly Commission argued that the reports signalled a radical change in the government's thinking about services exactly because the Monopoly Commission viewed insurance as a product which could be sold as a regular good while new regulation could protect consumers (Starke 1988).

Starke's interpretation may hold the answers as to how reform came about and may also point to how far reform is likely to go. The key is redefining protected services as regular tradable products which would experience efficiency gains from liberalisation while at the same time adopting new regulation to ensure that consumers and workers are sheltered against negative side effects of liberalisation. If such a redefinition is not possible then liberalisation becomes extremely difficult.

Postal reform

When the telecoms sector was opened to competition, the postal sector was expected to remain a public monopoly. The postal sector was a large employer, it had not encountered extensive technological changes, which encouraged reform, and its monopoly structure was seen as a requirement to ensure universal postal provisioning (Price Waterhouse 1997). Political opposition to reform was therefore likely to be massive. However, in spite of these obstacles it became increasingly clear that the organisation of the German postal sector suffered from a low product innovation rate, a small letter mail volume per inhabitant, below average labour productivity and high letter prices.

Prior to the 1997 reform the so-called 'reserved services' included letters under 1 kilo and priced under 10 DM while bulk mail was 'reserved' under 100 grams (Bundestag Committee for Post and Telecoms, 24 September 1997: 977). In reserved services Deutsche Post AG is the only operator allowed to collect, sort, transport and deliver mail. All other services were open to competition. Following the 1997 reform (which took effect on 1 January 1998), the reserved services segment was reduced to letters and addressed catalogues (direct mail) under 200 grams or costing less than 5.50 DM as well as bulk mail above 50 grams. Letters between 200 grams and 1 kilo were opened up to competition but required a licence.

AN INTEREST-BASED EXPLANATION

The interests of business users diverged initially. Supporters of reform included advertising and mail order firms as well as employer associations. However, the largest user group of postal services was newspaper producers who opposed reform because they feared that it would jeopardise universal service provisioning. Deutsche Post AG favoured the status quo because it obtained most of its revenue from the reserved letter services segment. Privately owned express and parcel service providers were interested in breaking into the mail business market and supported reform. Consumer organisations as well as the union found that reform proposals went too far because they feared that liberalisation would end the principle of universal service provision at affordable cost and lead to an increase in unemployment. Although business users and private providers largely favoured reform, substantial opposition to reform existed among consumers, the union and the incumbent provider. An interest-based explanation cannot account very well for reform. It therefore needs to be explained how opposition to reform was overcome in order to understand why and how part of the letter market was slowly opened up to competition.

THE IMPACT OF EU MEMBERSHIP

EU proposals for liberalisation were severely constrained by domestic politics. First, the Commission had long attempted to push reform of postal services on the agenda but refrained from using Article 86.3 (ex Article 90.3) to create competition. Second, the ECJ determined that competition rules apply to postal services but on the other hand the ECJ also ruled that Member States could protect postal providers operating in the 'general interest'. The ECJ left it up to national courts to determine which services meet such criteria.[9] In order for major reform of the postal sector to be undertaken in the EU, key Member States had to support such changes. The sharing of power between Member States and other actors such as EU institutions as well as the erosion of Member State influence predicted by the multi-level governance approach is not useful for explaining reform of the postal sector. How then did the German government change its views on postal sector reform from opposition to support?

THE BREAK IN GERMAN GOVERNMENT OPPOSITION

The economic success of Deutsche Post AG following the initial postal reform in 1989 constituted a central reason for why the German government sought to open up postal services to competition (Committee for Post and Telecoms, 7 October 1997). However, it was very difficult for the government to devise a proposal for postal reform, which would be accepted in the Bundesrat by the social democrats as well as the federal states.

The main issue for the CDU/CSU was whether postal liberalisation could be combined with universal service provision. The CDU/CSU feared that if letter services were opened up to competition then postal operators would only be interested in providing services in the most profitable areas such as city centres and would not be keen on offering services in rural areas. However, during the hearings about the new postal reform, studies were presented which proposed solutions on how to maintain the principle of universal service provisioning. One solution entailed the establishment of an equalisation foundation (Ausgleichsfond) paid for by licence holders. This solution formed the crux of the CDU/CSU reform proposal. By setting up such a licence system CDU/CSU core constituents in rural areas would be sheltered from potentially negative side effects of market reform.

On 16 May 1997 the Bundesrat turned down the government's proposal. The party most against the proposal, and who had a majority in the Bundesrat was the SPD. That party feared that postal jobs in the private sector would be less well paid and more stressful. The SPD therefore demanded that a social clause be inserted in the new postal legislation. This clause should ensure that jobs in the privately owned postal operators were 'equal' to jobs in the Deutsche Post AG (Committee for Post and Telecoms, SPD statement, 7 October 1997: 93–94). Many federal states also feared that lower prices and service improvements in the metropolitan areas would result in a decline in service and higher prices in rural areas (*Frankfurter Allgemeine Zeitung*, 17 May 1997, no author: 14).

Because of substantial opposition in the Bundesrat the legislative proposal was submitted to the Vermittlungsauschuss (conciliation committee) to be discussed on 11 December 1997. A compromise was found which allowed a continuation of part of the DPG monopoly. Universal service provision was guaranteed by creating a licence system, which required licencees to fund universal services. The proposal satisfied the SPD and the Bundesrat.

Summarising, in postal services substantial reform has taken place even beyond what was expected only a few years back. The government convinced the opposition that sheltering of jobs and service provisioning would be guaranteed. However, extensive opposition to full reform both in Germany and in the EU prevented complete liberalisation of postal services.

Section two has shown that a crucial aspect to liberalisation was the ability of the government to reinterpret services as regular tradable products where economic gains from trade were expected and at the same time adopt legislation to protect customers and employees from potential harm.

Enlargement and services liberalisation

According to the European Commission, 'an integrated policy in the services sector is vital if an enlarged EU is to benefit fully from all opportunities offered by new technology and ways of doing business' (DG internal market website 11 January 2002 at www.europa.eu.int/comm). If the hypothesis proposed in this chapter concerning how and why services are opened up to competition is correct, what are the lessons from Germany and Brussels concerning the prospects for a single market in services in an enlarged European Union?

The German case examined an interest-based explanation, which emphasised pressure from users and producers. The case also examined a multi-level governance approach, which stressed pressure for reform from EU institutions. While both explanations offered important insights, government support for reform was most important combined with legislation to shelter exposed groups from potential harm.

Liberalisation of services such as post and telecoms has obviously reduced government control in these sectors in Germany, yet services liberalisation also requires domestic institutional capacity to ensure implementation of the new liberal regime. A key difference between Germany and the new Member States is at times a less-developed institutional capacity in the latter to ensure proper implementation of the liberalisation directives. Furthermore, EU directives embed market reforms in legislation to continue the universal service provision in post and telecoms, protect insurance customers against insolvency, etc. This legislation also requires implementation. In Germany social clauses are put in place to ensure job quality and possibly shelter jobs. EU services directives leave room for adoption at the Member State level of social clauses. Social partners such as unions and employers' associations have an important role to play in securing agreement about social clauses. However, agreement on social clauses will be difficult to reach in the new Member States because they lack strong unions and employers' associations. The new Member States have increasingly focused on national-level market making but 'most of the institutions that could make markets more inclusive, and/or support the process of catch-up growth of these economies, are weak or absent' (Bruszt 2002: 123). The combination of strong states and weak social and economic actors could become a major obstacle to Europeanisation in the new Member States (Bruszt 2002).

Liberalisation of telecoms, postal and insurance services
in the new Member States

The German case showed that the government was instrumental in bringing services reform successfully to a close. Previously protected services were reinterpreted as tradable products and protection of consumers and employees was crucial. This section analyses the implications of this finding for services reform in an enlarged EU. It first examines the extent of service liberalisation in applicant countries and the government's role in securing reform. Second, it explores the possibility of adopting regulation in applicant countries to protect exposed groups. The focus is first on the services that have already been liberalised in the EU such as telecoms. Next, we turn to examining services that have not yet been opened up to competition in the EU including the letter market.

THE EXTENT OF SERVICES REFORM IN EASTERN EUROPE

The role played by governments in Eastern Europe is different from the role played by the German government concerning services liberalisation in one major respect: applicant countries do not have a choice regarding whether post, telecoms and insurance services should be liberalised. New Member States according to the criteria for accession laid down at the Copenhagen European Council in June 1993 have to accept the *acquis communautaire*, which means that they must adopt the entire body of existing EU law.

Concerning telecoms the accession chapters were successfully closed ahead of time with all applicant countries. Governments in the new Member States favoured reform because of a need to modernise a crucial part of the infrastructure and because of the need to raise cash in a difficult economic situation. A range of West European and US telecom investors now operate in applicant countries. In the Czech Republic, 27 per cent of the capital of the national operator SPT was sold in 1995 to a Swiss-Dutch consortium. The Hungarian telecoms company Matav was separated from the Post Office on 1 January 1990 and partially privatised and 30 per cent of the capital is held by a German-United States consortium (International Labour Organisation 1998). Market reform encourages the presence of large international investors and their presence fortifies liberalisation because foreign investors do not accept that the former monopoly receives special favours.

The chapter on the free movement of postal services was also provisionally closed ahead of time. Certainly in postal services applicant countries still maintain a reserved area for domestic mail, typically with a weight limit of 350 grams and with a price cap of five times the standard rate (see for example the Czech Postal Act available at www.mdcr.cz/text/archiv/nzps.rtf). The reserved market segment is in accordance with the latest EU postal directive. Foreign direct investment is also taking place in postal services in the new Member States. For example the Czech postal office parcel division is now part of Deutsche Post AG's growing European network. One reason for the support for reform in applicant countries is that reforms to reduce or end subsidies from the state budget are attractive to governments in an economically tight situation.

INSUFFICIENT IMPLEMENTATION OF EU DIRECTIVES

Securing effective implementation of liberalisation schemes in the new Member States will be a key challenge in the coming years. It is crucial that institution building to secure legal frameworks to protect competition and embed markets is undertaken. However, according to Laszlo Bruszt, '[T]he emerging capitalism in CEE countries looks like an institutional desert, at least in comparison to the form(s) of capitalism evolving within the European Union' (Bruszt 2002: 123).

According to Alexander Spachis, Adviser on Enlargement and Financial Institutions in the Internal Market Directorate General, in financial services for example much needs to be done to achieve accepted standards in the supervisory authorities (presentation at the UNICE workshop in Athens 7–8 November 2003. See http://europa.eu.int/comm/internal_market/en/index. htm). Spachis argues that the challenge in financial services is to deepen the legal framework and institutions that underpin financial stability (http://europa.eu.int/comm/internal_market/en/index.htm).

Implementation of the postal directive in applicant countries remains problematic. EU express mail carriers represented by the European Express Association (EEA) complain about inadequate implementation of competition rules in applicant countries and the Commission agrees with the EEA complaint (interview EEA, 13 February 2002; interview European Commission Directorate General for the Internal Market, 14 February 2002). Some applicant countries such as the Czech Republic enforce stringent licence requirements for express carriers even though the Postal Directive of 1997 explicitly states that licences are not required in this market segment and that only an authorisation by national authorities is needed. Furthermore, some countries – most notably Hungary – demand that express carriers must contribute to a compensation fund in order to assist the universal service provider Magyar Posta in the event it is unable to fund the cost of a universal postal service. However, according to the 1997 Postal Directive only providers of universal services are required to contribute to such a fund and express services are not part of the universal service requirement (interview EEA, 13 February 2002; EEA letter to the Hungarian Prime Minister 8 January 2002). Another problem is inefficient transit arrangements for trucks carrying postal deliveries across borders into Eastern Europe (interview International Express Carriers Conference, 11 June 2002).

A study by Dieke and Campbell revealed two additional causes for concern in respect to the provision of a universal postal service in the new Member States (Dieke and Campbell 2003). First, each country according to the Postal Directive sets firm requirements for monitoring of quality of service. Each country is expected to set standards for quality of service, to provide independent monitoring of performance and to publish the results (Dieke and Campbell 2003: 117). So far in August 2003 only three countries met these standards (the Czech Republic, Hungary and Slovakia). According to Campbell and Dieke, '[U]ntil objective quality of service standards are set and independently monitored, the actual quality of service provided in some [accession] countries must be considered open to question' (Dieke and Campbell 2003: 117). Furthermore, only the Czech and Slovak universal service providers keep separate accounts as required by the Postal Directive for the reserved services and the non-reserved services respectively.

Concerning the telecoms sector, the European Commission has prepared regular reports monitoring the implementation of the EU regulatory framework.

The most recent report was released in November 2003 (see *Monitoring of EU Candidate Countries (Telecommunication Services Sector)* at http://europa. eu.int/information_society/topics/ecomm/all_about/international_aspects/ main_areas_work/eu_enlargement/index_en.htm). According to the report, a major problem in all countries is that governments too closely control the regulatory bodies. Examples include ministers controlling the appointments, regulations needing ministerial approval, and the government controlling the regulator's budget. However, all countries need to develop regulatory rules and undertake the necessary institutional reforms for separation of powers between government and the regulatory authority to enable the regulatory authority to commit to its rulings.

EMBEDDING MARKETS

The German case highlighted the need for the government to offer some protection to exposed groups. Governments in Eastern Europe are likely to face the same pressures. Concerning regulation to shelter exposed groups, EU directives guarantee a universal service obligation in telecoms as well as postal services. However, applicant countries have trouble meeting this requirement. Possibly the prohibition of traditional cream skimming from telecom services to postal services as well as from letter services to parcel services has left the already financially strapped applicant countries in trouble. The fact remains that financing of the universal service obligation is not an easy task for applicant countries.

Furthermore, to what extent have the rights of workers in telecoms and postal services been protected? Eurofedop,[10] which represents postal and telecoms workers in EU Member States as well as applicant countries, strongly supports employment protection schemes in applicant countries. However, it is difficult for financially strapped applicant countries with relatively high unemployment rates to afford such protection. If investors insist on drastic job cuts in order to improve profitability the cost of protectionist schemes may become too vast (interview Eurofedop, 12 February 2002). As a result a worst-case scenario could entail drastic job cuts, which could lead to strikes and could destroy employee morale and ultimately customer satisfaction. Scarce resources to secure universal services and employment protection make postal reform in applicant countries a difficult endeavour.

New Member States lack strong unions and employers' associations. This is a weakness when they seek to ensure social inclusion, e.g. by securing employment, good working conditions, retirement schemes etc. (Interview UNICE 26 November 2003; interview ETUC 13 July 2004). A labour-intensive sector such as the post relied heavily on the social partners when the post was liberalised in Germany. Weak social partners could therefore constitute a major impediment to reform of the postal sector in the new Member States. Foreign investors in the new Member States are increasingly seeking to establish relationships with fledgeling social partners in order to build relationships that may facilitate dialogue about necessary reforms within firms, but this remains a major challenge (interview Confederation of Danish Industries 24 November 2003).

Services that have not yet been liberalised in the EU

What are the likely implications of enlargement for those services, which have still not been fully liberalised within the EU, such as most of the letter market? With unemployment on the rise in the EU, Member State governments in France, Germany and the UK have recently expressed greater reluctance to liberalise the letter market (interview Eurofedop, 14 February 2002; www.senat.fr/rap/r01-176/r01-176.html). Enlargement may also slow the process of further service sector liberalisation in the EU simply because it takes longer for twenty-five or more governments to convince their constituents of the benefits of reform than it would take fifteen. Following enlargement it could therefore become more difficult to adopt new directives to liberalise politically sensitive services. Finally, concerning the EU's ability to negotiate international agreements to liberalise services within the WTO framework, the Treaty of Nice (which was signed on 26 February 2001), introduces qualified majority voting in services. This measure to enhance efficiency in decision-making in the Council of Ministers could be important as the number of EU Member States rises. Yet the atmosphere of consensus in the Council of Ministers could mean that formally introducing qualified majority voting might not have much of an impact on decision-making (Golub 1999).

Conclusion

Liberalisation of services such as post, insurance and telecoms represents a paradigm shift, as these services have traditionally not been considered as tradable products. In Germany pressure from users and from EU institutions was important to successfully conclude reforms. The government's ability was especially important to reinterpret services as tradable products while offering protection in the form of a universal service obligation and employment protection schemes. Eastern European governments, however, have to accept the acquis. Weak institutions in the new Member States mean that efficient implementation of EU directives is lacking. Building institutions to enforce implementation of EU directives is crucial to ensure the efficient running of an enlarged single European market in services. Governments without large financial assets may, however, find it difficult to finance universal services and employment protection schemes. Finally, embedding services liberalisation in social protection schemes can be problematic in these countries because social partners are weak. If social partners are weak they cannot contribute as they have done in existing EU Member States to shaping constructive solutions about how best to reduce the negative consequences of market reform.

Notes

1 I would like to thank the Danish Social Science Research Council as well as Harvard University's Program for the Study of Germany and Europe for funding parts of the research. I benefited from extensive research visits at the Max Planck Institute for the Study of Societies in Cologne and the Centre for European Policy Studies in Brussels. I wish to thank Suzanne Berger, Torben Iversen, Andrew Moravcsik and Ken Oye for advice on parts of the argument. Last but not least, I wish to thank the reviewers for their very helpful comments. All faults of course remain my own.

2 On the impact of insurance reform, see Schmidt 2001.

3 Knudsen 'Breaking with Tradition: Liberalisation of Services Trade in the EU', unpublished Ph.D. thesis, Department of Political Science, MIT, January 2001.

4 See for the liberal intergovernmentalist argument, Hoffmann (1966), Milward (1992), Moravcsik (1993) (1999). The multi-level governance approach has been developed respectively in Marks, Hooghe and Blank (1996), Sandholtz (1993), Sbragia (1992), and Pierson (1996). A review of the debate can be found in Caporaso and Keeler (1995).

5 Knudsen (2001).

6 The detailed stenographic protocols from the hearings held in the German Bundestag's committees such as the committee for post and telecoms provided a key source of information concerning the preferences of users and providers of telecoms services. Another key source consists of the extensive written statements provided by the various actors prior to the hearings. Academic articles, interviews with key actors involved in the reforms, business and government studies and reports, newspapers, etc., also constituted useful sources.

7 Case 205/84 Commission v Federal Republic of Germany [1986]; Case 206/84 Commission v Ireland [1986]; Case 220/83 Commission v France [1986]; Case 252/83 Commission v Denmark [1986]. See Pool (1990) and Dehousse (1998) for more information on ECJ rulings in insurance services.

8 The government in 1987 set up a Deregulation Commission (Deregulierungskommission) to estimate the cost of existing regulations in the German economy as well as to develop proposals for reform concerning how regulations could be removed.

9 Case C320/91 Procureur du Roi v Paul Corbeau.

10 Eurofedop is a Christian Democratic Trade Union Association. The socialist trade union association for postal workers is Union Network International.

ELFRIEDE REGELSBERGER AND WOLFGANG WESSELS

6

The evolution of the Common Foreign and Security Policy: a case of an imperfect ratchet fusion

Common Foreign and Security Policy: an institutionalist perspective

Political relevance and academic offers

The Common Foreign and Security Policy (CFSP) and its evolution since the 1960s are of high political and academic relevance: the Second Pillar of the European Union (EU) constitutes a key element of the European construction as well as one cornerstone of the national foreign policies of its Member States. It is increasingly perceived as an important though strange actor within the international system. The CFSP, as it stands today, after the signing of the Treaty of Nice, does not, however, automatically document a clearly designed and commonly accepted master plan. On the contrary: to avoid doctrinal debates the 'founding fathers' of European political cooperation (EPC) and later the creators of the Second Pillar of the EU system opted for a pragmatic and ambiguous institutional construction open to different interpretations (Nuttall 1992, Rummel and Wessels 1978). Consequently, various concepts of the aims and methods of a joint international presence of the EU and its Member States continue to exist.

Institutional and procedural reforms and adaptations as concluded in several treaty amendments since the 1980s have not overcome this fundamental ambiguity.

To grasp this rather unique phenomenon various schools of thought have emerged over the years, which offer helpful approaches to explore, explain and evaluate its main features (Weiler and Wessels 1988, Pijpers, Regelsberger and Wessels 1988, Ginsberg 1999, 2001).

Thus the classical (neo-)realist approach interprets the structures and results of the CFSP as a typical product of behavioural patterns of nation states in times of interdependence and globalisation (Link 2001). In order to secure their national interests, governments participate in a European regime of coordination. Among sovereign states it offers attractive policy options for specific issues and within certain periods. CFSP thus remains a primarily inter-governmental framework – despite its procedural differentiation, its enlargement of scope and increasing links with the EC Pillar. The constraints of the inter-national environment may increasingly force individual governments to 'speak with one voice'. However, they remain the sole 'players' in a 'game' in which sover-eignties are pooled only as long as vital national interests converge. In such an understanding, EC institutions may have no say at all. The EC bodies should be subservient to the 'high politics' (Hoffmann 1966) of the key national leaders. Instead, an institutional structure and procedures will be constructed in which unanimity reigns and decisions are taken by those traditionally in charge of foreign policy. Legitimate rule can only be exercised by representatives of the nation states. Depending on the dynamics of the international system, the EU might need to become a 'superpower', but it should not and will not turn into a 'superstate' (Blair 2000). The institutional evolution would thus clearly be limited to marginal adaptations and fine-tuning of intergovernmental 'modes of govern-ance' (for the term, see Wallace 2000a: 28–35, Kohler-Koch 1999: 20–26, Wessels and Linsenmann 2002).

In an opposing view, the CFSP is understood as a part and as a result of a comprehensive and fundamental integration process leading to a *finalité* in the shape of a federal state – even if in a distant future (see also the chapters by Crum (11) and Kohler-Koch (3), this volume).

Based on the assumption of functionalist spill-overs the formerly loose and intergovernmental EPC/CFSP diplomacy is expected to gradually move towards a system with clear supranational elements. In this neo-federalist perspective (Pinder 2001a, 2001b) EC institutions are constructed to turn into relevant actors inside the CFSP system. Through constant treaty revisions by intergov-ernmental conferences their roles would thus be strengthened to the detriment of the traditional actors which might even be replaced by supranational institutions one day. The vision of a European federation expects procedural adaptations with greater competences for those European organs that are not dominated by the nation states, i.e. the European Commission and the European Parliament. Increased success of such a communitarised foreign policy system would enhance a common European identity as an actor not only in the international system but inside the EU for its citizens as well. Loyalties are shifted to the EU level in a 'process whereby political actors in several dis-tinct national settings are persuaded to shift their loyalties, expectations and political activities towards a new centre, whose institutions possess or demand jurisdiction over the pre-existing national states. The end result of a process of political integration is expected to lead to a new political community, superim-posed over the pre-existing ones' (Haas 1958: 16, see also Monnet 1976, Hallstein 1972). Legitimation is then achieved by an effective output perfor-mance (Scharpf 2000).

Our approach: testing a ratchet fusion

Within this set of divergent and analytical explanations, our approach starts with the core assumption that the process and the products of intergovernmental conferences (IGCs) like Maastricht, Amsterdam and Nice are milestones in the European unification process in general and also in the area of foreign and security policy. They produce history-making decisions (Peterson 1995: 72) as critical junctures and formative events; at those focal points key actors of Member States as 'masters of the treaty' (German Constitutional Court 1993, 1995) create and revise opportunity structures, with incentives and constraints for both themselves and for Community actors. These institutional and procedural arrangements offer access to and influence on the preparing, taking, implementing and controlling of political decisions (Maurer and Wessels 2002) over an increasing scope of common foreign policy activities.

In a historical retro perspective, we thus observe a nearly regular treaty-making – some kind of a hidden constitutionalisation – in the area of the CFSP since the last 1980s. One IGC sets up subjects and dates for the following one. The latest IGC that started in October 2003 was unique insofar as it debated a Draft Constitutional Treaty (European Convention 2003) that had been designed before in a broad public debate among both parliamentarians and government representatives from the EU Member States and the applicant countries as well as representatives from the EU (European Parliament, European Commission). However, Heads of State and Government of 25 Member States failed to reach consensus on the text in December 2003 despite an Italian Presidency eager to find solutions to the most contested issues (Conference 2003). The Brussels failure does not mark the end of shaping and fixing the final institutional and procedural configuration of the EU system over all and the CFSP Pillar in particular. In the area of CFSP and in particular for ESDP the reform process will continue, if not via another IGC in 2004, at least through Council or national decisions for specific subjects.

To explain the evolution of the CFSP in a comprehensive way, however, the analysis of legal provisions must be confronted with real patterns of the 'living constitution' (Olsen 2000: 6, Maurer and Wessels 2002) over a considerable time span. In particular, links between treaty-making and the normal patterns of political actors in institutions need to be considered (Scharpf 1997). In such a dynamic perspective we understand the EPC/CFSP evolution as part of a 'fusion' (Wessels 1997) in a 'ratchet' process (Wessels 2001b: 6–7) of a cascade integration ladder (Maurer and Wessels 2002).

Via IGCs in particular national actors have step by step created, amended and revised institutional and procedural incentives and constraints. National and European actors increasingly employ these opportunity structures to use EU instruments for coping with external challenges perceived by all as common problems. By relying on a limited set of legal and real integration indicators (see earlier works by Lindberg and Scheingold 1970, Grabitz et al. 1988, Stone Sweet and Sandholtz 1998, Pollack 2000), we can identify recurrent patterns which indicate a process of a *de facto* stronger involvement of national and EC actors in a kind of 'Europeanisation' (Olsen 2002: 4) or 'Brussellisation' for joint activities and pressure in the international system.

In a fusion perspective, this move towards an EU location means a shift of political attention and personal resources to the Brussels arena (Maurer, Mittag and Wessels 2002) without necessarily implying a direct communitarisation in strict legal terms. The thesis of a ratchet fusion assumes and predicts that this evolution is irreversible: 'plateaux' of a certain status quo might be reached from time to time and for a longer period (see figure 6.1). A spill-back from these levels, however, would falsify the major argument of our thesis.

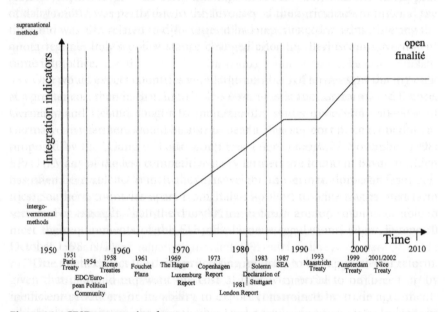

Figure 6.1   CFSP construction dates

Constructing the rules: the evolution of the legal constitution from the 1950s to Nice 2000

In line with our evolutionary approach we shall now analyse the basic texts to identify how the 'masters of the treaty' (German Constitutional Court 1993, 1995) have created opportunity structures for national and Community actors in this policy field. The institutionalisation of a common foreign and security policy at the European level can so far be described as an incremental process, which led to the formulation of aims, norms, methods and institutions of the envisaged cooperation; each step towards a new plateau was caused by a specific European and international context and by a set of multiple motives of the participating governments.

*Failing forerunners 1951–62: the federal European Defence Community
versus the intergovernmental Fouchet plans*

In the immediate aftermath of the Second World War plans to integrate key
sectors of national sovereignty – such as the former war industries coal and steel
and also defence – in a new European framework found considerable support in
the countries which were to become the founding fathers of the Paris Treaty on
the Coal and Steel Community (1951) and later on of the Rome Treaties (1957).
Plans for the creation of a European Defence Community (EDC) on the basis of
proposals from the then French Prime Minister, Pléven, in 1950 suggested a far-
reaching integration of military forces under a joint command structure, a single
budget and joint armament programmes. Integration in the military field and the
European Coal and Steel Community in 1951 were supposed to develop under a
common 'roof' in the form of a European Political Community. The latter was
supposed to constitute the over-arching integrated structure enabling the
Member States to consult each other on their foreign policies in a permanent
manner and within common institutions including modes of a joint external
representation. However, due to French worries about a loss of sovereignty the
already signed EDC treaty provisions in the end were not ratified by the Assemblée
Nationale (1954). The strategic concept of achieving supranational political integration in Europe by focusing on defence and foreign policy therefore remained
merely a visionary concept (Schoutheete 1986: 11, Wessel 1999: 1–4).

Similarly unsuccessful ideas, again with a French connotation, to initiate
cooperation among the signatories of the EC treaties emerged in the early 1960s.
In contrast to the integrationist approach of the earlier concepts, the Fouchet
Plans, named after a spokesman of de Gaulle, suggested the opposite institutional strategy. Traditional intergovernmental cooperation was seen as the preferred mode for foreign policy issues as matters of defence had already been
transferred to NATO and the revised Brussels Pact, which was transformed into
the Western European Union (WEU) during the years 1954/55. Gaullist policy
annoyed the partners of France and provoked a 'no' to the Fouchet proposals,
which were increasingly perceived as French means of 'invading' the supranational character of the EC institutional set-up, to produce competition with
NATO and to prevent the United Kingdom from participation, as desired by
other EC countries.

One lesson of the two failures was that no consensus was possible on a comprehensive master plan with a clear institutional *finalité*, which would be installed
by a constitution-like jump into a new legal framework. Incremental and modest
steps were apparently the only strategy to advance.

The EPC reports: the period of political commitments
between 1969 and 1983

Not until the transformation of the international and European context at the
end of the 1960s did the formerly six EC governments decide to again reflect on
ways to enhance the process of political unification in Europe.

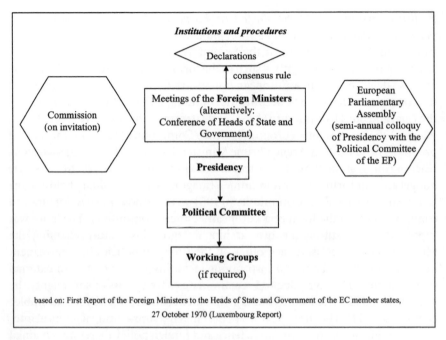

Institutions and procedures

Declarations

consensus rule

Commission
(on invitation)

Meetings of the **Foreign Ministers**
(alternatively:
Conference of Heads of State and
Government)

European
Parliamentary
Assembly
(semi-annual colloquy
of Presidency with the
Political Committee
of the EP)

Presidency

Political Committee

Working Groups
(if required)

based on: First Report of the Foreign Ministers to the Heads of State and Government of the EC member states,
27 October 1970 (Luxembourg Report)

Figure 6.2   Early EPC: institutions and procedures

The summit of The Hague in 1969 then launched a new but modest start (see figure 6.2) to the process of finding a way that Europe could contribute to events and developments in the world in a corresponding to its responsibilities: the foreign ministers and their top diplomats, the political directors, now defined the first principles and procedures to cooperate in this field (Rummel and Wessels 1978, Schoutheete 1986, Nuttall 1992). Due to the experiences of the past and basic differences among the 'founding fathers' of EPC about the nature of such an undertaking, a cautious and ambiguous approach prevailed. The objectives and mechanisms were prudently formulated and laid down in a legally non-binding agreement known as the Luxembourg or Davignon (the then Belgian Political Director) Report of 27 October 1970. This text expressed that 'Europe must prepare itself to exercise the responsibilities which to assume in the world is both its duty and a necessity on account of its greater cohesion and its increasingly important role' (Luxembourg Report 1970: point 9).

Pressure from outside, most obvious in the oil embargo of the early 1970s and in the fourth Middle East war, but also first positive experiences of the participants with the new system produced a second text, the Copenhagen Report of 23 July 1973. Again, the paper reflected nothing but a political commitment of the foreign ministers to consult each other on foreign policy issues 'to ensure . . . improved mutual understanding' and 'to strengthen solidarity between Governments . . . and, wherever it appears possible and desirable, joint action' (Copenhagen Report 1973). The agreement cautiously formalised what had emerged in practice as useful mechanisms for involving foreign ministers and diplomats. It documented a commitment to a loose and soft method of cooperation, nothing more – but also nothing less.

The same applies to the third report, named after the city in which it was agreed upon by the foreign ministers of the then ten Member States (after the Greek accession to the EC): the London Report of 13 October 1981. Driven by the nine's, respectively ten's poor collective performance in international crises in the late 1970s, like the Soviet invasion of Afghanistan or the seizing of US hostages in Iran, steps were undertaken to re-enforce the concertation reflex among the participating governments by a crisis mechanism, which was to enable them 'increasingly to shape events and not merely to react to them' (London Report 1981). For the first time the ten recognised the usefulness of the Commission's participation in the EPC at all levels and broadened the EPC agenda prudently towards the 'political' aspects of security. Their approach, however, remained intergovernmental, consensus-based and outside an EC-linked legal framework.

Attempts by two integrationist foreign ministers of that time, the German Hans-Dietrich Genscher and his Italian counterpart, Emilio Colombo, to translate the achievements of EPC into legal provisions and to bring them closer to the Community structure for the sake of efficiency and greater consistency of Europe's international performance failed in the early 1980s (Genscher and Colombo 1981). At that time no consensus for such a qualitative leap could be reached, and the passing of another political agreement, the Solemn Declaration of Stuttgart, named after its place of signature under the German Presidency in 1983, was perceived as the ultimate compromise. Even this modest outcome could not satisfy all of the ten: the Greek government, the 'enfant terrible' in EPC at that time after the Socialist victory in Athens, issued a general reserve on the obligations of the EPC, which could be perceived as a loss of national sovereignty, while the Danish 'no' referred 'only' to the extension of EPC to 'political and economic' aspects of security.

From the SEA over Maastricht and Amsterdam to Nice and beyond: formalisation via treaty-making, 1986–2003

THE SINGLE EUROPEAN ACT:
LEGAL CONFIRMATION OF PREVIOUS PRAGMATISM
In the wake of the southern enlargement of the Community in 1986 the Member States wished to give new impulses to the integration process, which focused on the creation of the Single Market. However, the EPC, too, had become a central element for foreign policy formulation at national level and from the perspective of its participants deserved a further strengthening (Forster and Wallace 2000: 465). As part of the overall debate on reforming the institutional set-up from 1984 to 1986, the EPC received its first legal basis in the first comprehensive intergovernmental conference to amend and reform the treaties. Title III, Art. 30 of the Single European Act (SEA) of 17/28 February 1986 stated that '[T]he High

Contracting Parties being members of the European Community' – an explicit hint at the exclusion of third countries from the 'club' – 'shall endeavour jointly to formulate and implement a European foreign policy' (Art. 30, point 1 SEA). Compared to the earlier reports, the treaty text speaks more clearly of the Member States' obligations to consult each other before their own positions were fixed and to refrain from national decisions 'which impair their effectiveness as a cohesive force in international relations or within international organisations' (Art. 30, point 2 SEA). In the case of deviant behaviour of member countries, however, no sanction mechanisms were foreseen. The SEA widely confirmed the institutions and procedures of the daily EPC business (Art. 30, points 3–4, 10 SEA), which remained intergovernmental and required decisions based on consensus. A new item was the creation of a small administrative unit located at the General Secretariat of the Council in Brussels, which was to assist the presidency in the management of the EPC (Art. 30, point 10g SEA). With regard to the gradual enlargement of scope of the EPC, it is important to note that the treaty not only reaffirmed the need for cooperation in the 'political and economic' matters of security but that achievements in this field were seen to essentially contribute 'to the development of a European identity in external policy matters' (Art. 30, point 6 SEA). Finally, the treaty contained the first revision clause for the EPC, i.e. to examine the provisions five years after the entry into force of the SEA (Art. 30, point 12 SEA). This formula paved the way for the quasi-regular construction of legal and institutional adaptations from the middle of the 1980s till the first decade of the third millennium.

MAASTRICHT: FROM A DIPLOMATIC 'CLUB'
TOWARDS A FORMALISED PILLAR OF THE EU

Dynamic forces inside the Communities, e.g. progress towards the internal market and EMU, as well as a changed international environment, most obvious with the end of the Cold War and German unification, were the driving forces for a further strengthening of the EPC in the early 1990s. As a part of an expressed common will on behalf of the signatories of the EC treaties to achieve an 'ever closer Union of the peoples of Europe' (Art. A Treaty on European Union (TEU), Maastricht Version (MV)) the twelve were ready to enter a qualitatively new stage in their cooperation in foreign policy. The transformation of the EPC into a Common Foreign and Security Policy of the European Union (CFSP) signals a leap forward in various respects, as the CFSP is incorporated into 'one single institutional framework' (Art. C TEU MV).

The new provisions set out the general objectives and rules of the European construction and created the three Pillars under a common roof. The closeness of EC and CFSP structures is obvious in so far as an EC organ, i.e. the Council, became the central decision-making body in the CFSP (Art. J.2, J.8,2 TEU MV) and the roles of the European Commission and the European Parliament were confirmed. Art. C TEU also demanded the coherence of all foreign policy activities for which the Council and the Commission were made jointly responsible.

On the administrative level, the Political Committee remained the central body for the preparation and implementation of CFSP policies. However, it entered into a competitive situation with the Committee of Permanent Representatives (Coreper), which is traditionally in charge of the Council's work (Art. 151 TEC MV) and which acts as a gate-keeper towards CFSP attempts to 'invade' the Community Pillar. The administrative set-up of the CFSP was to be covered by the Community budget.

Furthermore, for the first time majority voting was introduced to the CFSP. Compared to EC rules there are, however, certain specific modalities: majority decisions not only require 62 weighted votes but they must at the same time comprise two-thirds of the Member States (Art. J.3,2 TEU MV). Majority voting is applicable only in specific cases, i.e. the implementation of joint actions, while the objectives, means and duration of the concrete measures were to be defined by prior consensus.

Questions of security and defence are no longer taboos on the CFSP agenda. Especially the Western European Union, so far the relatively independent defence component of Europe, was to be understood as an integral part of the development of the European Union (Jopp 1997). The Twelve attributed considerable weight 'to include all questions related to the security of the Union, including the eventual framing of a common defence policy which might in time lead to a common defence' (Title V, Art. J.4 TEU MV) and undertook specific measures to improve the liaison between the CFSP institutions and those of the WEU. Thereby they emphasised a particular guiding role for the European Council. A revision clause was inserted to review the CFSP provisions and present the results to the European Council in 1996 'with a view to furthering the objective of this Treaty, and having in view the date of 1998 in the context of Article XII of the Brussels Treaty' (Art. J.4 point 6 TEU MV).

AMSTERDAM: A RATIONALISED INTERGOVERNMENTALISM

Soon after the Maastricht provisions had taken shape, new external challenges like the growing conflict in the EU's immediate neighbourhood in ex-Yugoslavia and, moreover, its weak performance in this crisis re-opened the debate on the appropriateness of the CFSP. So did the EU's image of an anchor of economic growth and political stability, as the emerging democracies surrounding the EU twelve/fifteen members (as from January 1995 on with the accession of Austria, Finland and Sweden) often perceived it.

Another IGC leading to the European Council of Amsterdam 1997 produced procedural amendments to improve the EU's internal efficiency and external visibility and effectiveness (Dumond and Setton 1999, Monar 1997a: 249, Griller et al. 2000: 373, Regelsberger and Schmalz 2001: 249). Among the novelties were: a provision to move from the consensus requirement towards the possibility of constructive abstention (Title V, Art. 23 TEU Amsterdam Version (AV)); new ways to achieve an extension of majority votes through the introduction of the instrument of 'common strategies' (Arts. 13 and 23 TEU AV) though national safeguard and fall back clauses were inserted, i.e. a national veto is made possible in case of 'important and stated reasons of national policy' (Art. 23.2 TEU AV). Besides, the office of a High Representative for the CFSP (Art. 18.3 and 26 TEU AV) was created to assist the presidency in both management and external representation. Modifications of the old troika system towards more continuity (Art. 18 TEU AV) were introduced, as was the installation of a Policy Planning and Early Warning Unit (PPEWU) at the Council Secretariat under the authority of the High Representative for the CFSP (see figure 6.3a).

The Amsterdam Treaty (Monar and Wessels 2001) also renders the security and defence aspects of CFSP more precisely. It introduces the 'Petersberg tasks' (Art. 17 TEU AV), i.e. the EU's competence for humanitarian and rescue tasks, peace-keeping, crisis management including peace-making and combat forces.

The institutional and procedural amendments and revisions illustrate the clear preference of the Member States to improve the efficiency of these

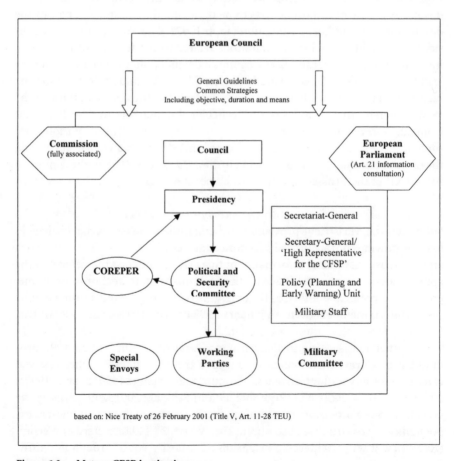

Figure 6.3a Mature CFSP institutions

procedures without giving up their ultimate say. The coordination became more legalised, but the heads of governments did not introduce any 'hard' sanctions against non-compliant members. They rationalised their intergovernmental set-up without a qualitative move towards a communitarisation. In contrast, such a step was taken in justice and home affairs by moving asylum and immigration issues from the Third to the First Pillar (Monar 2001).

NICE: SCOPE EXTENSION TO MILITARY TASKS – (C)ESDP:
EUROPEAN SECURITY AND DEFENCE POLICY
Shortly after the provisions of the Amsterdam Treaty came into force in May 1999, another debate started on revising and amending the treaties just signed. It was driven mainly by the 'leftovers' of Amsterdam, i.e. fundamental questions on EC institutional provisions, which had remained unsolved in the earlier IGC but which were pressing in view of the forthcoming Eastern enlargement of the EU (see also the chapter by Laursen, this volume). At the beginning, the need to consider another reform of the CFSP provisions was widely felt to be premature and only slight legal adaptations seemed necessary. These would reflect recent dynamism in certain areas of CFSP without, however, provoking a debate on sensitive issues, particularly in the area of security and defence.

However, matters of European security and defence were not completely out of sight. The EU's experience with the Kosovo crisis and the altered course in British policy towards an autonomous European capacity produced unexpected dynamism in CFSP practice (Jopp 2000: 243, Regelsberger 2000: 233). The fifteen entered into intensive deliberations on an EU Rapid Reaction Force and on institutional and organisational adaptations (military committee, military staff). As in the early days of EPC these new steps started informally and were then gradually transformed into Council decisions.

The outcome (Regelsberger 2001b, Algieri 2001, Wessels 2001b) of the third IGC, which ended with the Nice European Council in December 2000 and the signature of 26 February 2001, offers for the CFSP a modest extension of majority voting (see figure 6.3b) in the case of the appointment of the High Representative for the CFSP – as the Secretary General of the Council – (Art. 207 EC Treaty Nice Version (NV)) and of nominating special envoys (Art. 23,2 TEU NV). In institutional terms again the treaty revision takes up real developments: the Political Committee, traditionally already the central CFSP body to prepare and implement ministerial decisions, plays a growing role particularly in cases of crisis management operations (Art. 25 TEU NV). Its new function is also reflected in a change of name to Political and Security Committee (PSC), while other details, such as its composition, location or the chair, are by intention not fixed in the treaty itself but through a Council decision (Council Decision 01/78/CFSP of 22 January 2001).

Furthermore, the Nice treaty foresees adaptations in Art. 17 TEU which correspond to an earlier decision of the WEU Council to transfer major functions of this organisation to the EU (except for the mutual military assistance clause

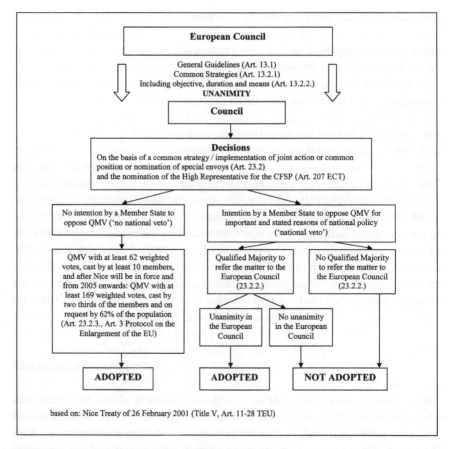

Figure 6.3b   Mature CFSP decision-making procedures

of the contracting WEU parties) – an almost revolutionary development if one recalls the massive disputes among the fifteen even over the gradual integration of the WEU bodies into the EU before 1998.

Finally, it is worth mentioning that the Heads of State and Government agreed to introduce some sort of an 'enhanced cooperation' also to the Second Pillar (Art. 27a–e TEU NV, Regelsberger 2001b: 159, Wessels 2001a: 205), based on the conviction that in an enlarged EU situations might occur where a group of the 'willing' could go ahead with a specific policy serving the common interests and objectives of the CFSP. The articles mentioned suggest an enhanced cooperation of at least eight Member States in those cases where the implementation of a joint action (Art. 14 TEU AV) or a common position (Art. 15 TEU AV) cannot be taken up by all. However, enhanced cooperation 'shall not relate to matters having military or defence implications' (Art. 27b TEU NV). This limitation to specific cases counters the initial ideas of some governments to make the provisions applicable also to the sensitive area of security and defence where unanimity at fifteen plus might be difficult to arrive at. However, the modest compromise reached in Nice after much controversy also had to take account of the concerns of several small Member States which feared to be marginalised and excluded from the core groups – an experience they had witnessed already in the course of the Bosnia Contact Group and the Kosovo crisis (Algieri 2001: 162, Regelsberger 2001b: 160).

THE EUROPEAN CONVENTION 2002-3:
A NEW ARCHITECTURE FOR CFSP IN THE DRAFT CONSTITUTIONAL TREATY

Nice by no means signals the end of the CFSP reforms. On the contrary, the prospect of EU enlargement and other external challenges like 11 September 2001 and the war against Iraq in 2003 forced the fifteen to redefine their 'place' as that of a European 'power' capable of assuming an active role in a global world (European Council 2000, 2001). Intensive debates in the newly established European Convention between January 2002 and July 2003 resulted in the Draft Constitutional Treaty which was to become the basis of the Intergovernmental Conference, the necessary legal framework to revise the existing TEU provisions. Though initially accepted as a 'good basis' for the IGC negotiations the Brussels European Council in December 2003 failed to achieve an agreement on the future European Constitution. While fundamental divergences of views on the voting system could not be overcome the CFSP provisions though modified during the IGC compared to the proposals of the Convention did not provoke the failure.

The Draft Treaty Establishing a Constitution for Europe (CONV 850/03) has both confirmed and reformulated major provisions of the EU's 'legal constitution'. The 'preamble', the 'Union's values' (Art. I-2) and the 'Union's objectives' as well as the 'principles and objectives' (Art. III-194) of the 'Union's external action' (Art. III-193) strongly advocated an active role dominated by the idea of a 'civilian power'. More than before, opportunities are presented to pursue these goals by acting as a 'peace power' but also by means of 'combat forces' (Arts I-40; III-210). In order to improve the operational capabilities of the EU the draft text introduces new modes of flexibility in the area of security and defence. In contrast to the Nice version of the TEU the new provisions offer 'structured cooperation' (Art. I-40; III-213) for those among the Member States most advanced in military capabilities and able and willing to implement the most demanding ESDP missions. A Defence Union with mutual military guarantees is, as previously, not put forward. The standard formula of a 'progressive framing of a common defence policy, which might lead to a common defence' (Arts. I-15, 40) is repeated. Remarkably enough, however, the Convention proposes to establish 'closer cooperation' (Art. I-40,7) in case a Member State has become victim of an armed aggression on its territory.

Concerning the evolution of the institutional architecture of the CFSP the Constitutional Treaty follows traditional lines of the past and adds some innovations. First of all, it reinforces the overarching weight of the European Council

(Arts. I-20–21; III-194–196) which is to identify the strategic interests and objectives of the Union which relate to both the CFSP and to other areas of the external action of the Union and to decide about the general guidelines, including matters with defence implications. Institutional innovations like the establishment of an extended Presidency of the European Council and explicit competences for the chair to represent the EU externally at this level and to convene extraordinary sessions if the international situation so requires will add to the enlarged responsibilities of the EU political top. Simultaneously the new provisions are not free of ambiguities and signal potential conflicts with the also newly established post of a Union Minister for Foreign Affairs (Art. I-27). He is the major institutional invention of the Constitutional Treaty. Compared to the existing High Representative for the CFSP, his successor will not only have a formal right of initiative for the whole CFSP/ESDP business but will act as the key spokesman towards the outside and exercise important functions for the internal formulation, mediation and decision-making in CFSP matters since he/she will permanently chair the Foreign Affairs Council (Art. I-23.2). Besides, and after different experiences with various persons speaking (Presidency, Commission, High Representative, Troika), the Convention proposals foresee the fusion between several areas of external action, i.e. Second Pillar issues and the EC's external relations in even one person, i.e. the Union Minister for Foreign Affairs who is to become Vice-President of the Commission simultaneously. Though these provisions could open a broad and multifunctional scope of opportunities, at the same time they might also create a set of inter-institutional and intra-institutional constraints on this new post.

Compared to the innovative steps described above progress in the field of majority voting has been rather modest in the area of CFSP. The protagonists of its extension widely failed against massive opposition from the traditional supporters of the unanimity principle like the United Kingdom. The Draft Treaty (Arts I-24; III-201) confirms the existing rules and suggests to go beyond these principles if the European Council defines new items for this procedure (ESDP matters will remain excluded) or the Union Foreign Minister takes the initiative on specific issues and in close collaboration with the Heads of State and Government in the European Council.

Using the treaty rules: evolutionary patterns of the living constitution

After several steps of constructing an institutional and procedural set-up, the EU and its Member States today dispose of a unique 'legal regime' (Smith 2001) or 'CFSP legal order' (Wessel 1999) to jointly formulate and implement a Common Foreign and Security Policy including matters of European Security and Defence. It evolved over more than thirty years from a loose set of vague and ambiguous political commitments towards a system based on a differentiated set of legal provisions within a formal framework. This construction of the 'legal constitution' indicates an institutional growth and considerable differentiation of the rules of cooperation in the foreign policy of the EC Member States.

We have, however, to observe and to analyse the real modes of governance. Since the 1980s, a considerable evolution towards a more and more sophisticated system, in which national politicians and diplomats are interlocking with the Community actors, becomes obvious. This living constitution is documented in the patterns of engagement of actors as well as the use of the procedures, in particular for producing policy outcomes.

Involvement of actors

As constitutional developments above illustrate, both the number and variety of actors in the CFSP and ESDP of today have little in common with the early days of the EPC and are beyond the already more sophisticated system of the early 1990s (Bretherton and Vogler 1999). More and more national and community actors use an ever growing institutional set-up.

Today, the Second Pillar of the EU finds at its hierarchical top the European Council with meetings at least twice a year, according to the EU treaty (Art. 4 TEU NV), while in reality at least the same number of informal sessions are convened in addition. Its task is to give overall guidance and to define the principles of the joint endeavours including those on defence. In time of crisis the European Council will meet at a short notice.

The Council in its composition of foreign ministers and, if needed, including the ministers of defence – a clear novelty since 2000 – prepares the discussions of the European Council and is politically responsible for all main decisions in CSFP. What had seemed unthinkable in the first two decades of the EPC has become normal by now, i.e. foreign ministers meet in the Council at monthly intervals at the sites of the EC institutions to discuss all foreign and security issues. Above all, its work is no longer exclusively prepared by the Political Committee/PSC but in cooperation with the Committee of Permanent Representatives, which is according to Art. 207 EC Treaty (NV) traditionally in charge of the Council preparations. Not surprisingly, this shared responsibility at the administrative level occasionally creates unproductive conflicts over the distribution of competencies.

At the administrative level we witness a 'Brussellisation' of the diplomatic apparatus and thus the creation of a 'core network' (see for the term Wessels and Linsenmann 2002): the constant broadening of the CFSP agenda has given rise to an intensive use of a great number of working parties for regional subjects, like the Middle East or Latin America, as well as for functional topics, e.g. human rights issues (Wessels 2000: 181). Other expert groups, like the one on civil crisis management, were established only recently for improving the fifteen's performance in ESDP. Another category of groups deals with the proper functioning of the CFSP itself, like the European Correspondents of the national foreign ministries, and its close association with the Community business, especially the group of Political Councillors in the permanent representations of the EU

Member States in Brussels. The working parties meet at regular intervals, twice per presidency at least, and report regularly to the Political and Security Committee, the key institution at diplomatic level in CFSP.

Since its inception under the Swedish presidency in the first half of 2001 this body works at high intensity, i.e. in twice-weekly meetings. The fact that the members of the PSC are by intention permanently placed in Brussels and that they are composed of high level officials/ambassadors from the permanent representations of EU Member States to the Union (according to Council Decision 01/78 CFSP of 22 January 2001) has accelerated the decision-making process and opened the way not only for a better daily coordination between the CFSP and EC Pillar for the sake of consistency but also for a strengthening of the common European interests. However, these positive effects of 'Brussellisation' have found their limits so far in certain international crisis situations like the Iraq war in 2003 and partly in the events of September 11 2001 where fundamental national interests were concerned and questions of national security and peace or war occurred. Despite the fact that the intensive contacts among the CFSP staff in Brussels might have occasionally limited or at least changed the influence of traditional actors in the national foreign ministries the work of the PSC cannot successfully be done without a constant link to the diplomats 'at home'. It needs to be supplied both with information and instructions from the capitals. Besides, the political directors, forming the previous Political Committee, are not out of the game. On the contrary, the PSC in the above mentioned composition has to tackle the daily business while the Political Directors meet at certain intervals to concentrate on selected key issues and to define mid-term perspectives for important areas.

The dynamics in ESDP matters have also massively contributed to the institutional growth since the mid-1990s, most obvious in the installation of the EU Military Committee, from 2001 onwards as a permanent structure, and the establishment of the EU Military Staff in the Secretariat General of the Council at a size of 130 officers (as of 2001 onwards). Most recently and as a consequence of the first crisis management operations of the EU since 2003 (EU Police Mission in Bosnia to be followed by a military operation to take over from SFOR; EU Military operation 'Concordia' and Police Mission 'Proxima' in Macedonia; EU Military Operation 'Artemis' in Congo) preparations are underway to establish an 'Agency in the field of defence capabilities' (Council Press Release 2003) and a 'cell with civil/military components' (Presidency Conclusions 2003: point 89), i.e. some sort of military Headquarters under the roof of the Council Secretariat and under the authority of the High Representative for the CFSP (Presidency Conclusions 2003), which will add to the complexity of the present institutional structure of the CFSP.

In view of our trend analysis also this part of the 'Brussellisation' could bear similar socialisation results as the EPC in the first two decades of its existence did, especially as many actors have already shared experiences within NATO bodies. However, the very different administrative cultures and working methods of the military and those in the Council Secretariat and Foreign Offices could produce some dividing lines in the day to day work. Some experts even speculate that there is something like a 'Fourth Pillar' in the making by the military establishment. Others predict a strengthening of intergovernmentalism which might even spill-over into the Community Pillar. The fact that the European Commission is not (yet) admitted to the Military Committee, although it is fully associated with the CFSP at all levels according to the treaty provisions (Art. 27 TEU NV), could indicate a trend into such a direction.

The post of the High Representative for the CFSP, for which the former NATO Secretary General Javier Solana has been appointed in 1999, represents another major feature of the institutional innovations of the late 1990s (Verderame 1999: 22). Formally, the position of the High Representative is clearly subordinated to the Council and its members: he 'shall assist the Council . . . in particular through contributing to the formulation, preparation and implementation of policy decisions, and, when appropriate acting on behalf of the Council at the request of the Presidency, through conducting political dialogue with third parties' (Art. 26 TEU NV). In CFSP practice Solana has managed to use these functions extensively in close cooperation with the presidencies. He enjoys considerable authority both among the fifteen and outside the EU borders (Frisch 2000). He has been frequently charged with specific mandates and takes part in the formulation of key issues of CFSP and also ESDP. Also in the internal CFSP hierarchy Solana managed to clarify and strengthen his position. This applies towards the special envoys who have to carry out their tasks under his authority and partly towards the PSC which he might chair in crisis situations after consultation with the presidency (Council Decision 01/78/CFSP of 22 January 2001).

The role of the Commission has also been strengthened in the CFSP over the years: in particular, its co-responsibility for a coherent approach in foreign policy (Art. 3 TEU NV) and for implementing CFSP decisions especially when it comes to a distribution of funds give importance to the Commission's participation. With the 'rise' of other actors in CFSP, and especially of the High Representative for the CFSP, however, also competition has emerged for the Commission as the spokesperson of the EU. This competition applies primarily to the Commissioner in charge of external relations and CFSP, who sees an overlap in competences in the area of civil crisis management and perceives institutional complications with the post of the High Representative for the CFSP.

As stated above, it was and still is the explicit intention of the EC Member States to prevent the European Court of Justice from jurisdiction over CFSP acts. To the extent, however, that the Second and First Pillar issues become inter-related, e.g. in the case of sanctions, situations might occur where the CFSP could interfere with the competences of the EC, thus provoking a violation of the EC treaties for which the Court's ruling could be demanded (Smith 2001). Another example of genuinely Community actors 'invading' the CFSP scene points at the fact that in CFSP actions financed through the EC budget the European Court of Auditors can exert control over the Second Pillar. This has happened several times meanwhile, e.g. in the case of the EU administration of the Bosnian city of Mostar, and with a rather negative result on not only how the earmarked money was spent but also with regard to inefficient internal coordination between Council and Commission (Court of Auditors 2001).

Use of procedures

TRENDS IN THE CFSP OUTPUT

For a systematic overview on the patterns of real activities we will take a look at the published policy results. As table 6.1 illustrates, the policy output of today's CFSP has largely increased compared to what the EPC produced before. Both in terms of quantity (i.e. agenda according to regional and functional issues) and quality (i.e. differentiation of instruments and contents) the differences are obvious.

In contrast to the early days of the EPC when 'speaking with one voice' focused on the Arab-Israeli conflict and the Conference on Security and Cooperation in Europe, the CFSP agenda of today has a really global outlook (Durand and de Vasconcelos 1998, Holland 1997, Regelsberger 2000, 2001a, 2002, 2003). It is largely determined by the course of events and the fifteen (plus the ten applicants which participate at all CFSP levels since the signature of the Accession Treaty in April 2003) undertake considerable efforts to respond to them in a fast and precise manner.

Declarations have remained an adequate tool to do so despite the harsh and often unjustified criticism of a 'mere' declaratory European diplomacy. As reactions of the third parties concerned often confirm 'words' may have a significance in foreign policy though they may not always be enough to demonstrate the EU's self-claimed capacity to act. Compared to earlier texts those of today reflect a far more sophisticated '*acquis politique*' which is constantly adapted to new circumstances and which interferes in very concrete terms with the affairs of the addressees. This is true not only for issues in the immediate neighbourhood of the EU, like the CFSP statements on the domestic political system in the EU candidate countries or towards developments in the Western Balkans, but also for other world regions as the CFSP statements on political events, e.g. in Asia or Africa demonstrate.

Interventions against the violation of human rights also belong to the traditional arsenal of the fifteen's foreign policy instruments and show considerable growth rates in recent years (rise from 175 demarches by the presidency in third countries in 2000 to 487 demarches in 2002; see Council of the European Union 1999, 2000, 2001a; Regelsberger 2000, 2001a, 2002, 2003). They are frequently undertaken as silent diplomacy but it is also the EU's explicit understanding to work towards a strengthening of the human rights at international fora like the United Nations. In the UN bodies in New York – except in the Security Council – and elsewhere the 'voice' of the fifteen is widely accepted by

Table 6.1 EPC/CFSP, 1970–2003, forms of output

	1970	1972	1973	1986	1987	1990	1994	1997	1998	1999	2000	2001	2002	2003	Total
Declarations	–	2	10	54	63	115	110	123	141	123	184	196	197	150	1468
Common positions[1]	–	–	–	–	–	–	8	13	22	35	33	20	24	24	179
Joint actions[2]	–	–	–	–	–	–	14	15	20	20	21	19	20	32	161
Common strategies[3]	–	–	–	–	–	–	–	–	–	2	1	–	–	2[8]	5
Decisions[4]	–	–	–	–	–	–	–	–	–	–	5	6	–	3	14
Conclusion of international agreement[5]	–	–	–	–	–	–	–	–	–	–	–	2	3	16	21
Enhanced cooperation[6]	–	–	–	–	–	–	–	–	–	–	–	–	–	–	–

Source: Own calculations based upon the Bulletins of the EC/EU and Annual Reports of the Activities of the EC/EU. Legislative acts according to http://ue.eu.int/pesc/.

the other participants and the EU countries have successfully improved their profile by tabling joint drafts in the negotiations, by letting the presidency speak on their behalf and by voting unanimously in around 75–80 per cent of the resolutions put to a vote in the period 1996–2002 (Sucharipa 2003: 796) while consensus had remained with 46 per cent in the 1970s and had declined in the early 1980s to 39 per cent (Sucharipa 1999, Stadler 1993).

In order to become more pro-active in its performance the Maastricht treaty introduced the new instruments of 'joint actions' and 'common positions'. After some time of misperceptions of the proper use of the one or the other the following practice of these new so-called legislative acts has emerged: 'common positions' reflect an overall approach of the EU towards a third country, and so far mainly those of the ACP group, or contain specific sanctions against a state which have to be implemented afterwards either via Community regulations or national law. 'Joint actions' are to express a particular interest of the EU and its Member States towards a country or region which manifests itself in visible activities 'at place' (Art. 14.1 TEU NV). They refer to geographical zones (see figure 6.4) close to the EU, such as the former Yugoslavia, Russia or the Middle East. Examples of such very concrete decisions limited in time and staffed with operational resources were the election observations in Russia, in South Africa and the Occupied Territories in the first half of the 1990s. Today joint actions cover among others the work of the EU's Special Representatives who help to bring stability and peace to the Middle East (Moratinos, Otte), to South East Europe (Hombach, Busek), Macedonia (Léotard, Le Roy, Brouhns), Bosnia (Lord Ashdown), Afghanistan (Klaiber, Vendrell), the Great Lakes Region in Africa (Ajello) and most recently (2003) for the South Caucasus (Talvitie). Other joint actions of the day contain the EU's support for the UN administration of Kosovo, assistance to the setting up of police forces in Albania and the EU Monitoring Mission in the Federal Republic of Yugoslavia.

The other new instrument, the common strategy, introduced with the Amsterdam Treaty only in 1999, has been used only three times so far. Designed to express the EU's vital interests towards a country or a region by formulating a comprehensive approach, it is not surprising that Russia, the Ukraine and the Mediterranean were among the priorities, but strangely enough not yet the Balkans. Prepared by the Council and formally passed by the European Council these common strategies have received considerable criticism. They are seen as reflecting nothing but a shopping list without indications on the fifteen's major fields of interests and recall what has been determined and implemented already elsewhere, some also inside CFSP argue (Solana 2001). Besides, critics point at the fact that the publication of a common strategy works against its use in times of crisis as a sanction instrument and therefore reduces its value as a whole. Furthermore, common strategies have not produced the expected majority decisions in CFSP when implementing the relevant parts of it by common positions and joint actions. However, common strategies seem to play a helpful role in terms of coherence of EC, CFSP and national policies (Schmalz 1998) because

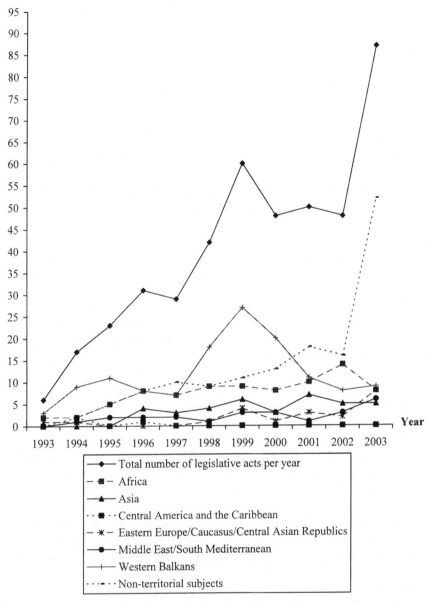

Source: General Secretariat of the Council as of 30 January 2004, http://ue.eu.int/pcsc/

Figure 6.4   CFSP output, 1993–2003: geographical distribution of issues

the formulation of the text requires much concertation among the actors involved at the different levels and fosters a harmonisation of views among them.

MAJORITY VOTING: DEAD TREATY LETTERS

In comparison to an increasing output, the real patterns of CFSP decision-making remain characterised by the traditional intergovernmental style. The consensus rule was the guiding principle of the old EPC and it has remained so even in the mature CFSP. Protagonist hopes to accelerate the decision-making process through majority votes have not been fulfilled yet. The respective treaty provisions (Art. 23 TEU AV) are admittedly modest and limited to the implementation of common strategies, joint actions and common positions; however, these opportunities have not been seized by governments. Even the idea of using them as a 'threat potential' to find a common line more rapidly has revealed no evidence so far. The German presidency in the first half of 1999 was keen on setting a sign after the Amsterdam provisions had come into force but had to accept considerable resistance on the part of several partners. Subsequent presidencies traditionally more sceptical of the value of majority voting did nothing to promote the application of procedures. These patterns of no-use documents the irrelevance of some of the major treaty provisions.

FINANCING CFSP VIA THE EC BUDGET

Despite the variety of procedural modes and the inherent opportunities for a greater efficiency of the decision making, the fifteen continue to prefer the intergovernmental procedures practised now for decades. However, there is one area where Community rules also reign into the CFSP Pillar: the budget. As the masters of the Maastricht Treaty wished to see a more visible and operational CFSP, the question of financing such concrete activities became obvious. It was at first tackled in a rather vague mode offering either Community resources to be decided upon unanimously in the Council or requiring national contributions from the Member States which they were to specify according to a system yet to be defined (Art. J.11 TEU MV). Since money was scarce in the capitals even the most energetic supporters of an intergovernmental CFSP Pillar were ready to take recourse to the EC budget to finance some of the first joint CFSP actions. What they were eventually not aware of was that this implied the acceptance of the EC rules for the budgetary procedure with the Council and the European Parliament acting as the budgetary authority on an equal footing. Year-long disputes (Monar 1997b: 57) followed until the next intergovernmental conference. In Amsterdam the existing treaty provisions were amended (Art. 28 TEU AV) and improved (Griller *et al.* 2000: 417) stating that CFSP operational expenditure is covered by the EC budget except for CFSP decisions with military or defence implications. Besides, in May 1999 an inter-institutional agreement was signed by the Council, the European Parliament, and the European Commission which defines the procedures and categories of the CFSP expenditure. In this specific area parliamentary participation and some sort of control is probably most direct since the Council is obliged to inform the EP regularly on those actions which imply financial commitments. The importance, however, is limited since one also has to be aware of the fact that CFSP expenditure (47 million euros in 2000) only comprises around 0.05 per cent (in 2000) of the total EC budget and roughly 1.0 per cent (in 2000) of all those budget lines covering external EC policies (in total 4825 million euros). This marginal expenditure limits the direct influence of the European Parliament which has to improve its still rather modest participation in the formulation of the CFSP policies (as laid down in Art. 21 TEU).

Conclusions and perspectives

Dynamics and limitations of the fusion process
In testing the thesis of a ratchet fusion we observe the following trends: First, the evolution of formal provisions documents a ratchet process. IGCs have regularly revised the legal constitution upwards on the integration ladder in incremental steps (see figure 6.5). We would locate the CFSP in its Nice version at the higher end plateau II. However, compared to other policy fields like EMU and certain policies belonging to the field of Justice and Home Affairs, treaty changes have not yet moved it onto the third major level, that of supranational communitarisation, and the draft Constitutional Treaty of 2003 doesn't either.

Second, the evolution of real patterns in the living constitution shows a trend towards an intensive use of institutions and procedures to produce an increasing and more differentiated output. However, the mainly supranational elements have largely remained dead letters. Third, the analysis of both dimensions signals

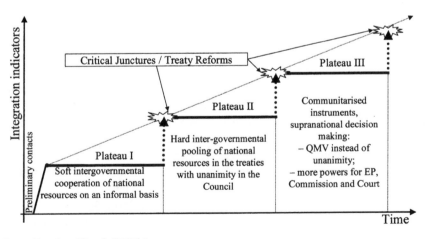

Source: Based on Wessels (2001b).

Figure 6.5 The integration cascade: a micro view of ratchet fusion

that political attention and personal resources have been shifted to Brussels. The fusion process increasingly links national actors in a differentiated horizontal intergovernmental set-up but national resources are not yet communitarised as in other policy fields. And in international crises national actors even tend to re-emerge to run the machinery among themselves and/or in specific alliances among the EU Member States.

The trend of this imperfect ratchet process is based on fusion dynamics which are created by mutually reinforcing learning processes and treaty-making, i.e. legal and real evolutions are closely linked. The argument starts from a counter-intuitive finding that several national actors in different periods of the postwar history, including post-1989 times, and in an ever-increasing number of European countries have invested their time, attention and human resources into the EC/EU system, including increasingly the CFSP and since the late 1990s also the European Security and Defence Policy (ESDP). Faced with external shocks from the international system, national actors of different generations and party political orientations have looked again and again for an efficient and effective problem-solving framework. The original 'choices for Europe' (Moravscik 1999) were thus reiterated at several occasions.

In creating opportunity structures by treaty articles, national actors tried to keep their formal autonomy and national sovereignty especially in foreign and security policy. The search for efficiency was matched by the continuous effort to keep key decisions of the CFSP under ultimate national control.

A key body for analysing this process is the European Council. The Heads of State and Government and the President of the Commission identify their problems collectively and push for effective actions. Once perceived as a major problem-solving framework for foreign policy new and additional challenges were increasingly allocated to this set of institutions. Thus not necessarily 'objective' internal or external events and developments were the causes for the trends we observed, but the way actors in Member States learned to esteem the use of the CFSP for their own purposes. These mechanisms and processes work to a considerable degree because they are perceived as serving the self-interest of national and Community actors. The competition by actors for access and influence in the EU policy cycles is a major incentive to move upwards in the ratchet fusion. Thus, all actors try to profit from a positive-sum game.

This general role attribution to EU institutions also supports the fundamental legitimacy of the EU system. The often claimed deficits in the accountability and transparency would then be only of an 'academic' nature. The steps for creating legal provisions and using them intensively might be more an indicator of the fact that at least the political establishment has identified the EU as their system in the deep sense of a fundamental political community (Easton 1965: 177) as a major arena for dealing with vital issues. Thus this move to Brussels explains the complexity of the procedures, the diffusion of responsibilities and the lack of transparency, but also the pooling of legitimacy resources – all phenomena well known in federal systems.

The institutional and procedural evolution and their intensive employment that we described with some data are thus both dependent and independent variables. Once started, the process generates itself. The socialisation within daily interactions shapes a European way of thinking which leads to new or reformed institutional arrangements.

As a consequence, the choice for Europe is no longer an option to be taken or refused freely by national leaders at whatever occasion. The scope of national autonomy gets narrower and the range of options becomes more EU oriented with each treaty amendment. The corridor for national policy options becomes narrower, though for the CFSP it remains still broader than for other sectors, e.g. monetary policies.

National and supranational Community actors share responsibility and accountability in mixed and merged structures and with policy instruments pooled from both national and EU level. Such a collective decision-making with a continuous enlargement of the political scope does, however, imply a hybrid institutional set-up with an unclear distribution of roles and instruments. In such a complex and multilevel system transparency is lacking and the need for institutional adaptations and reforms emerges. The inefficiency and ineffectiveness of the system is thus a built-in driving force for further constitutional engineering. Thus we can observe fusion dynamics in which institutional revisions each time create new pressing needs for further reforms.

TOWARDS A NEXT STEP IN THE FUSION LADDER?

Will these trends of an ever-closer fusion by a step by step ladder be broken? Or will the process go on 'forever' towards an unknown destiny, i.e. towards an open *finalité*? The key to this question is the common perception among national actors that this set-up serves one's own problems in whatever way.

DYNAMICS FOR A REAL STEP FORWARD

The overall dynamics of the EU system and the difficulties of the present institutions and procedures will create sufficient incentives for the Heads of State and Government to take a decisive step towards some kind of a supranational/federal set of rules for running an efficient and effective Common Foreign and Security Policy. Challenges and shocks from the international system will be perceived as pressures to push national politicians on the fusion cascade towards the third mode of governance (see figure 6.5) – perhaps at the beginning with another rather incremental but real transfer of powers – especially in the area of defence; this would lead to an upgrading of ESDP/CSDP to some kind of collective defence alliance.

ANOTHER REFINING OF THE INTERGOVERNMENTAL STATUS QUO

Foreign and especially defence policies remain in the intergovernmentally oriented mode, which gives national actors sufficient opportunities to use autonomously their own resources if perceived as necessary. This 'high politics' area would stay resistant to the usual spill-over pressures. The Heads of State and Government might take steps towards a further rationalisation of the intergovernmental coordination of national instruments in the next IGC, but they would not cross the borderline towards supranational procedures to use methods of communitarised resources. Even more: the greater focus on essential defence issues at the European level with a strong preoccupation on behalf of national actors and traditional consensual procedures could even spill-back towards the management at the lower end of the conventional CFSP. This scenario is supported by proposals such as nominating a permanent president of the European Council among its peers.

AN ONGOING FUSION

In this scenario the dilemma between institutionalising an efficient machinery for an effective international EU role and the guarantee for an ultimate national, say, will continue. The Convention and the subsequent IGC will produce further ambitious procedures. The search for a 'superpower without a superstate' will push the 'masters of the treaty' to look for modes of governance which will strengthen the EU as an actor without really transferring sovereignty. The proposal of a 'double hat', i.e. to entrust one person with both the office of the Union Minister for Foreign Affairs and the Vice President of the Commission, would follow this set of expectations.

Imperfect as it is, CFSP and its younger relative, the ESDP, will remain of high relevance for both the political world and academic research. Even more than thirty years after its inception under 'EPC' the CFSP has not yet reached its final stage neither in the form of the legal nor the living constitution.

Notes

1 Introduced in Maastricht (Art. 15 TEU AV).
2 Introduced in Maastricht (Art. 14 TEU AV).
3 Introduced in Amsterdam (Art. 13 TEU AV).
4 On CFSP institutional aspects.
5 According to Art. 24 TEU.
6 Introduced in Nice Treaty 2001 (Art. 27 a–e TEU NV).
7 This includes only the European Union statements and presidency statements on behalf of the European Union which were published from January until November 2003.
8 These are common strategies amending earlier common strategies in order to extend the period of their application.

SANDRA LAVENEX

7

Governance in an enlarging 'area of freedom, security and justice'

Introduction

Justice and Home Affairs (JHA) is one of the most recent areas of cooperation in the EU – and has rapidly moved from the sidelines to the centre stage of the European integration project. Spurred by the progress made through 'closer cooperation' in the Schengen framework, an impressive number of measures have been developed which relate to the management of the EU's external borders, immigration and asylum policy, and police and judicial cooperation in civil and criminal law matters. With the call for an 'Area of Freedom, Security and Justice' (AFSJ), the Treaty of Amsterdam has given these policy fields a prominent place in the Union's architecture. This rapid evolution of JHA from an initially marginal issue to a central focus of European unification has prompted some commentators to compare the work programme contained in the Amsterdam Treaty with the 1992 programme for the creation of the Single Market (Boer and Wallace 2000: 517, Monar 2001a: 294).

Whilst JHA cooperation is indeed 'booming business' (Boer 1999: 319), this expansion occurs in quite a different fashion than the modes of governance developed in the traditional Community Pillar. Many issues falling under the title of JHA address sensitive questions of domestic politics which touch the core of state sovereignty. A transgovernmental mode of policy-making has established itself which may allow for cooperative problem-solving without strong engagement of supranational actors. This chapter analyses the tension between partial communitarisation and intensive transgovernmentalism and reflects on the implications of Eastern enlargement for institutional and policy developments in JHA. It is argued that Member States' genuine interest in including the accession countries of Central and Eastern Europe (CEECs) in their efforts to safeguard internal security and stability has implied an early extension of cooperation to the East, which challenges established modes of transgovernmental cooperation.

The chapter starts with an analysis of the emergence of JHA on the EU agenda and highlights the challenges posed by Eastern enlargement. The relationship between transgovernmentalism and communitarisation under the Treaties of Amsterdam and Nice is investigated in the second section. The conclusion interprets these developments in the light of the recent enlargement.

Traditional modes of policy-making in JHA

Accounts of JHA often point at the role of the Single European Act (SEA) of 1986 and explain the emergence of this new field of European integration as a consequence of the determination to realise freedom of movement for persons. According to this logic, the abolition of internal border controls in the EU threatened to create a security deficit in the Member States which had to be compensated for by the elaboration of common policies at the EU's external borders. A look beyond particular developments in the EU, however, shows that the emergence of cooperation in JHA was very much influenced by the successive espousal of domestic security concerns by transgovernmental fora already prior to the SEA, and their consecutive linkage with the single market project. These groups, which emerged from the mid-1970s onwards, had some important features in common:

- they had a smaller and more homogeneous constituency than the already existing fora of cooperation;
- they worked on a more informal and flexible basis;
- they were primarily driven by the dynamic interchange between ministerial officials and law enforcement professionals at the operational level rather than by high-level political decisions (Anderson et al. 1995, Bigo 1996).

According to Helen Wallace (2000), the resulting networks of interaction may be characterised as a structure of 'intensive transgovernmentalism' which rests 'mainly on interaction between the relevant national policy-makers, and with relatively little involvement by the EU institutions' (Wallace 2000: 33). In contrast to intergovernmentalism, the term transgovernmental refers to the activities of governmental actors below the level of Heads of State or Government such as ministerial officials, law enforcement agencies, and other bureaucratic actors. These officials act with a certain degree of autonomy from chief executives and develop their own policy agenda (Keohane and Nye 1974). In the EU context transgovernmental cooperation may occur both outside the Treaty framework and within, and often takes the form of informal, not legally binding, agreements. In any case, the roles of the Commission, the Parliament and the Court are limited, and the impetus for cooperation comes rather from the transgovernmental networks than from supranational or governmental actors. A second difference with the intergovernmentalist approach to European integration is that the notion of transgovernmentalism does not reject the idea that integration does take place, but this occurs with different means than the Community method or neofunctionalism would predict. It will be shown that whilst intensive transgovernmentalism continues to be the main institutional mode of policy-making in JHA, the prospect of Eastern enlargement has favoured the introduction of more supranational elements, reflected in the provisions adopted in the Amsterdam Treaty.

The transgovernmental sources of JHA cooperation

The first steps towards cooperation in criminal and penal matters were made in the framework of the Council of Europe and Interpol. In the 1970s the lead was taken over by new transgovernmental groups composed of representatives from national home ministries, partly with the participation of non-EU countries (Bigo 1996: 79ff.). The most influential forum became the so-called Trevi group founded in 1975 which shaped to a considerable degree the development of what became later the Third Pillar including the Europol Convention.

Starting with the problem of terrorism, Trevi's mandate was subsequently widened to include the issues of international (organised) crime, drugs, external borders, fraud, immigration and asylum. This evolution corresponded with the conjuncture of internal security preoccupations in influential Member States and was marked by the proliferation of informal consultation fora among them. In this context the reinvigoration of the single market project in the SEA provided an opportunity for linking domestic internal security concerns with the broader project of European integration and in particular the free movement of persons. A salient example for such a linkage is the reform of the asylum law in Germany, in which domestic calls for a restriction of the constitutional asylum right of Art. 16 (2) Basic Law were justified from the mid-1980s onwards as necessary consequences of the abolition of internal borders in the EU (Lavenex 2001a). Germany was equally influential in the area of police cooperation with ex-Chancellor Kohl's initiative to create an FBI-like 'Central European Investigation Office', an initiative which ultimately led to the establishment of the European Police Office, Europol (Bigo 1996: 208ff., Fijnaut 1993). The coupling of existing transgovernmental JHA cooperation with the questions of freedom of movement and European integration became most explicit in the Schengen group which, founded originally by five Member States in 1985 (the Benelux countries, France and Germany), framed its cooperation as 'compensatory' for the realisation of free movement of persons.[1] This logic was taken over by the Maastricht Treaty which included questions related to the crossing of external borders, immigration, asylum, drugs, fraud, customs, judicial and police cooperation in civil and criminal matters as 'matters of common interest' for the realisation of the free movement of persons in its Third Pillar (Title VI TEU old version). Whilst the Schengen group continued to operate outside the EU framework, Maastricht's 'Third Pillar' formalised the existing structures of transgovernmental cooperation, keeping the influence of supranational actors to a minimum: a shared right of initiative for the Commission, unanimous voting in the Council, an often disregarded consultation procedure with the Parliament (Curtin and Meijers 1995), and no judicial review by the Court of Justice (Bieber and Monar 1995).

The main achievement of the Maastricht Treaty was to conglomerate the various forums of cooperation among JHA officials into one common institutional framework and to connect them to the general interests of the Union. More important steps bringing JHA to the centre of EU 'governance' were made with the Amsterdam Treaty. The Schengen Agreement was included in the EU framework. Parts of what used to be the Third Pillar were transferred into the Community Pillar (asylum, immigration, external borders and judicial cooperation in civil law matters, Title IV TEC) and the decision-making procedures of what was left of the new Third Pillar were transformed and renamed 'police and judicial cooperation in criminal matters' (PJCCM, Title VI TEU). Issues with important overlap with Community competence such as financial fraud and customs cooperation were given a legal basis in the 'mainstream' EC Treaty (Art. 280 TEC and Art. 135 TEC respectively). Whilst implying a diversification between policy fields which would eventually come under full Community competence and those maintained under transgovernmental procedures, the Amsterdam Treaty gave these issues a certain symbolic unity as constituents of an 'Area of Freedom, Security and Justice' (Art. 2 TEU, Art. 61 TEC).

The diversification of JHA in the Amsterdam Treaty mirrors on the one hand the different degrees of domestic sensitivity of the various issues pertaining to JHA, since those issues which relate closest to the core of state sovereignty, the maintenance of internal security and public order, remain in the sphere of transgovernmental cooperation. On the other hand, it is interesting to see that this diversification does not reflect the intensity of cooperation, with police cooperation and organised crime being the busiest area of cooperation in the late 1990s (Boer and Wallace 2000: 503). According to Monica den Boer the lack of more incisive institutional reforms is paradoxical since this is also 'the area with the most pressing need for international cooperation' (Boer 1999: 308). However this development might also be a sign that the needs for cooperation could be matched by governance structures which differ from the traditional Community method.

A look at the wide range of measures included in the definition of the JHA *acquis communautaire* at the end of the 1990s confirms this interpretation, even if the cumbersome procedures and the lack of tangible policy output of the Third Pillar have faced much criticism (e.g. O'Keeffe 1995). The reason behind this apparent paradox is that the vast majority of these measures did not take the shape of formal instruments provided by the EU Treaty and were not legally binding. Whilst this loose form of cooperation allowed for a maximum degree of sovereign discretion over both decision-taking and implementation on parts of the Member States, the determination of the *acquis* in the wake of the Amsterdam Treaty represented a stronger formalisation and codification of JHA cooperation, and was mainly induced by the prospect of an Eastern enlargement of the EU.

Eastern enlargement as a challenge for transgovernmentalism

The coincidence of the opening up of the Eastern bloc in 1989 with the intensifying cooperation against the potential threats resulting from an abolition of internal borders exacerbated existing fears of 'porous borders', and added a sense of urgency to that cooperation. Yet the fact that the Second Schengen Agreement of 1990 which laid down the agenda for the further years was already drafted by 1988 shows that the perception of new security threats at the EU's Eastern borders acted more as an additional source of justification than as a causal determinant of JHA cooperation.[2] Whilst developments in Central and Eastern Europe were thus not the main reason driving cooperation forward, the wish to include the CEECs into this cooperation and the latter's linkage with the procedural framework of EU enlargement led to a stronger formalisation of JHA and favoured the introduction of supranational elements into this policy field.

The prospect of an Eastern enlargement challenged the existing structures of transgovernmental cooperation in several ways:

- the number of participating countries would double;
- the strong divergence and heterogeneity of JHA in the accession countries challenged the informal and flexible mode of cooperation and called for stronger compliance mechanisms;
- the asymmetry of interests and professional expertise at the operational level questioned the efficiency of transgovernmental networks, leading to a stronger politicisation of cooperation.[3]

The first move in including JHA in the enlargement process was made by the European Commission in 1994, when it urged the JHA ministers to take a decision on the procedures for consulting and informing the CEECs within a more structured and hence formal relationship (Commission 1994). In fact transgovernmental cooperation between individual Member States and the accession countries was already well under way, both in bilateral and multilateral activities. The lead was taken by the countries sharing borders with the CEECs. Shortly after the fall of the Berlin Wall, Germany and its *Länder* developed a wide range of bilateral activities geared at the export of high standards of border control infrastructure and technology as well as police training and equipment to the CEECs. The Nordic countries concentrated on the Baltic states; Austria on Hungary and Slovenia. France too provided different CEECs with police training and border control technology, whilst the UK focused especially on the issue of organised crime (Bort 2000: 15ff, Eisl 1999: 179, Langdon 1995: 19ff). At the multilateral level the Schengen Group extended its purview. In 1991 it concluded a model readmission agreement with Poland which provided for the obligation to readmit own and third country nationals having entered a Schengen member without authorisation from Poland. In Berlin in the same year the Germans took the initiative at a conference on illegal immigration to launch the so-called Budapest process. Counting forty participating countries, today, the Budapest process has developed into a leading forum for pan-European cooperation in questions relating to internal security (see Lavenex 1999: 75ff.).

Against this background the Commission's call in 1994 to include JHA in the formal pre-accession strategy must be interpreted as an attempt to bring activities falling in the ambit of Maastricht's Third Pillar closer to the EU institutions and to ensure a stronger coordination of the various bilateral and multilateral processes. Yet Member States avoided giving JHA an important place in the structured dialogue which shaped the pre-accession process between 1994 and 1997. It was only with the launch of the 'accession partnerships' that the ongoing transgovernmental cooperation gained a more formal basis in the enlargement framework. This timing coincided with two developments: the first (informal) determination of the JHA *acquis* in a letter of the Irish Presidency to the CEECs in 1996, and the intergovernmental conference leading to the Amsterdam Treaty.

The publication of the list of measures which the CEECs would have to adopt in JHA revealed for the first time the wide range of reforms which the CEECs would have to fulfil in order to join the Union. This list was significantly extended three years later with the inclusion of the much broader Schengen *acquis*, which was determined only one month before the coming into force of the Amsterdam Treaty in May 1999. Whilst the opaque legal nature of cooperation under the Third Pillar and the selective approach adopted by the Member States had long obscured the role of JHA in relations with the CEECs, the extensive definition of measures which the latter would have to adopt turned this policy field into one of the most difficult aspects of the enlargement process (Eisl 1999, Lavenex 2001b, Reflection Group 1999). In addition to the formal conventions and other legally binding instruments adopted by the Member States, and informal, non-binding ones such as resolutions and conclusions, it was agreed that the CEECs also have to adopt 'the agreed elements of draft instruments which are in negotiation' (Commission 1997: B.3.7) as well as the full Schengen *acquis* including 'further measures taken by the institutions within its scope' (Art. 8, Schengen Protocol, TEU).

This extensive definition of measures which the CEECs would have to adopt challenged the existing forms of bilateral and multilateral exchanges and made a more coordinated strategy inevitable. This is due to both the internal situation with JHA in the accession countries and the characteristics of the JHA *acquis*. Whilst within the EU, transgovernmental cooperation in JHA could build on a certain degree of common heritage with regard to the rule of law, the organisation of the judiciary, professional police and border guards, data protection, or independent asylum systems, the post-communist CEECs lacked this common tradition and thus need a much greater degree of institutional, legislative and administrative change in order to fulfil the necessary adaptations. Apart from the scope of institutional change required, the interests of the CEECs are not necessarily congruent with those of the EU Member States. Examples of conflicting interests are the tension between tight visa regimes and relations with ethnic minorities in other countries, cross-border trade or general political relations (Grabbe 2002), or the costs involved in establishing tight border regimes and acting as gate-keepers for refugees and other migrants heading towards the more affluent countries of Western Europe (Lavenex 1999, Wallace and Stola 2001).

In addition to the situation in the CEECs several features of the JHA *acquis* call for a stronger communitarisation in the face of Eastern enlargement. The first and most tangible point is the opaque legal nature of most measures included in the *acquis* and the circumstance that they are binding on the accession countries but not on the Member States. The second problem is the dynamic nature of the *acquis* and the fact that the accession countries have to adopt measures which are currently under negotiation. They face a moving target and a great degree of insecurity over the exact direction of the necessary adaptations. A third crucial problem is the fragmented and patchy nature of the JHA *acquis* and the continuity of a large degree of divergence among the Member States themselves as to e.g. the organisation of the police forces, the functioning of the judicial system, the approach towards legal immigration, or the criteria for granting refugee status. Finally, this fragmented, diverging, and 'multilevel' nature of the JHA *acquis* is complicated by the conflicts of values involved in balancing internal security considerations with respect for the rule of law, data protection, or fundamental rights.

The structure of the JHA *acquis* and the difficulties implied in transferring it Eastwards opened a window of opportunity for a greater involvement of supranational actors in this transgovernmental policy field. On the basis of a commissioned study on the priorities for JHA cooperation in the CEECs (the so-called Langdon Report of 1995), the Commission addressed these issues in its opinions on the preparations for EU membership included in the Agenda 2000. The Commission has since actively promoted adaptation in JHA through different pre-accession instruments (such as the allocation of Phare money or the financing of specialised programmes such as Grotius, Oisin or Falcone, see Eisl 1999); the launch of the twinning programme between national administrations; and the partial involvement of the CEECs in common specialised bodies such as CIREA (asylum), CIREFI (immigration), PAPEG (organised crime), or Europol. Although the structures of transgovernmental cooperation continue to dominate the pre-accession process (Lavenex 2001b), another way to cope with the challenge of enlargement in JHA is the reform of the institutional modes of policy-making in the EU. The next section analyses the changes introduced with the Treaties of Amsterdam and Nice and scrutinises the scope for supranational policy-making in this hitherto predominantly transgovernmental policy field.

Policy-making in an area of freedom, security and justice

The Amsterdam Treaty and the special European Council meeting on JHA in Tampere in October 1999 laid the basis for the adoption of supranational EC law in central aspects of JHA. This incremental communitarisation of questions relating to the entry and stay of third country nationals, the police and the judiciary is not uncontroversial in the Member States, as it represents a new dimension in the integration process. In contrast to the main body of predominantly economic integration, these questions touch core aspects of national identity and sovereignty and affect Max Weber's notion of the 'monopoly of the legitimate use of force' in the Member States. This section scrutinises the relationship between intensive transgovernmentalism and communitarisation in recent reforms of JHA against the background of the challenges posed by Eastern enlargement. In the light of the problems of diversity emanating from the accession of ten or more new Member States, particular attention is paid to the questions how far recent reforms establish a coherent and comprehensive work programme in JHA, provide institutional modes for overcoming an impeding deadlock in decision-taking and implementation, and put the outcomes of this cooperation on a more rigorous legal basis.

The scope of cooperation in JHA

As mentioned above the JHA *acquis* is not really an expression of a common, harmonised policy but rather the result of a patchwork of measures adopted in different fields related to internal security and third country nationals.[4] Before the Amsterdam Treaty came into force cooperation was largely responsive and *ad hoc*, reacting to perceived threats and public anxieties in the Member States (Boer and Wallace 2000: 495). This view corresponds to the statement of the JHA Ministers responsible for immigration in the wake of the Maastricht Treaty, namely that 'harmonisation has not been regarded as an end in itself but as a means of reorienting policies where such action makes for efficiency and speed of intervention' (Ministers Responsible for Immigration 1991: 3). In asylum and immigration matters cooperation focused mainly on the fight against abusive asylum claims and illegal immigration, the approximation of visa policies, the adoption of common standards for controls at external borders, expulsion and the conclusion of readmission agreements with third countries. Although the Amsterdam Treaty and the Tampere European Council laid down a clear timetable for establishing a 'common European asylum system', the adoption of minimum standards for asylum procedures, the harmonisation of the refugee definition, or common rules relating to the long-term immigration of third country nationals have been much more difficult to achieve (see Guild, this volume). In the face of the great diversity in national immigration systems and the sensitivity of these issues, the Commission has proposed to adopt an 'open method of coordination' in order to reach an incremental approximation and coordination in immigration policy (Commission 2001b). However, the Council has hitherto opposed this initiative.

The area of *police* cooperation has seen a steady expansion since the European Police Office, Europol, became operational in July 1999. The Tampere Presidency Conclusions extended police cooperation to 'all forms of crime'

(Tampere European Council 1999: 40), and new issues were added to Europol's mandate.[5] Cooperation was extended to operational powers and information exchange. This extension is also important with regard to the law enforcement authorities covered by the Third Pillar which now include, apart from the police and customs organisations, fiscal inspection authorities and secret intelligence services. The Tampere Conclusions also provided for the creation of a Task Force of Chiefs of Police and a European Police College. Yet the domestic policing systems vary greatly between the Member States as the EU has never aspired to create a common European police force. A somewhat different situation emerges with regard to those police forces entrusted with the control at the EU's external borders. The strict control standards laid down in the Schengen *acquis*, and the high burden resting on the EU's southern and new Eastern Member States have spurred plans to set-up a common border police at the European level.

Judicial cooperation in civil and criminal matters was slower to develop, but became one of the most dynamic areas of integration in the recent years. Major triggers of this development were the entry into force of the Amsterdam Treaty and the initiative by France's Justice Minister Elisabeth Guigou to create a European Judicial Area as well as the work of the European Judicial Network starting in 1998. Important steps were taken at the Tampere European Council. Heads of State and Government called for an enhancement of access to justice and request the Council to establish minimum standards for an adequate level of legal aid in cross-border litigation and for the protection of the rights of victims of crime. Considering the great diversity in domestic judicial systems, a potentially path-breaking decision was the endorsement of the principle of mutual recognition of judicial decisions in cases of cross-border litigation in both civil and criminal matters. A Communication on mutual recognition was also adopted for final decisions on the expulsion of third country nationals at the JHA council meeting in May 2001. Notwithstanding this decision in favour of mutual recognition, an approximation and harmonisation of national laws has started with regard to fast track extradition procedures and legislation on civil matters. According to Article 31 (e) TEU, some minimum rules relating to the constituent elements of criminal acts and penalties in the field of organised crime, terrorism and drug trafficking may be expected. Another important new development is the creation of the new Eurojust cross-border prosecution unit composed of national prosecutors and magistrates (or police officers of equivalent competence) detached from each Member State. According to the new Article 31(2) TEU included in the Nice Treaty, this unit has the task of facilitating proper coordination between national prosecuting authorities and of supporting criminal investigations in organised crime cases. Of course, the events of September 11, 2001 added a sense of urgency to this cooperation, reflected among other things in the adoption of an action plan in the fight against terrorism and a European arrest warrant.

Notwithstanding this clear expansion of activities the exact finality of cooperation in the different sub-areas of JHA is left unclear. The treaties mention at no point the aim of developing a common 'policy' in any of these areas. Despite the inclusion of very specific objectives and deadlines, some of these objectives date back from several years or cover only specific aspects of a policy, whilst excluding others. A good example is the area of asylum and immigration policy, where most objectives were in fact already agreed in the working programme of the JHA ministers prepared for the Maastricht Treaty (Ministers Responsible for Immigration 1991). At the Tampere Summit the EU Heads of State and Government called for the establishment of a 'Common European Asylum System', not 'Policy' (Council 1999b). A similar wording is included in Articles 30 and 31 TEU which list the elements of 'common action' – not 'common policy' with regard to PJCCM. National responsibility for domestic policing is clearly acknowledged in Article 33 TEU, which states that Title VI 'shall not affect the exercise of the responsibilities incumbent upon Member States with regard to the maintenance of law and order and the safe-guarding of internal security'. Another example is judicial cooperation in civil matters which, by virtue of Article 65 TEC, is limited to a range of areas having 'cross-border implications', whilst excluding other important areas such as customs and administrative law. According to Jörg Monar, this selective access 'favours piecemeal problem solving rather than a comprehensive policy-making approach' (Monar 2001a: 274). Another important constraint to an expansion of EC/EU policy-making in JHA is the linkage of this field with the overarching goal of free movement of persons. This linkage is salient in Article 2 TEU where JHA cooperation is justified in terms of assuring the free movement of persons (see endnote 7) and reappears in Title IV TEC 'Visas, asylum, immigration and other policies *related to free movement of persons*' (emphasis added). Herewith, the rationale of 'compensatory measures' first adopted in the Schengen Agreement has gained a firm basis in the European treaties and may limit the scope of cooperation in the different sub-fields of JHA to those aspects where the Member States see a direct link with freedom of movement. A look at some domestic reforms in the area of asylum or immigration in the Member States confirms the continuity of mainly national perspectives on these problems and one finds little reference to the new European context set by the Amsterdam Treaty.

New instruments and old procedures

The expansion of JHA cooperation was facilitated by the institutional reforms of the Amsterdam Treaty. The transfer of asylum, immigration and judicial cooperation in civil matters to the First Pillar prepared the ground for a greater involvement of supranational actors and the adoption of EC law in these areas. However important elements of prior transgovernmental cooperation persist. The clearest indication of this collaboration is the *transitional period* of five years in Title IV TEC during which the Maastricht rules of interaction are basically maintained. After five years, in 2004, the only guaranteed change is the sole right of initiative for the Commission. The Nice European Council did not significantly alter this structure of cooperation. The main change is the introduction of the qualified majority voting rule (QMV) with regard to judicial cooperation in civil law matters, with the exception of family law (Art. 65 TEC). For some issues the procedures for introducing QMV and the co-decision procedure with the European Parliament were clarified. From 1 January 2004 onwards the Council may decide on the basis of unanimous vote to introduce QMV for measures relating to the free movement of third country nationals (Art. 62(3) TEC); illegal immigration (Art. 63(3)(b) TEC); and external borders controls (Art. 62(2) TEC). In contrast there are two areas where the Nice Treaty does not facilitate the introduction of QMV but, rather, makes it more difficult to achieve. The modified Article 67(5) TEC states that for measures relating to asylum and minimum rules on temporary protection QMV may only be introduced 'provided that the Council has previously [unanimously, SL] adopted . . . Community legislation defining the common rules and basic principles governing these issues'. In absence of such an agreement before 2004, the accession of ten new 'front-line' Member States will make decision-taking by consensus much more difficult.

New decision-making procedures were also introduced in the Third Pillar which now extends the Commission's right of initiative to all areas of cooperation in Title VI TEU (PJCCM), although the Commission has to share this right with the Member States. The opaque legal instruments of the Maastricht Treaty were replaced by well established, legally binding legal instruments, but some of these, the framework decisions, are excluded from direct effect, which may be 'contrary to the legal protection of the citizen' (Boer 1999: 317).

Another impetus for communitarisation in JHA may be the new powers attributed to the European Court of Justice (ECJ). Limitations were however put on the preliminary ruling procedure (Art. 234 TEC) which has been described as the cornerstone of Community law establishing its primary principles and ensuring its uniform application and interpretation throughout the Union (Fennelly 2000). The Amsterdam Treaty limits the power to make references for preliminary ruling under Title IV TEC to courts of the Member States against whose decisions there is no judicial remedy under national law (Art. 68(1) TEC) and precludes jurisdiction in cases relating to 'the maintenance of law and order and the safeguarding of internal security' (Art. 68(2) TEC). The third limitation is contained in Article 68(3) TEC which excludes the retroactive impact of ECJ rulings on (previous) rulings by national courts. A similarly cautious expansion of the ECJ's role occurred under the Third Pillar which provides for an optional preliminary ruling procedure only if and when the Member States have decided so previously (Art. 35(2) TEU). An important limitation of the Court's jurisdiction is also included in Article 35(5) TEU: the Court shall not 'review the validity or proportionality of operations carried out by the police or other law enforcement services of a Member State or the exercise of the responsibilities incumbent upon Member States with regard to the maintenance of law and order and the safeguarding of internal security'. This means that the Court's jurisdiction covers only regulation and not operational law enforcement activity flowing out from Third Pillar cooperation (Boer 1999: 318).

Another manifestation of the high degree of Member State discretion implied by the institutional framework of cooperation in JHA are the various elements of *flexibility* included in the treaties. The clearest manifestations of flexibility are the opt-outs of Denmark, Ireland and the UK from parts of cooperation in JHA. According to Article 69 TEC and the respective Treaty protocols, these three countries are not bound to cooperation under Title IV EC, but may opt-in on individual measures. Whilst Denmark participates in the free movement area and may adopt relevant European provisions as international law (avoiding the direct effect of EC law and ECJ jurisdiction), Ireland and the UK maintain their opt-out from the lifting of internal frontier controls but wish to adhere to the flanking measures of the JHA *acquis* such as asylum, PJCCM, and the Schengen Information System (SIS) (Kuijper 2000: 354). Together with the limitations imposed on the ECJ's jurisdiction (see above), these opt-outs represent a departure from the established principle of uniform jurisdiction in the Union (Fennelly 2000). This *à la carte* jurisdiction is equally visible in the Third Pillar, where each Member State is free to make a declaration accepting the Court's competence and to define the type of national courts which may make references to the ECJ (Art. 35 TEU, Gormley 1999: 63). In addition to this variable geometry of JHA, both Title IV TEC and Title VI TEU allow for the introduction of closer cooperation (Art. 11 TEC and Art. 40 TEU). This option, which was usually justified in terms of allowing a deepening of the Union in the wake of the 2004 Eastern enlargement has been significantly simplified with the Treaty of Nice (Title VII TEU). Finally a sort of enhanced cooperation 'through the back door' is included in PJCCM with the 'rolling ratification' provision of Article 34(2)(d) TEU which rules that unless otherwise provided, conventions shall, 'once adopted by at least half of the Member States, enter into force for those Member States' (Boer 1999: 308).

These deviations from the traditional Community method of policy-making reflect the strong reluctance of the Member States against a full communitarisation of these core issues of state sovereignty. This reluctance is also visible with regard to the intergovernmental bodies set-up in JHA such as Europol. Member States have hitherto opposed measures which would gradually transform Europol from an intergovernmental institution into a Community agency subject to some degree of control through the European Parliament. This became clear in a negative decision of the Council against a Commission proposal which would have established a legal base for the funding of Europol out of the EC budget at the end of 2002.

Much more far-reaching reform proposals were elaborated in the Convention preparing the Draft Constitution for the European Union during which JHA turned out to be one of the most prominent themes for the future of Europe. First of all, the Pillar structure separating some aspect of JHA between the first and the third Pillar (PJCCM) would be abolished. The convention agreed that all measures concerning border controls, immigration and asylum would shift to a qualified majority vote in the Council. Furthermore, in all cases except one (emergency asylum decisions) there would be also co-decision with the European Parliament. The same would apply to the majority of legislation concerning criminal law and policing, excluding only the creation of the European Police Prosecutor, cross-border actions by police and operational police measures. Furthermore, in those areas where the Commission does not have the exclusive right to propose legislation, the dominant role of the Member States would be lessened through the rule that a proposal may only be submitted by a quarter of the Member States. Finally, also judicial control would be expanded by applying the normal rules of the Court of Justice's jurisdiction to all JHA matters in all Member States, with the exception of the validity and proportionality of policing actions, where this is a matter of national law.

The wider geography of JHA cooperation

While the convention will indeed strengthen Communitarian elements, another difficulty in the establishment of supranational structures in JHA is the extension of this cooperation beyond the territorial borders of the EU. The same holds for the formal endorsement of a genuinely cross-pillar approach (Tampere European Council) which consists of linking JHA objectives with the Union's general foreign policy as well as making use of CFSP instruments and traditional First Pillar instruments such as trade and association agreements (Art. 300 TEC, see Lavenex 2002). A look at policy developments after Amsterdam shows that this foreign policy dimension is one of the most dynamic aspects of JHA cooperation. This external dimension has been included in all relevant policy documents and figures prominently in the Action Plan of the Council and the Commission 'on how best to implement the provisions of the Treaty of Amsterdam on an area of freedom, security and justice' (Council 1999a). However, the view back onto the emergence of cooperation in JHA shows that the involvement of third countries is all but new. As mentioned in the first section, the origins of JHA cooperation lie in the activities of international organisations with a wide constitution, the Council of Europe and Interpol, and in particular the more informal activities of more selective transgovernmental fora. Whilst the latter were created in part as a means to circumvent the organisational rigidity of those overarching institutions, their membership was from the onset designed to fit perceived functional needs. The Trevi group, for instance, gathered seven associated members (Austria, Canada, Morocco, Norway, Sweden Switzerland, USA), besides the EU Member States (see Bigo 1996: 162). A cross-continental organisation in the area of migration is the IGC which was created in 1985 and gathers representatives from the EU Member States plus Switzerland, Norway, the USA, Canada and Australia. Finally, one of the clearest examples of the functional rather than geographic scope of JHA cooperation is the association in 1998 of two non-EU Member States to the Schengen Agreement, Norway and Iceland.

Although the Maastricht Treaty brought most of these transgovernmental activities under one 'roof', the networks established in the 1970s and 1980s between law and order officials from EU and non-EU Member States have prevailed. Willy Bruggeman, Deputy Director of Europol, has said 'Europe can be considered, in policing terms, as being made up of a series of concentric and overlapping circles' which contend the role of the EU as a leading actor in this area (Bruggeman 2000). The influence of these networks is very important in the relations between the EU and the new Member States of Central and Eastern Europe, where the inclusion of JHA in the official pre-accession agenda was predated by a dense web of bilateral and multilateral activities at a purely trans-governmental level (see above).

Whilst JHA cooperation has always extended beyond the limited circle of EU Member States a relatively new development is the heightened focus on preventive activities with a clear foreign policy dimension. A prominent example of this new emphasis on foreign policy in JHA is the scoreboard of the European Commission on progress in the fulfilment of Treaty objectives, which placed 'Partnership with countries of origin' at the top of the chapter on EU asylum and immigration policy (Commission 2001a). Other examples are the strategy papers released after the Amsterdam Treaty, for instance the action plan 'on how best to implement the provisions of the Treaty of Amsterdam on an area of freedom, security and justice' (Council 1999a) and the action plan 'to combat organised crime' (Council 1997). Under the title 'relations with third countries and international organisations', the first document calls for intensifying the dialogue in JHA with 'an increasing number of third countries and international organisations and bodies (e.g. Interpol, UNHCR, Council of Europe, G8 and OECD)' (Council 1999a: section 22). Similarly, the action plan on organised crime stresses the need for 'working closely with the countries that are candidates for the membership of the Union, with the Union's transatlantic partners, with other countries such as Russia and Ukraine and with the major international players active in the field of the fight against organised crime' (Chapter 2, § 5a). This focus is also salient in the strategy developed towards the countries of South-Eastern Europe, with cooperation in JHA figuring prominently in the Stabilisation and Association Agreements concluded with Macedonia and Croatia in 2001. Migration-related clauses and readmission agreements were also included in the newer association agreements between the EU and the Maghreb (Morocco and Tunisia) and ACP countries. Another more organisa-tional expression of this foreign policy dimension in JHA is the creation of the transgovernmental High Level Working Group on Asylum and Migration (HLWG) which has elaborated action plans for Albania and the region, Afghanistan and the region, Iraq, Somalia and Sri Lanka (Selm 2002). Finally, this expansion of cooperation beyond the EU's borders is also important in the activities of other specialised bodies such as the migration-related clearing houses CIREA and CIREFI and Europol which, since March 2000, have been given the mandate to enter into negotiations on 'Model Cooperation Agreements' with non-EU States and non-EU related bodies (Europol 2000).

The logic supporting such a wider geographical perspective on JHA cooperation is the blurring of boundaries between the notions of 'external' and 'internal' security (Boer 1997) and the fact that the 'security' problems addressed by JHA are seen to originate from sources outside the EU. From this perspective, the extension of JHA cooperation is justified with the need to prevent 'spill-over' effects to neighbouring countries, including EU Member States' (Stability Pact Organisation 2000). Another dynamic behind this extension may well be that it is easier to reach consensus on actions relating to third countries than on an approximation and eventual harmonisation of JHA policies 'at home'.

Conclusion: the AFSJ between transgovernmentalism and communitarisation

The 2001 scoreboard published by the European Commission on the realisation of the AFSJ illustrates the tension between transgovernmentalism and communitarisation in the area of JHA:

> There is indeed a widespread recognition (both public and political) that the most challenging issues facing our society, such as migration and crime, can only be usefully addressed at the level of the Union rather than by Member States acting alone. In addition, the establishment of networks has led to a new culture of European cooperation at both the political and operational level. (Commission 2001a: 4)

The establishment of transgovernmental networks and the widening of their agenda of cooperation is without doubt a clear sign of an intensifying integration of JHA. It is also the sign of a particular form of governance which contrasts with the traditional, supranational Community method of European integration. Not only are the competences of EU institutions constrained, reflected in the continuity of unanimity voting, the shared right of initiative of the Commission, or the limits on the powers of the Parliament or the Court. Other factors that limit full communitarisation are the selectivity and limitation of policy objectives, the abundant presence of 'safety clauses' preserving sovereign control, and the fragmentation of cooperation through both flexible cooperation and the division of relevant provisions across political Pillars of the EU. The analysis of the broader scope of JHA cooperation and its gradual extension towards third countries shows that the use of transgovernmental policy-making procedures is not limited to intra-EU cooperation, but expands well beyond the limited circle of EU Member States.

In this context, the impetus for a deepening of JHA cooperation and the potential for fulfilling the idea of an AFSJ seems to stem from two sources: the internal demand for a more democratic, 'free', 'just' and 'secure' Union inside, and the need for political leverage in the relations with the accession countries. A look at the political context of the IGC leading to the Amsterdam Treaty shows that the broad definition of the *acquis* that the CEECs have to adopt and questions of transparency, accountability, and the links between the people and the

Union were major factors behind the transfer of important parts of the Third Pillar to the first (Reflection Group 1995, Devuyst 1998). The issue of democracy and legitimacy was particularly pertinent in the area of JHA which – whilst touching sensitive issues of domestic politics and civil liberties – was characterised by a clear dominance of executive policy-making, secretive modes of operation and the by-passing of the European and national parliaments (Curtin and Meijers 1995, O'Keeffe 1995, Monar 1995). The emerging discourse against the creation of a 'Fortress Europe' mobilised popular attention for the deficiencies of cooperation in this area, including its focus on restrictive measures, the lack of implementation, and the absence of democratic and judicial control. At the same time politicians in the EU institutions and in national capitals discovered the growing popular support for European solutions to the problems of undocumented migration, asylum, organised crime and drugs trafficking, which was partially fuelled by fears linked to the prospects of Eastern enlargement. Internal security cooperation and its connection with the realisation of freedom of movement offered 'a means of locking in popular support for the Union' (Twomey 1999: 358). In the Amsterdam Treaty this legitimising strategy found its verbal expression in the framing of JHA cooperation as a means to create an 'Area of Freedom, Security and Justice' (Art. 2 TEU, Art. 61 TEC).[6] Recalling basic democratic traditions and values in the Member States and linking citizens' freedoms with internal security and the rule of law, this metaphor provides a powerful rhetorical tool for a dynamic development of JHA cooperation (Monar 2001b, Twomey 1999). It provides legitimacy to the extensive obligations placed on the accession countries.

The pace of developments in JHA and their strong affinity to external, contextual influences make it difficult to judge whether the transgovernmental structures of cooperation which predominate to date are a transitory phenomenon, or will become a distinct mode of governance in EU politics. In any case the accession of ten new Member States will have a significant impact on the future shape of this policy field, and, in the light of persisting national apprehensions, is likely to act in favour of more supranational elements in the realisation of an 'Area of Freedom, Security, and Justice'.

Notes

1 After the signature of the Second Schengen Agreement in 1990, which lays down the compensatory measures for abolishing internal border controls, all Member States with the exclusion of Ireland and the UK joined the Schengen Group.
2 See the draft Second Schengen Agreement reprinted in Hailbronner (1989).
3 The impact of diversity and heterogeneity on transgovernmental cooperation was already illustrated with the accession of Italy and Greece to the Schengen Agreement. These Member States had to implement wide-ranging reforms and waited for seven years until they were fully admitted into all operational parts of the system (from 1990 to 1997 and 1992 to 1999 respectively).

4 For the full list of measures adopted see the JHA Council's website at http://ue. eu.int/jai/ default.asp?lang=en and the scoreboard of the European Commission on the creation of an AFSJ at www.europa.eu.int/comm/dgs/justice_home/pdf/scoreboard_30oct01_en.pdf.

5 Europol's original mandate included drug trafficking, immigration networks, vehicle trafficking, trafficking in human beings, trafficking in radioactive and nuclear substances, and associated money-laundering activities. In 1998 and 1999, terrorism, forgery of money and other means of payment, and child pornography were added.

6 The metaphor of an AFSJ was included at several prominent places in the Amsterdam Treaty. It is now included in the Preamble of the TEU ('Resolved to facilitate the free movement of persons, while facilitating the safety and security of their peoples, be establishing an area of freedom, security and justice in accordance with the provisions of this treaty'); in the list of objectives of the Union in Article 2 TEU ('to maintain and develop the Union and an area of freedom, security and justice, in which the free movement of persons is assured in conjunction with appropriate measures with respect to external border controls, asylum, immigration and the prevention and combating of crime'); in Article 29 TEU on police and judicial cooperation in criminal matters, in Article 40 TEU on closer cooperation; and in Article 61 TEC on cooperation on 'visas, asylum, immigration and other policies related to the free movement of persons'.

8

Changing the ground rules: reframing immigration, asylum and security in the European Union[1]

Introduction

The Amsterdam Treaty changed the legal framework of the European Union regarding third country nationals, that is, nationals of countries other than the Member States of the European Union itself. It moved from the intergovernmental Third Pillar of the Union responsibility for coordination of immigration and asylum as regards third country nationals and provided powers to adopt binding measures regarding these two fields and a timetable within which to adopt them. The expression of intention of the European Council at Tampere, Finland, October 1999, sets out the objectives for the implementation of the new powers on immigration and asylum given to the Community by the Amsterdam Treaty as follows:

> The aim is an open and secure European Union fully committed to the obligations of the Geneva Refugee Convention and other relevant human rights instruments and able to respond to humanitarian needs on the basis of solidarity. A common approach must also be developed to ensure the integration into our societies of those third country nationals who are lawfully resident in the Union.

Faced with the new challenge of a general competence in the fields of immigration and asylum, the first step for the Community is to draw conclusions from its experiences in using the powers provided to it in these fields. A useful starting place is from the perspective of the migrant him- or herself. The perspective of the migrant must always be informed by what the law permits or prohibits her or him from doing. In the field of immigration, the question is one of the possibilities to move, reside, exercise economic activities and enjoy protection from discrimination and expulsion. The first thing a migrant wants to know is whether there is a right to move, a right to reside and a right to engage in economic activities.

The Community objective of free migration

The initial immigration law of the Community was founded on the realisation of the objective of the abolition of obstacles to the free movement of persons within the territory of the Community (Article 3 European Community Treaty, hereafter EC). This was given particularity as regards workers (Article 39 EC), the self-employed (Article 43 EC) and service providers and recipients (Article 49 EC). The Community chose to define its legal order by reference to a direct relationship between individuals resident within it and Community law without, necessarily, the intermediary of national law.[2] Further, it established the supremacy of Community rules which seek uniformity of result in their application across the diverse territory of the Union, over contrary national rules (26/62 *Van Gend & Loos* [1963] ECR 1).When applying this legal framework to the objective of free movement of persons, the Community legal order created a system based on a right of choice to the individual, supported by the full power of Community law, taking precedence over national rules or the exercise of national discretion.

What then were the keys that the original Treaty gave to the individual to exercise free movement rights? First and most importantly was the need for the individual to exercise an economic activity in order to access the movement right. In the definition of economic activity and its adequacy or otherwise for the purpose of accessing the right, the Community ring-fenced the defining capacity as one reserved to the Community itself and not available to the Member States. The reasoning for this was not only to ensure that persons in similar situations anywhere in the Union would be able to enjoy the same right defined in a consistent manner, but also expressly to avoid the risk of Member State attempts to limit the rights of individuals and make them subject to more narrow national rules. The specified economic activities were work, self-employment or service provision or receipt. The legislator intentionally included the first three, the Court found the last implicit in the third (286/82, 26/83 *Liusi & Carbone* ECR [1984] 377). By so doing, the right of movement and residence extended to both active and passive economic activity. According to one interpretation (186/87 *Cowan* ECR [1988]195) as everyone is a service recipient in one way or another almost all the time, there is no moment when a person is not exercising a right which is a prerequisite to free movement. The second criterion was the application of a nationality requirement on the exercise of the free movement right. An individual was entitled to access the right of free movement in his or her capacity as an economic actor provided that he or she also held the nationality of one of the Member States, but his or her family members of any nationality were entitled to accompany the principal family and to engage in economic activities (Article 10, Regulation 1612/68).

In this regime of easy circulation with rights and guarantees extending even to the access to social security benefits, in a Community of fifteen Member States, including States with development levels as different as Greece and

Denmark, what has the result been? Only 1.7 per cent of the population of the Member States consists of nationals of other Member States (Eurostat 1997). While many people move across the Union on holiday, for business, or for a short trip, very few people actually stay and exercise a longer-term economic and residence right. What might seem a perverse result of the right of free movement of persons and the increasingly complete regime to encourage migration within the Community is the fact that fewer people use their right than in pre-1968 when there were greater controls (the end of the transitional provisions on free movement of workers in the EC Treaty). It would appear that movement of persons in the European Union is not necessarily affected by legal measures designed to make movement easier. It must then be asked whether legal measures designed to make movement more difficult are in fact different in their result.

From as early as 1961 the European Community was extending the rules of its internal immigration regime to third country nationals through the settlement of agreements with third countries granting work, residence and protection from expulsion rights to their nationals resident in the Union (Staples 1999). The first such agreement was with Greece in 1961, the second with Turkey in 1963 followed by numerous others. In doing this the Community used the same structural tools as it had done in respect to Community nationals. The categorisation of persons remained constant: workers, self-employed and service providers and recipients. The approach remained constant: the creation of rights accessible to individuals to make choices about the migratory patterns of their lives, to the limitation of the exercise of discretion by the Member State authorities. What differed was the scope of the provisions. In only one case were full free movement rights secured for third country nationals on the basis of a multilateral agreement between the Community and the states of origin (the European Economic Area Agreement). The regime developed in a somewhat haphazard manner, but in general was characterised by the extension of some immigration related rights to nationals of states on the borders of the Community.

The Community legislator recognised the value of this immigration law and has used the technique to develop a new series of immigration rights for nationals of the Central and Eastern European countries, the Baltics and Slovenia (Guild 1996). In the negotiation and settlement of agreements with these states from 1991 to the present, the Community has consistently included provisions on workers which promise, at least, non-discrimination in working conditions. Further they have included in all the agreements provisions creating a right of self-employment for nationals of those states, whether natural or legal persons, in the Member States. This right, worded similarly to Article 43 EC on the right of establishment for Community nationals, provides a mechanism to permit lawful migration for economic purposes from countries on the borders of the Community and from which, particularly during the period from 1990 to 1994, were perceived as a source of substantial migration flows into the Community. Beneficial regimes which give them rights and guarantee non-discrimination do not appear to result in increased flows of persons. Indeed, in respect to the Central and Eastern European countries (CEECs), after the settling of agreements with those countries, all of which include a legal route for economic migration, it appears that actual numbers of nationals from those states seeking to remain in the Member States have decreased (Eurostat 1994, 1995, 1996; see also table 8.1).

Table 8.1   The European agreements: Central and Eastern European Countries, Baltic States and Slovenia

Country	Date of signature	Entry into force
Bulgaria	08.03.1993	01.02.1995
Czech Republic	04.10.1993	01.02.1995
Estonia	12.06.1995	01.02.1998
Hungary	16.12.1991	01.02.1994
Latvia	12.06.1995	01.02.1998
Lithuania	12.06.1995	01.02.1998
Poland	16.12.1991	01.02.1994
Romania	08.03.1993	01.02.1995
Slovakia	04.10.1993	01.02.1995
Slovenia	10.06.1996	01.03.1999

The European Court of Justice confirmed in September 2001 the direct effect of the self-employment right of nationals of the Central and Eastern European Countries in the territory of the Member States (*Kondova* 27 September 2001, *Jany* 30 November 2001). This is of critical importance for enlargement as it means that even if free movement for workers is delayed many years, nationals of all the accession countries have an immigration right to reside on the territory of the Member States during that transitional period in the capacity of self-employed persons even though they are excluded from the labour market.

The intergovernmental period: changing the structure of norms

From 1985 to 1999 the Member States engaged in a variety of attempts at coordination of immigration and asylum policy outside the structures of the European Community (Papademetriou 1996). The moves were at least nominally associated with the decision to complete the internal market and abolish intra-Member State controls at borders on the movement of persons. This objective caused consternation in a number of ministries in the Member States, particularly those engaged in the control of aliens. The prospect that other Member States' unwanted aliens would come to their country over 'open' borders raised doubts which found popular voice in many Member States. One immediate result was a pressure for increased involvement of security services in the Member States in the internal market project regarding the movement of aliens (Bigo 1996). Another was the political decision to seek to coordinate if not harmonise some aspects of external border control in order to achieve the abolition of internal border controls (Guild 2001).

At the same time the Member States began coordination of their substantive immigration and asylum laws first through international conventions settled exclusively among themselves, such as the Dublin Convention on responsibility for asylum applications, and then through rather ill-defined instruments called resolutions, recommendations and conclusions (Guild and Niessen 1996). These developments were the subject of substantial and well justified public criticism on grounds of lack of transparency, democratic legitimacy and uniform judicial supervision. These intergovernmental activities were brought within the scope of the Union by the Maastricht Treaty which established a new venue, the Third Pillar, for coordination of activity in the fields of immigration and asylum. This intergovernmental approach was also pursued to abolish border controls on persons between some of the Member States through the Schengen Agreements of 1985 and 1990 (den Boer 1997). Both the Schengen experiment and the Third Pillar provided venues for the Member States to discuss and approximate ideas about immigration and asylum. However, the result was not coordination. For example, the division contained in the Treaty on European Union (TEU), which created a Community competence for visas – their form and the countries whose nationals must have them – and the underlying immigration and border policy which was placed in the Third Pillar highlighted the problematic relationship created not only within the Union, dividing the Council, Commission and Parliament in separate legal actions before the Court of Justice. It also showed the difficulties between the positions of the individual, the subject of the measures, and the Community. The direct relationship which had characterised Community law in immigration was lost. These intergovernmental experiments were of qualified success. At the time of the Intergovernmental Conference that led to the Amsterdam Treaty, Member States (with the exception of Denmark, Ireland and the UK) were ready to change the mechanisms and grant substantial powers to the European Community in the field of immigration and asylum.

The Amsterdam compromise: powers without concrete objects

The Community has now been granted extensive powers in the fields of immigration and asylum by the new Title IV EC albeit with diminished jurisdiction to the European Court of Justice (Peers 1999). The question arises, how should these new powers be exercised, and what lessons should be learnt from the Community's engagement with immigration so far? I will look at the broad areas of competence only in the fields of borders and immigration policy. These two policy areas are of the vital importance to enlargement. The accession countries must gradually be transformed from being external EU border states to being internal ones. Their nationals must be changed from being seen as third country nationals subject to exclusionary policies designed to protect the EU labour market to being considered fully free to move and work throughout the Union.

Control of the crossing of external borders

From the inception of a border control free internal market the concept of the abolition of intra-Member State border controls has been linked to that of external border controls. Thus, the definition of the territorial scope of external borders must be resolved. The immediate image is one of the outer line around the territory of the Member States to which one then must add the international airports, train stations, etc. However, the matter has not proved so simple. The status of Gibraltar for instance long remained disputed between Spain and the UK: is it an internal or external border and of which states (Hedemann-Robinson 1996)? This discussion which held up the signing of the Draft Convention on External Borders was only resolved between the UK and Spain shortly before the European Council was to vote in June 2000 on the UK's application to participate in the Schengen Information System. Spain, as a participating member had the power to veto the UK's request. It did not.

The next question, what a control is and where it takes place, has to do with the territorial scope of the external borders. In the context of the Schengen Implementing Convention and its subsidiary legislation, checks take place, for instance within a 20 km zone inside the formal borders of a number of the Schengen states by police and border guards on a random basis. Do such checks also constitute a form of external border control insofar as they relate to persons who have crossed an external border irregularly? A further question arises regarding the detection of a person who has arrived illegally in a Member State. Where such a person has never gone through a check at the new external border, is their detection, for instance at the offices of a Member State's public assistance authority a first external control, an internal control or an investigation unrelated to borders?

More than one Member State has sought to define third country nationals as still at the external frontier awaiting a control over when those persons have been present on the territory of the Member State for not inconsiderable periods of time. France, for instance, was condemned by the European Court of Human Rights for seeking to maintain that asylum seekers within French territory, but held in the international zone, were not within French territory for the purposes of the application of the European Convention on Human Rights (*Amuur* [1996] 22 EHRR 533).

One final issue regarding the territorial scope of the external border also relates to where that border is in reality for persons seeking to cross it. For all of those persons, nationals of countries on the common visa list, the main border control effectively takes place at the point when they apply for the visa. At that point an investigation is undertaken into their eligibility for admission to the territory of the Member State. Under the rules of the Schengen common visa (which will now apply to the common visa under new Title IV EC) once a visa is obtained, unless disputed, it is valid for admission to any Member State and across the external border in any part of the European Union (leaving aside those Member States which have opted out: Denmark, Ireland and the UK). With the issuing of a visa a EU Member State consular post in fact is giving a visa to cross the EU external border. In effect the assessment and decision on whether the person should be allowed to cross the external border is made in the individual's state of origin. Thus, the crossing of external borders is, in fact, inextricably linked with the issuing of visas and the conditions which apply (Guild 2001).

This issue has important consequences for the accession countries in the light of the enlargement process. One Member State border official told an expert audience in July 2001 that, in his opinion, the lifting of border controls on candidate states for participation in the frontier free area would need to be the subject of very lengthy transitional periods, even up to twenty years. Should there be such long transitional periods for the abolition of border controls with these countries, it would likely cause substantial political difficulties. Accession countries have been advised that they must adopt all of the EC border rules before becoming members, including the visa list. The application of the visa list will cause friction with the candidates' Eastern neighbours, such as Ukraine and Belarus, not to mention Moldova. Nationals of these states will be made subject to visa requirements in many cases for the first time to enter the Eastern European countries that they previously could travel to without visa. . If nationals of the candidate states cannot even enjoy frontier-free travel within the Union after accession, some will undoubtedly question the high price paid for participation in the system.

What are the new powers?
Within five years of the entry into force of the Amsterdam Treaty the Council must adopt measures on the crossing of external borders of the Member States. Because of the highly complicated arrangement contained in the Schengen Protocol it is unclear what will remain to be done within five years of the date of entry into force. Following the Council's agreement on the legal basis of the Schengen *acquis* in relation to all the aspects of the crossing of external frontiers now inserted into the EC Treaty there may be little to be done unless the Parliament should wish to mount a challenge to the legality of the 'automatic' transfer of the Schengen *acquis* into the EC Treaty.[3] The specific measures which must be adopted are:

- standard procedures to be followed by the Member States in carrying out checks on persons at such borders: Article 62(2)(a) EC; this means that the Community will now be responsible for adopting a measure which spells out uniform procedures for persons at the external borders. This is in effect the rules on access to the territory of the Union; these rules should be drafted or adapted, in the event that a Schengen provision is deemed to cover this, to give effect to the Community's best interests in promoting movement of persons for cultural, educational and recreational activities;

- rules on visas for intended stays of no more than three months which include the list of third countries whose nationals must be in possession of visas when crossing the external borders and those nationals who are exempt from that requirement: Article 62(2)(b) (I) EC. It is important to note here that one demand of the European Parliament as regards this visa list, that it includes both a 'white' list (countries whose nationals are exempt) as well as 'black' list (countries whose nationals must have a visa), has been achieved through this Treaty amendment;

- the procedures and conditions for issuing visas by Member States: Article 62(2)(b)(ii) EC; this will be very important as it is here that common rules which are the background to access to the territory of the Union will be found. As the primary immigration control is moved by the Schengen arrangements to the country of origin specifically for those countries which are on the common visa list, the conditions for obtaining a visa become determinative of whether an individual will have access to the territory;

- a uniform visa format (subject of an existing Regulation) Article 62(2)(b) (iii) EC; the importance of a uniform format visa is that it defines the document to which certain rights attach;

- rules on an uniform visa: Article 62(2)(b)(iv) EC; these are the rules which are critical to the value and meaning of a common format visa; for instance if the common format visa does not give a right of entry to the territory from wherever the individual starts or seeks to enter the territory, then its value is highly circumscribed.

A number of major concerns have been expressed. First, as is the case in all areas of the new Title, ensuring transparency is critical. It is the link of information between the other institutions of the Community and of those who live in the territory of the Union. The protection of individual liberty by restricting the collection and unjustified access to personal data held under the Schengen Information System remains far from achieved. The second regards accountability. Since the Amsterdam Treaty entered into force the provisions relating to the list of third countries whose nationals must be in possession of a visa and the uniform visa format are subject to qualified majority voting in the Council and consultation with the Parliament. The Regulation on the uniform visa format has already been adopted. The important contents of the next necessary measures relate to how a third country national may obtain a visa, what requirements that would be subject to, and what the visa entitles the person to do.

There are three concerns regarding international human rights obligations. The first relates to persons fleeing persecution, torture or inhuman or degrading treatment. Under the Schengen *acquis* all parties are required to apply sanctions on carriers for transporting to a Schengen country persons who do not have the correct documents. However, it is inevitable that persons fleeing persecution and torture may have incorrect or incomplete documents or lack of them altogether. Even if they are in possession of a passport, the rules applied as regarding the acquisition of a Schengen visa, including requirements of resources and intentions to leave the territory within the three month permitted period, make it impossible for them to obtain that part of the required documentation (Vedsted-Hansen 1999).

A second area of concern deals with the application of visa requirements which renders it virtually impossible for family members of third country nationals to visit relatives within the territory of the Union. The right to protection from interference with private and family life contained in Article 8 ECHR has not been extended to require states to permit the admission and residence of family members where family life could be enjoyed in some other state. However, the application of common visa rules which have the effect of preventing short visits by close family members, particularly if the relative resident within the Union is not able to travel to the third country, raises the question of whether this aspect of private and family life comes within the spirit of the concept as contained in Article 8 ECHR.

Finally, there is the 'minimum standards' versus 'maximum protection' issue. It must be resolved because the purpose of the introduction of the common rules on crossing of external borders is to provide assurance to Member States that the persons entering the Union at one border post are the same ones those that would be admitted at a border crossing point on their own territory. There is a strong temptation to apply rules which encapsulate the most restrictive elements of all the Member States and do not provide any margin to a Member State to apply a more relaxed regime. This tendency should be countered. Member States should be permitted the flexibility to continue to issue national visas on grounds which reflect their traditions and needs. It must, however, be subject to the common floor of rights. Member States should not be permitted to fall below the common standard.

Immigration policy regarding nationals of third countries

A variety of different regimes apply to third country nationals resident within the territory of the Member States as opposed to those coming to reside. There is a need to look carefully at the different categories of third country nationals whose situation may be regulated by Community law and to determine the source of that regulation in Community law. For instance, third country national family members of migrant Community nationals, in principle, are not subject to the new Title IV, as their rights derive from the implementing measures of Articles 39-49 EC. Similarly, special provisions apply to EEA nationals, Turkish workers and their family members and nationals of the CEECs (Central and Eastern European Countries) who are self-employed. Different groups of third country nationals enjoy different levels of protection under Community law in accordance with provisions of the Treaty and agreements with third countries which are outside the ambit of the new Title (Antalovsky: 1998).

A survey of the different groups of third country nationals with specific admission, stay, residence and economic activity rights in Community law distinct from the new Title indicates the following groups:

1   *Family members of Community nationals.* Spouses, children under 21 and over 21 when dependent on the family, all dependent relatives in the ascending and descending line of the worker and his or her spouse. There is also a duty on the state to facilitate admission of a wider group of family members who are either dependent on the family or lived under the same roof in the country whence they came (Article 10, Regulation 1612/68). The Commission has proposed amendment of this Regulation, which will widen the group of family members entitled to admission, stay, residence and employment or self-employment).

2   *Employees of a Community based enterprise providing services in another Member State.* This is the result of the interpretation of Article 49 EC by the European Court of Justice culminating in the decision of *Van der Elst* [1994] ECR I-3803. This is also the subject of a proposal for a directive from the Commission (COM(1999) 3 Final of 27.1.99) regarding third country nationals established in one Member State and providing services in another. The power to adopt a measure giving effect to this right was included in Article 49 EC as a result of the Single European Act, but a proposal from the Commission for an implementing directive was only published in January 2001.

3   *EEA (European Economic Area) nationals other than citizens of the Union exercising free movement rights.* This applies to nationals of Iceland, Liechtenstein and Norway who, although they remain third country nationals for the purposes of Community law, are entitled to rights of entry, stay, residence and employment which are co-extensive with those of Community nationals by virtue of the agreement between their states and the EC. Similarly the Swiss will benefit under the Agreement signed with that state in February 1999.

4   *Turkish workers and their family members protected by Decision 1/80 or other provisions of the EEC Turkey Association Agreement.* The rights which have been clarified on a number of occasions by the European Court of Justice include a right of continued employment and residence, rights of residence and employment for family members who have been admitted to the territory under national law, and protection against expulsion. As the Court has stressed on more than one occasion, first admission to

the territory of the Member States remains a matter for national law (Gutmann 1995).

5   *Maghreb workers to the extent they are protected under the EC agreements with their states* (Algeria, Morocco and Tunisia). These rights are limited to non-discrimination in working conditions and social security but the European Court of Justice has recently held that the equal treatment in working conditions right can have consequences for the residence right where an existing right of employment continues (*El Yassini* [1999] ECR I-1267).

6   *African, Caribbean and Pacific (ACP) Agreement States' nationals in so far as they are protected under the ACP Agreement.* Again the rights here are limited to non-discrimination in working conditions and social security and are contained in an Annex to the Agreement; the effect of the Annex has yet to be clarified by the European Court of Justice.

7   *CEEC nationals who are self-employed or key workers (as defined in the Agreements) protected under the Europe Agreements.* These are the most recent rights created for third country nationals and include a right of entry, stay, residence and either self-employment or employment depending on the category of the Agreement relied upon (Guild 1996).

In addition to these rights, third country nationals may fall in and out of the competence of Title IV. For instance third country national family members after majority or dissolution of a marriage may fall outside the protection of Regulation 1612/68. They may need to look elsewhere for a right to stay. CEEC nationals admitted for self-employment who take employment can no longer rely on their establishment right in the agreement between their state and the Community. The regulation of third country nationals will be highly complicated as a result of the piecemeal development of Community law in the field. This situation will continue unless there is an upward harmonisation to the highest standard for all. The Parliament may feel that it is premature to advocate a full upward harmonisation which would include - for instance, the extension of the right to admission to any Member State for the purpose of self-employment for all third country nationals.

What are the new powers?

The new powers of the Community in Title IV EC are to adopt measures on immigration policy regarding:

- conditions of entry and residence, and standards on procedures for the issue by Member States of long-term visas and residence permits, including those for the purpose of family reunion: Article 63(3)(a) EC (the subject of a number of Third Pillar measures and the Commission's proposal for a convention on admission of third country nationals OJ C 337, 7.11.97);

- illegal immigration and illegal residence, including repatriation of illegal residents: Article 63(3)(b) EC – the subject matter of numerous Third Pillar activities (Guild and Niessen 1996);
- measures defining the rights and conditions under which nationals of third countries who are legally resident in a Member State may reside in other Member States: Article 63(4) EC (Groenendijk 1998).

What is also important is the division of powers into those relating to general rights of admission regarding *immigration policy* and those relating to the treatment of third country nationals already resident in the territory of the Union. These rights *define the rights and conditions* of their free movement within the Union. Measures on policy are not necessarily ones which have direct effect and regulate the position of third country nationals vis-à-vis the Member States. This policy power could be interpreted as doing no more than setting a framework for national measures to make sure that the Member States are moving in the same direction. Such an interpretation would have various shortcomings. Unless there is agreement on who gets rights of residence and admission in one Member State it may be difficult to agree who gets to move throughout the territory of the Union, to reside and work. The scope of immigration policy is less than clear regarding illegal immigration and illegal residence, including repatriation of illegal residents. The power in respect to third country nationals legally resident in a Member State is slightly fuller. It is a power to adopt measures to define rights, therefore addressing the relationship of third country nationals who reside in the Union with all of the Member States.

Purpose of inclusion in the constitutional framework of the Union

The purpose of the new powers is critical to understanding how they should be exercised. As the objectives of the Title are somewhat Delphic, further assistance from Community law in general and its position in an international framework may be necessary. The provisions on third country nationals are aimed at the fulfilment of the objective of establishing an area of freedom, security and justice. They are not aimed specifically at the abolition of intra-Union border controls.

CONDITIONS OF ENTRY AND RESIDENCE

These words in the context of measures on immigration policy should be interpreted as including the Community's objectives in the field of the common commercial policy. Care must be taken that measures adopted by the Community in one field do not nullify or impair the effectiveness of measures and policies adopted elsewhere. The Community's commitment under the World Trade Organisation Agreement to liberalisation of trade in services (the General Agreement on Trade in Services) includes a framework for the movement of natural persons for the purpose of service provision (Guild 2001a).

STANDARDS AND PROCEDURES
FOR THE ISSUE OF LONG TERM VISAS AND RESIDENCE PERMITS
This is a very concrete power which requires more than mere coordination through a loose interpretation of immigration policy. Not least for this reason the term immigration policy may need to be interpreted as giving rise to a power to adopt measures which are substantive, binding and sufficiently clear, precise and unconditional regarding the obligations to give rise to rights to individuals. The creation of common standards and procedures is necessary to give effect to rights for individuals which are consistent throughout the Community. Unless the processing of applications meets common minimum procedural criteria of care, impartiality and legitimacy no matter which Member State embassy or authority is considering them, the common Community rules will not in fact be common.

FAMILY REUNION
Community law has long recognised the importance of family reunion to the dignity of migrant workers and as an indispensable element to their successful integration into the host community, according to the preamble to the Regulation 1612/68. It is one of the first areas where the Commission has proposed legislation. Unfortunately that legislation already contains the principle of discrimination between the rights of migration Community nationals and those of third country nationals resident in the Union (Brinkmann 2001).

ILLEGAL IMMIGRATION AND ILLEGAL
RESIDENCE, INCLUDING REPATRIATION OF ILLEGAL RESIDENTS
The existence of illegal immigration and residence are the result of immigration laws and practices. Substantial and persistent numbers of persons in irregular positions in the Member States may be seen as evidence of the inappropriateness of the laws and practices of the Member States. The logic of the EU immigration policy is that people should be treated in such a way that: (1) they never become illegal; or (2) if this happens inadvertently they are regularised; or (3) they should be expelled. To this extent illegal immigration and residence are the tests of whether immigration policy as expressed in law and practice is appropriate. Where illegal immigration and residence are on the increase a reassessment of policy and its manifestations needs to be undertaken.

All the Member States are parties to the European Convention on Human Rights (ECHR). The position of the ECHR in Community law has been strengthened further by the Amsterdam Treaty amendments. Article 8 ECHR, the right to family and private life, has consistently been held by the European Court of Human Rights to include the right of long resident foreigners not to be expelled. The adoption of a Community policy on expulsion must give full effect to the Member States' obligations under Article 8 ECHR as interpreted by the European Court of Human Rights. Indeed, the object of the policy should be to implement in a consistent and uniform manner the right to protection from expulsion expressed in Article 8 ECHR. The purpose of this power should be understood in this context.

RIGHTS OF LEGALLY RESIDENT THIRD COUNTRY NATIONALS TO RESIDE IN OTHER MEMBER STATES

The purpose of including this power in the EC Treaty should be understood as necessary to reduce differential rights between migrant nationals of the Member States and third country nationals who, in many cases, may have been born and lived all their lives within the Union. As the Member States are not willing to agree to harmonise their nationality laws so as to create uniform laws that stipulate how third country nationals may become citizens of the Union, it is then incumbent to agree to extend the benefits of Community free movement rights to long resident third country nationals as a compensatory measure to reduce discrimination between persons whose objective situation is similar. Only by such measures can a genuinely single labour market be created.

What must be done?

Only measures with respect to illegal immigration, illegal residence and repatriation of illegal residents must be taken within the five year deadline from entry into force of the Amsterdam Treaty. The other two areas are not subject to time limits. The Commission and Council's joint work programme of December 1998 promises early action with respect to these persons, even though this is not required under the Amsterdam Treaty amendments. A proposal has now been made for legislation on long-term resident third country nationals. The Commission's draft would provide a secure residence right in Community law for all third country nationals who have resided lawfully in a Member State for five years or more (students are an exception; they must complete ten years unless pursuing doctoral studies). Under the draft, they would also have a right of residence in any other Member State provided they have a job offer there. Another proposal has been made on access to employment and to the territory for third country nationals. It provides that work and residence permits shall be issued for a third country national candidate where a job has remained unfilled for a specified period of time.

This field is likely to be problematic in light of enlargement. On the one hand, far reaching proposals for legislation are under active consideration in the Council at the same time as enlargement discussions are progressing. It is not clear for the candidates what they are signing up to under this heading. They are required to give a blank cheque to the EU that they will implement whatever is adopted by the Council in this field while they remain outside the discussions. On the other hand, CEEC nationals will be subject to new migration legislation if they seek to go to the Member States during the transitional period when free movement of workers is delayed. Thus the CEEC governments will be applying EU rules on access for employment to Ukrainians and others while these same rules are being applied to their nationals by the EU Member States (Nyiri, Toth and Fullerton 2001).

Conclusions

It is not yet clear whether there has been a substantial change in direction or approach from the introduction of the Third Pillar powers in the field of immigration and asylum into the First Pillar. The measures proposed by the Member States, inevitably follow the Third Pillar style, even though proposed in the First Pillar. How many of them are likely to ever be approved is uncertain. Of greater interest are those measures which have been proposed by the Commission that will have the exclusive right of initiative in the field in 2004. Thus the Commission's approach is perhaps more important in the longer term in determining the strength of the intergovernmental legacy in the field.

There are a number of indicators which would suggest that the First Pillar is being influenced strongly by the Third Pillar approaches and measures. The wholesale incorporation of the Schengen *acquis* would point in this direction. However, the resistance to the Schengen *acquis* and the stated intention to replace all of it with Community measures as expressed in the Commission's staff working paper (supra) would indicate greater independence from the legacy of the past. If indeed there has been no change then the EU is looking at a system of control over immigration which excludes the individual as holder of rights in favour of the state which now holds the powers (jointly with the other Member States) but has incorporated the right to act arbitrarily into the supra-national framework against any right of the individual to object.

What are the benefits of a rights-based approach? Four of them are immediately apparent:

1   Clarity of rights reduces administrative delay and cost as the rules and do not require senior officials to weigh up discretionary elements in order to reach decisions.
2   The individual alone can regulate his or her life in accordance with clear rules with a degree of security as to the consequences of any particular choice or action.
3   The alien and the society benefit from security as to who is and who is not entitled to reside, leave, return and exercise economic activities.
4   The suspicions of the host society that the alien is 'abusing' the immigration laws should be diminished by the application of transparent rules agreed by the fifteen Member States.

The disadvantage of the elimination of discretion is perhaps that Member States do not want further progress on rights for third country nationals. As has been seen in the context of the Third Pillar, it is easy to agree rules which one does not intend to apply. If the reason for retaining discretionary control over the entry, residence and economic activities of third country nationals is because Member States want to be able to refuse easily these rights then it is likely at Community level there will be a strong temptation to implement an exclusionary regime with a power of the Member State to make exceptions. This would not necessarily be in the interests of the Community.

In terms of the moral duties of the Community, the first field which needs to be regulated on a 'rights' basis is that of free movement rights for third country nationals lawfully resident in the Union. The upward harmonisation of the rights of all third country nationals resident in the Union is the fairest and most equitable way to implement this new power in Article 63(4) EC. The second category which needs urgent implementation is family reunion, the rules of which should reduce discrimination between third country nationals and Community nationals. The development of a primary immigration law for Europe should respect the rules of liberalisation of trade which the Community has promoted. It is not acceptable to seek to force other countries to open up their frontiers to permit European consultants access to their markets yet retain closed access to Europe. Building on the existing Community and international framework to develop the Community's new immigration law will be the easiest route and the most politically acceptable. It will also impose the least new administrative burdens on the Member States.

This perspective also needs to inform the common rules on visas and crossing of borders. The administrative discretion which currently renders it a time consuming and degrading activity for many third country nationals to seek a short stay visa for the EU needs to be limited and made subject to clear rules. Where a person, on account of his or her nationality, is subject to mandatory visa requirements there should be a presumption in favour of the visa's issue; refusal should be only on the basis of motivated reasons which fulfil specified criteria which are capable of withstanding a transparency test. In this way the increasing and unfortunately also accurate characterisation of the European Community as closed to outsiders other than those coming from the developed (white) world can be dispelled.

The most important lesson which the European Community's history of regulating immigration teaches is that there are real benefits to the adoption of clear, easily implemented rules which allow the individual dignity and freedom in the choice of movement and economic activity. A generous approach to the accession countries is also a requirement. The Community already has the experience of enlargements which in no case led to a disruption of the labour market. The political benefit of a generous approach will be important to the legitimacy of the CEEC governments which have pursued accession to the EU and to diminish the appeal of nationalistic trends in those countries. Such an approach is consistent with the EC's traditional approach to movement of persons, but it would constitute a substantial change of approach in comparison with the intergovernmental, which has characterised pre-Amsterdam immigration and asylum policy in the Union. The coming years will determine whether the Union is capable of learning from its own history or whether it will become caught in the logic of freedom as protection from choice, security as inimical to substantive rights for individuals and justice as divorced from judicial interference.

Notes

1　This paper was current as of early 2002.
2　In those cases where such an intermediary was necessary the Community defined for itself the remedies for the individual against the failure of the national authorities to give definition in national law C-6/90 & 9/90 *Francovich & Bonifaci* [1991] ECR I-5357.
3　However, the European Commission in a staff working paper on visa policy consequent upon the Treaty of Amsterdam and the integration of the Schengen *acquis* in the EU (SEC (1999) 1213, Brussels, 16.07.99) makes it clear that the Commission's view is that there is a requirement under the new Title to propose and adopt new measures in accordance with the five year time limit. To leave the Schengen *acquis* applicable under the protocol is not satisfactory.

PART III

Institutional change

Finn Laursen

9

The Amsterdam and Nice IGCs: from output failure to institutional choice

Introduction

This chapter analyses the institutional issues that came to the fore in the European Union in the latter part of the 1990s as the Union started to move towards its fifth enlargement. We shall compare the two Intergovernmental Conferences (IGCs) of Amsterdam and Nice. Why did the 1996–97 IGC that produced the Treaty of Amsterdam largely fail to make the institutional reforms, which were considered necessary by many Member States, especially the larger ones, to prepare the European Union (EU) for enlargement? Why did the IGC 2000 that produced the Treaty of Nice succeed in producing those reforms? Which reforms were produced in the end? How do we explain these reforms?

Part of the answer to the question of the different outcomes of the two IGCs is timing. Although the Central and Eastern European countries (CEECs) had been offered membership by the Copenhagen European Council in June 1993 on condition of fulfilling certain economic, political and administrative criteria the pressure on the Heads of State and Government meeting in Amsterdam in June 1997 was insufficient to get them to make the difficult institutional changes deemed necessary. In a *protocol on the institutions with the prospect of enlargement of the European Union* the Member States committed themselves to reduce the Commission to one member per Member State and solve the question of weighting of votes in the Council before enlargement with up to a maximum of twenty members. A comprehensive review of the institutions would be required before the EU could enlarge beyond twenty members (Laursen 2002a).

As pressure for Eastern enlargement mounted the Cologne European Council in June 1999 decided to call another the IGC during 2000 'to ensure that the European Union's institutions can continue to work efficiently after enlargement' (European Council 1999).

We shall concentrate our description and analysis on the three issues singled out in Cologne. They are, the re-weighting of votes in the Council, the composition of the Commission and, to a lesser extent, the increased use of QMV in the Council. These issues were very much linked in the minds of the decision-makers. As they were not solved in the negotiations that led to the Amsterdam Treaty they became known as the Amsterdam 'leftovers.'

Efficiency became a key-word in the debate. With many more members the feeling was that decision-making would become more difficult. Questions of legitimacy were also considered to be very important. This part of the *problematique* had much to do with the balance between the big and small Member States. Many of the future new members were relatively small and the existing weighting of votes was relatively favourable towards the small members. Would it be fair that a coalition of small Member States would be able to dominate in the EU after enlargement? In the end the central question became one of capacity to control future developments in the EU after enlargement. It became a kind of 'constitutional' choice.

The context

The most important part of the context of the two IGCs then was the upcoming Eastern enlargement of the Union. Soon after the entry into force of the Maastricht Treaty in November 1993, the EU went through its fourth enlargement. The end of the Cold War made it possible for three formerly neutral countries, Austria, Sweden and Finland, to join the EU, which occurred on 1 January 1995. This enlargement took place on the basis of the Maastricht Treaty. It was, however, agreed at the time that further enlargements should await another IGC, in which institutions should be adapted so as to allow for enlargement without weakening the EU's institutional capacity (Laursen 2001a). Over the years, the EU had been enlarged from the original six to fifteen members without radical change in the institutions. By the time of the fourth enlargement ten Central and Eastern European Countries had applied for membership, as had Cyprus, Malta and Turkey. These applications opened the prospect of an EU with nearly twice as many members. How could such a Union be ensured of an adequate capacity to make and implement decisions? How would it affect the balance between small and big Member States? In the end this latter issue construed by many as a zero-sum game – turned out to be the most difficult.

Council voting
Until and including the fourth enlargement it would be decided how many votes the new Member States would get in the Council and what implications this new distribution would have for QMV and, by implication, how many votes would constitute a blocking minority.

Table 9.1 displaying the situation in EU-15 shows that the existing weights of votes are far from proportional. The big states are relatively under-represented, especially Germany. The small states are relatively over-represented, especially Luxembourg. Without changes to the system membership of smaller countries like Cyprus, Malta, Slovenia and the Baltic countries would make this situation more visible. Thus, the bigger Member States argued that there was a need for changes in the weighting of votes in the Council before the next enlargement.

Table 9.1   Council voting

	Number	Population (millions)	Citizens per vote (millions)
Germany	10	81.7	8.2
United Kingdom	10	58.6	5.9
France	10	58.1	5.8
Italy	10	57.7	5.8
Spain	8	39.1	4.9
Netherlands	5	15.5	3.1
Greece	5	10.5	2.1
Belgium	5	10.2	2.0
Portugal	5	9.9	2.0
Sweden	4	8.9	2.2
Austria	4	8.1	2.0
Denmark	3	5.2	1.7
Finland	3	5.1	1.7
Irland	3	3.6	0.9
Luxembourg	2	0.4	0.2
Total	87	372.6	
Qualified majority	62		
Blocking minority	26		

Source: Simon Hix (1999: 70).

Table 9.2 shows the votes the new members would get if the current system were extrapolated to the future members. In a Union of 27 members a blocking minority would be 39, a number of votes which could be reached by the ten CEECs.

Composition and role of the Commission
The composition of the Commission was also on the agenda. Already in the 1970s it was argued that the Commission was getting too large for the existing portfolios. After the fourth enlargement in 1995 the Commission had twenty members, two from each of the big Member States, Germany, France, UK, Italy and Spain, and one from each of the remaining Member States. Should each future member, even very small ones like Cyprus, Malta and the Baltic states, have one Commissioner? Might the big Member States accept having only one Commissioner? Or was it time to stop thinking in national terms? After all, once appointed the Commissioners are supposed to represent the European interest and not take instructions from their home countries. One could imagine other

Table 9.2　Extrapolation of the current voting system to a Union of 27 members

	Population (millions)	Votes
Union of 15 members	371	87
Poland	38.5	8
Romania	22.8	6
Czech Republic	10.3	5
Hungary	10.3	5
Bulgaria	8.5	4
Slovakia	5.3	3
Lithuania	3.7	3
Latvia	2.6	2
Slovenia	2.0	2
Estonia	1.5	2
Cyprus	0.7	2
Malta	0.4	2
12 future members	106.6	44
Union of 27 members	477.6	131
Qualified majority in EU-27		93 (70.99%)
Blocking minority in EU-27		39 (29.77%)

Source: Commission Doc SN 612/96 (C 4).

scenarios. Could the European Parliament appoint the Commission on the basis of political considerations rather than the current national representation? Alternatively, could a group of states share a Commissioner? Or should one move towards some kind of rotation?

The question of the right of initiative was also discussed prior to the 1996–97 IGC. It raised the issue of whether the First Pillar's rule of exclusive right of initiative of the Commission could be extended to the Second and Third Pillars, where the Commission shared the right of initiative with the Member States? What about the European Parliament, should it also have a right of initiative? After all, such a right is normal in national parliaments.

The European Parliament

In relation to the European Parliament (EP) the issue at hand is that of the relative representation of the Member States (see table 9.3). How big should the Parliament be allowed to become? What would be a just division of the seats?

A mini-reform took place in connection with the Brussels summit in December 1993 (*EC Bulletin* 12–1993). United Germany got an additional 18 seats, while Italy, the United Kingdom, France and the Netherlands got an extra six, Spain four, Portugal, Greece and Belgium one each. Ireland, Denmark and Luxembourg did not get additional seats. Maybe the most important development was that the principle of equal representation of the four largest members was broken, a principle so far especially emphasised by France. It was French insistence on the principle that had made this reform impossible at the time of the Maastricht negotiations. Eventually France accepted the idea that Germany should have more seats in the EP than the three other big states.

Table 9.3 European Parliament

Member State	Number of seats	Population (millions)	Citizens per EP seat
Germany	99	81.7	826,000
France	87	58.1	670,000
Italy	87	57.7	659,000
United Kingdom	87	58.6	675,000
Spain	64	39.1	613,000
Netherlands	31	15.5	500,000
Belgium	25	10.2	404,000
Greece	25	10.5	420,000
Portugal	25	9.9	396,000
Sweden	22	8.9	400,000
Austria	21	8.1	386,000
Finland	16	5.1	319,000
Denmark	16	5.2	331,000
Ireland	15	3.6	240,000
Luxembourg	6	0.4	67,000
Total	626	372.6	

Source: Based on Simon Hix (1999: 77).

The discrepancy between the representation of the big and small Member States, however, remained large also after the mini-reform in 1993. It took 66,000 votes to get elected to the European Parliament from Luxembourg, while it took 805,000 votes in Germany. This did not seem very just, and enlargement with many relatively small states would also make this problem more visible.

The 1993 reform increased the total number of members of the European Parliament to 567. The enlargement in 1995 added 22 seats to Sweden, 21 to Austria and 16 to Finland, taking the total to 626 members of the European Parliament (MEPs).

Another question in connection with the European Parliament was the many legislative procedures that involved the Parliament in various ways. For some questions, the Parliament is only consulted, for other questions the so-called cooperation procedure applies which involves two readings in the Parliament, but not a real veto for the Parliament. The Maastricht Treaty introduced the so-called co-decision procedure (Art. 189b), which gave the Parliament a veto on some legislation especially relating to the single market. There is also the assent procedure requiring the Parliament to accept certain decisions, especially enlargement and association agreements. For the budget there are separate procedures. It had all become very complicated, and various sides expressed the need for simplification (Best 1994).

Report of the Reflection Group

A so-called Reflection Group prepared the IGC 96–97. According to the Reflection Group institutional changes should increase the citizens' confidence in the European institutions. Reform should 'improve the efficiency, democracy, and transparency of the Union' (Reflection Group 1995: 4).

More concrete proposals were often drafted in very careful language. Concerning the European Parliament 'it seems appropriate to fix a maximum number of seats. A majority accept a maximum of 700 in an enlarged Union' (Reflection Group 1995: 30). With respect to procedures a large majority was in favour of simplification, reducing them to the following three: consultation, co-decision and assent. It would also be appropriate to simplify the co-decision procedure.

Concerning QMV: 'In the case of Community legislation, a large majority in the Group is prepared to consider making qualified majority voting the general rule, on grounds of efficiency, since it will facilitate decision-making' (Reflection Group 1995: 33). Concerning the weighting of votes, the Reflection Group was clearly split: 'Several members point to a gradual deterioration in popular representation in the weighting of qualified majority voting as a result of the underrepresentation of the people of the more populous states and the growing number of less populous states in the Union' (Reflection Group 1995: 34). 'In the view of some the answer is a new weighting of votes that takes greater account of population. On the other hand, a system of double majority of votes and population has been suggested.' But,

> In any event, several members have voiced objections to the arguments in support of greater account being taken of the population criteria in qualified majority voting. Some have pointed out that the entire integration process rests on the fundamental principle of sovereign equality of States, with the present system already representing a concession under that principle. Others have taken the view that the present voting takes due account of population, arguing that in any case the institution which represents the people is the European Parliament. These members also emphasize that the smaller and medium sized Member States do not act as a block and that there is little if any prospect of Governments representing a majority of the Union's citizens being outvoted. (*ibid.*)

The Reflection Group was in favour of maintaining the Commission's monopoly of legislative initiative. Concerning the composition of the Commission, the Reflection Group basically mentioned two options: (1) maintaining a system involving Commissioners from all Member States, which would promote a feeling of belonging on the part of citizens; or (2) 'fewer than the number of Member States'. The number of really necessary portfolios should determine the size of the Commission. The pros and cons of the two options were presented.

The agenda of IGC 96–97

When the IGC started in connection with the meeting of the European Council in Turin in the spring of 1996, the agenda was grouped in three main points: (1) a Union close to the citizens; (2) institutions in a more democratic and efficient Union; and (3) strengthened capacity for the Union's external action (*EC Bulletin* 3-1996, point I.5). Questions relating to the Third Pillar were included in the first group. Among institutional issues the following were mentioned:

1   extent of majority voting, weighting of votes, threshold for QMV;
2   commission efficiency and composition;
3   role of ECJ and Court of Auditors;
4   rules to 'enable a certain number of Member States to develop a strengthened cooperation'.

The last point became known as flexibility. The various institutional issues during the IGC were dominated by four aims:

1   to simplify and make the decision-making process more efficient;
2   to strengthen the democratic basis of the Union. This led to various negotiations concerning the role of the European Parliament as well as national parliaments;
3   to change the balance between the big and small Member States. Two issues were central: the composition of the Commission and the weighting of votes in the Council;
4   to clarify and limit the role of the European Court of Justice especially pursued by the UK, which, however, did not lead to any changes (Isaksen, Toft and Bødtcher-Hansen 1998: 120).

Actor positions

After the IGC had begun, the Belmont European Centre in Brussels started following the positions of the actors in the IGC, i.e. the Member States, the Commission and the EP.[1] A quick consultation of the Belmont tables will show that there were a number of different positions at the outset and that much convergence of positions was needed before agreement could be reached on the institutional issues (Belmont European Policy Centre 1996).[2]

With respect to the Commission we find that none of the actors except the UK stated that it wanted to reduce the Commission's powers. No one wanted to abolish the exclusive right of initiative of the Commission. On these points change should not be expected. Eight actors wanted to reduce the number of Commissioners to one per Member State, but seven were against that proposal.

Although seven actors were in favour of increasing the powers of the European Parliament and none were against, there were still ten who answered: 'Don't know.' Overall, however, it was not unlikely that the European Parliament might end up being one of the institutional winners from the 1996–97 IGC. A large majority supported the idea of increasing the involvement of national parliaments.

Concerning the Council there was a large majority in favour of increased use of QMV. The linkage to future enlargements probably had an effect here. Ten actors answered 'yes' to the question of introducing population-weighted voting, but seven small states answered 'no'. Since the question was very general, it could include a re-weighting of votes, as well as the possibility of a double majority, which would require a majority of the population in the EU as well. The idea of public legislative meetings was supported by eleven actors and opposed by none. All the talk about greater openness seemed to have had its effects, although there may have been more hidden opposition than the answers showed. Nine actors supported change in the Presidency system but their answers did not indicate what kind of changes these might entail.

Early agreements

More than seventy-five official documents submitted to the IGC 96–97 dealt with institutional issues. Certain institutional issues were solved relatively early during the IGC. This included the idea of an increased use of the co-decision procedure and a reduction in the number of decision procedures by eliminating the cooperation procedure (except for Economic and Monetary Union that was not dealt with by the IGC). There was also early support for the idea of simplifying the co-decision procedure. Finally, all Member States agreed to limit the number of seats in the European Parliament to 700. These early agreements were reflected in the draft treaty proposal presented by the Irish Presidency in December 1996 (Isaksen, Toft and Bødtcher-Hansen 1998, McDonaugh 1998, Dehousse 1999).

Small versus big: the difficult issues

When the Dutch Presidency took over in January 1997 the more sensitive issues remained. These were the issues which largely confronted the big and the small countries. The last months of the negotiations concentrated on three main issues:

1   the future size and composition of the Commission;
2   changes in the weights of votes in the Council and threshold of QMV;
3   expansion of the scope of QMV in the First Pillar (Isaksen, Toft and Bødtcher-Hansen 1998: 121).

With respect to the Commission, certain large Member States wanted to set a ceiling on the number of Commissioners. France in particular was pressing the issue, suggesting a ceiling as low as ten Commissioners. This reduction would be combined with a system of rotation. Most small Member States, however, insisted on retaining a Commissioner from their country.

Concerning weighting of votes, France, Italy, Spain and the United Kingdom were especially in favour of a re-weighting in favour of larger states. Germany suggested a system of double majority, where the current system would be combined with the requirement that a majority should include a majority of the citizens of the Union. The smaller Member States took a rather sceptical position on changing the voting weights.

On 11 February 1997 the Dutch Presidency presented a so-called 'Non-Paper' on re-weighting of votes and the threshold in the Council decision-making process (CONF/3815/97). This document included two tables showing the evolution of the qualified majority and the blocking minority in terms of minimum of population. The tables showed that moving from twelve to fifteen Member States the QMV declined from 63.21 per cent of the total population to 58.3 per cent. In a Union of 26 it would fall to 50.29 per cent if the current weighting system were extrapolated.

The Presidency's 'Non-Paper' in February was analytical. Only towards the end of the negotiations did the Dutch Presidency issue a note (CONF/3888/97 of 24 April 1997) which included in two annexes two variants of possible re-weighting of votes in a Union of 15 and 26 respectively. Table 9.4 includes the data for the EU-15.

Table 9.4   Variants of a possible re-weighting of votes in a 15 Member State Union

Member States	Variant I, EU 15	Variant II, EU 15
Germany	25	12
UK	25	12
France	25	12
Italy	25	12
Spain	20	9
Netherlands	12	6
Greece	10	5
Belgium	10	5
Portugal	10	5
Sweden	8	4
Austria	8	4
Denmark	6	3
Finland	6	3
Ireland	6	3
Luxembourg	3	2
Total	199	97
QMV	142	69
Blocking minority	58	30
QMV % pop.	61%	60%

Source: CONF/3888/97 of 24 April 1997.

The suggested re-weighting of votes was established by allocating votes to Member States in a decreasing scale subject to size of population. Both variants would result in a minimum level of support of ± 60 per cent of the total Union population and respect the current level of the threshold for the qualified majority (71.2 per cent).

The foreign ministers discussed the proposals on 29–30 April without any agreement (*Agence Europe*, 1 May, 1997). The Dutch chief negotiator during the IGC, Michiel Patijn, later told the press that the issue of re-weighting had 'raised a confrontation between small and large Member States without precedent in the Community's history' (*Agence Europe*, 16 May, 1997).

The question was left to the Amsterdam meeting of the European Council in June 1997. None of the variants were accepted. The Belgians did not like the idea of suddenly having fewer votes than the Dutch. They referred to the equal treatment of Germany and France, which was maintained in the variants. The Belgian Prime Minister Jean-Luc Dehaene is reported to have been upset with his Dutch counterpart Wim Kok and is said to have threatened to leave a European Council meeting (Kerremans 2002). There was also the Spanish problem. The Spanish claimed extra compensation for losing a Commissioner since they had accepted fewer votes than the other big Member States in exchange for two Commissioners when they joined (Duff 1997: 133).

According to one account, France and Spain had been the countries pressing the most for a re-weighting of the votes (Svensson 2000: 165). The solution of double majorities was also discussed in Amsterdam, but France and the UK were against this solution which would have been to Germany's advantage. President Chirac called the solution 'dangerous' (*Agence Europe*, 19 June, 1997).

Concerning the extended use of QMV, all states, with the exception of the UK, agreed to the idea, but disagreement on which areas to include remained until the final decision in Amsterdam. In the end the extension was not as large as expected since Germany at the last moment decided in favour of a shorter list.

The main failure of Amsterdam was the fact that no agreement was reached on the two most central issues of the composition of the Commission and the voting system in the Council (Dehousse 1999; see also Laursen 2002b). The Treaty included a *protocol on the institutions with the prospect of enlargement of the European Union* which stipulated that 'At the date of entry into force of the first enlargement of the Union . . . the Commission shall comprise one national of each of the Member States, provided that, by that date, the weighting of the votes in the Council has been modified, whether by reweighing of the votes or by dual majority, in a manner acceptable to all Member States, taking into account all relevant elements, notably compensating those Member States which give up the possibility of nominating a second member of the Commission.' Article 2 of the protocol further stipulated: 'At least one year before the membership of the European Union exceeds twenty, a conference of representatives of the governments of Member States shall be convened in order to carry out a comprehensive review of the provisions of the treaties on the composition and functioning of the institutions' (Duff 1997: 300). The protocol on institutions committed the EU to a new IGC to solve the unsolved institutional issues.

Summary of Amsterdam institutional changes

The widened scope of the co-decision procedure made the European Parliament the big winner of Amsterdam. Most of the areas covered by the cooperation procedure were transferred to co-decision.

QMV was extended to eleven new treaty provisions, including employment guidelines and incentive measures, social exclusion, transparency, countering fraud and customs cooperation, as well as to five existing treaty provisions, including research framework programmes. As mentioned this list was shorter than expected.

The co-decision procedure was simplified among other things by abolishing the third reading phase. If the Conciliation Committee fails to agree on a joint text, the proposal is dropped. Amsterdam did agree on the 700 seats maximum for the European Parliament.

Explaining the limited Amsterdam results

Although Amsterdam was supposed to have solved the institutional issues before enlargement, it did not. Institutional reforms, especially extended use of QMV, were minor. A number of factors contributed to the limited extent of the reforms, including lack of convergence in national positions, lack of leadership and the feeling that the issue was not yet so pressing. Andrew Duff states:

> The biggest surprise at Amsterdam was that Helmut Kohl pulled back from traditional German positions on QMV. Led by Bavaria, the Länder governments, which compose the SPD-led Bundesrat, were anxious to protect their prerogatives over areas of domestic legislation, particularly concerning the environment and immigration. (Duff 1997: 155)

He continued to say that the Chancellor was said to have been preoccupied with the single currency project and unable to forge either a coherent or progressive German policy on institutional questions (see also Beuter 2002).

Another factor was the shock election of a Socialist-Communist government in France on 1 June which led to incoherent French positions during the later stages of the IGC (Deloche-Gaudez 2002). Domestic politics in Germany and France affected the usual Franco-German joint formulation of positions before meetings of the European Council and joint leadership during the final stage of the IGC.

In the end the most important explanation was probably timing. The issue was simply not sufficiently urgent to be solved quickly that Tuesday night in Amsterdam when the Heads of State and Government finally got to that point on the agenda. Enlargement was still a few years ahead (see also Moravcsik and Nicolaïdis 1999).

On to Nice

Amsterdam thus finished undecided on the reweighing of votes in the Council and the composition of the Commission. There were some who felt that the increased use of QMV as agreed in Amsterdam was too limited. The Amsterdam 'leftovers' would be discussed again in the IGC 2000 (for background, see Best, Gray and Stubb 2000).

It took a lot of horse-trading in Nice in December 2000 to solve these issues. In many ways Nice was unique. Past IGCs had usually dealt with both substantive policy issues and some institutional issues. This time the agenda was largely limited to institutional issues. These were to include a fourth issue that was added during the conference, that is, 'closer (or enhanced) cooperation' or 'flexibility'. The Treaty of Amsterdam had introduced clauses allowing a group of Member States to go further in the integration process than the hesitant and slower Member States, but the conditions for such 'closer cooperation' were rather strict. The issue in the Nice negotiations was whether the conditions should be made less strict. An easing would make it easier for pro-integration members to move faster than integration-sceptical Member States – which indeed in the end took place. We shall limit this account of the Nice Treaty to the three main Amsterdam 'leftovers'.

Re-weighting of votes

The re-weighting of votes in the Council that was agreed after prolonged negotiations can be seen in table 9.5. The four largest states, which currently have 10 votes, will get 29 in the future. If we only concentrate on population Germany should have gained more votes. Spain, which currently has 8 votes, will get 27, a very good result for that country. Spain then pulled Poland up to the same level. We also notice that there will be a differentiation between the Netherlands and Belgium, with the former getting 13 votes whereas the latter would only have 12 votes. In the past these two Member States used to have the same number of votes, namely 5 (for more detail, see Galloway 2001, Bond and Feus 2001).

Less controversially the Treaty of Nice also assigned new number of seats in the European Parliament (see table 9.6). A differentiation between Germany and France had existed since the mini-reform in 1993. In the future Germany will retain its 99 seats but the other current Member States will have to accept reductions in their representation in the future. The differences in number of inhabitants per seat will remain large.

Qualified Majority Vote (QMV)

The second main issue was the increased use of QMV. When the IGC 2000 started there were about seventy areas left that still required unanimity according to the treaty. The IGC discussed about forty-five of these in view of possible transfer to QMV. In the end it was decided to transfer about thirty-five areas (exact number depends on how it is measured). Twenty-three areas will move from the entry into force of the treaty. This group includes international agreements under CFSP, anti-discrimination incentive measures, free movement of citizens of the EU (with some exceptions), judicial cooperation in civil matters, trade in services and commercial aspects of intellectual property (with exceptions),

Table 9.5   Council Votes in EU-27 (as of 1 January 2005)

	Present votes	Future votes	Population (millions)	% of Union population
Germany	10	29	82.03	17.05
United Kingdom	10	29	59.25	12.31
France	10	29	58.97	12.25
Italy	10	29	57.61	11.97
Spain	8	27	39.39	8.19
Poland		27	38.67	8.04
Romania		14	22.49	4.67
Netherlands	5	13	15.76	3.28
Greece	5	12	10.53	2.19
Czech Republic		12	10.29	2.14
Belgium	5	12	10.21	2.12
Hungary		12	10.09	2.10
Portugal	5	12	9.98	2.07
Sweden	4	10	8.85	1.84
Bulgaria		10	8.23	1.71
Austria	4	10	8.08	1.68
Slovakia		7	5.39	1.12
Denmark	3	7	5.31	1.10
Finland	3	7	5.16	1.07
Ireland	3	7	3.74	0.78
Lithuania		7	3.70	0.77
Latvia		4	2.44	0.51
Slovenia		4	1.98	0.41
Estonia		4	1.45	0.30
Cyprus		4	0.75	0.16
Luxembourg	2	4	0.43	0.09
Malta		3	0.38	0.08
Total EU 27	87	345	481.18	100
Qualified majority of votes	62	258 (as well as a majority of Member States)		Furthermore at least 62% of the Union population, if a Member State asks for control of this criterion
Blocking minority	26	88		

Source: Treaty texts and European Parliament, 'Draft Treaty of Nice (initial analysis)', Brussels, 10 January 2001. The final version of the Nice Treaty was published in the *Official Journal of the European Communities*, C 80, 10 March 2001.

appointment of Secretary-General and Deputy Secretary-General of the Council, and importantly, nomination and appointment of the President of the Commission and its Members. For twelve areas introduction of QMV is deferred until a later (unspecified) date. For some areas relating to free movement of third-country nationals and illegal immigration the date is 1 May 2004. For Structural Funds it will be 1 January 2007 or later (date applicable after adoption of the Financial Perspective for 2007–13). The latter decision was a *cadeau* to Spain and other cohesion countries. More than twenty areas, mainly

Table 9.6   Seats in the European Parliament (EU-27)

	Population (millions)	Population as % of EU	Seats per Member State under the present system	Seats per Member State under the Treaty of Nice	Reduction in numbers	Reduction in %	Number of inhabitants per seat
Germany	82.04	17.05	99	99	0	0	828,667
United Kingdom	59.25	12.31	87	72	15	17.24	822,875
France	58.97	12.25	87	72	15	17.24	818,972
Italy	57.61	11.97	87	72	15	17.24	800,167
Spain	39.39	8.19	64	50	14	21.88	787,880
Poland	38.66	8.04		50			773,340
Romania	22.49	4.67		33			681,485
Netherlands	15.76	3.28	31	25	6	19.35	630,400
Greece	10.53	2.19	25	22	3	12.00	478,773
Czech Republic	10.29	2.14		20			514,500
Belgium	10.21	2.12	25	22	3	12.00	464,227
Hungary	10.09	2.1		20			504,600
Portugal	9.98	2.07	25	22	3	12.00	453,636
Sweden	8.85	1.84	22	18	4	18.18	491,889
Bulgaria	8.23	1.71		17			484,118
Austria	8.08	1.68	21	17	4	19.05	475,412
Slovakia	5.39	1.12		13			414,846
Denmark	5.31	1.1	16	13	3	18.75	408,692
Finland	5.16	1.07	16	13	3	18.75	396,923
Ireland	3.74	0.78	15	12	3	20.00	312,000
Lithuania	3.70	0.77		12			308,417
Latvia	2.44	0.51		8			304,875
Slovenia	1.98	0.41		7			282,571
Estonia	1.45	0.30		6			241,000
Cyprus	0.75	0.16		6			125,333
Luxembourg	0.43	0.09	6	6	0	0	71,500
Malta	0.38	0.08		5			75,800
Total EU 27	481.18	100		732			657,351

Source: European Parliament, 'Draft Treaty of Nice (initial analysis), 2 Brussels, 10 January 2001.

constitutional or quasi-constitutional provisions were considered too sensitive from the outset. It was agreed early on not to touch them.

The more controversial areas in these discussions about increased use of QMV included visa, asylum and immigration, where some issues will be transferred to QMV in 2004 and others later. Another controversial area was trade policy where the introduction of QMV for trade in services and trade-related aspects of intellectual property rights (TRIPS) takes place with some exemptions, including culture and the audiovisual area. Social policy was also controversial. Some countries wanted to protect their labour market rules and regulations against EU interference. For sensitive social policy areas unanimity therefore survived the IGC. The treaty also leaves taxation policies untouched. Some countries insisted on keeping distribution policy at the national level.

Commission

Concerning the third issue, size and composition of the Commission, the Treaty of Nice only found a partial solution. From 1 January 2005 the Commission will consist of one national from each Member State. When the EU reaches 27 members a reduction of the size of the Commission will have to be agreed and a system of rotation found, all of this by unanimity. So, at some point in time the Member States will not always have a Commissioner of their own nationality.

Nice has also strengthened the role of the President of the Commission. In the future he may decide the internal organisation of the Commission and reallocate responsibilities among the Commissioners during the Commission's term of office. He may also call on a member of the Commission to resign after obtaining the collective approval of the Commission.

Explaining the Nice results

IGCs are, as the name suggests, above all conferences of the Member State governments. Many of the major decisions in the history of European integration have been made in such conferences. John Peterson talks about history-making decisions being made at a super-systemic level and suggests that we need macro-theories to explain such decisions (Peterson 1995). History-making decisions are different from policy-setting at the systemic level or policy-shaping at the sub-systemic level. Among macro-theories to explain history-making decisions liberal intergovernmentalism constitutes a simple yet powerful framework for analysis.

Andrew Moravcsik developed 'liberal intergovernmentalism' as an alternative to early neofunctionalist theories of integration (see also Laursen 1995). When he first developed his approach he suggested a two-step analysis of integration, first national preference formation and then interstate bargaining (Moravcsik 1993). Later he added a third step, institutional choice (Moravcsik 1998). We shall take a look at liberal intergovernmentalism as a possible explanatory framework of Amsterdam and Nice and then move on to discuss some specific problems in connection with the Nice bargain.

The first stage according to Moravcsik is to try to explain national preferences. The central question asked here is whether it is economic or geopolitical interests that dominate when Member States form their preferences. Moravcsik's answer based on major decisions in the European integration process is that economic interests are the most important.

The second stage, interstate bargaining, seeks to explain the efficiency and distributional outcomes from EU negotiations. Here two possible explanations of agreements on substance are contrasted: asymmetrical interdependence or supranational entrepreneurship. Moravcsik arrives at the answer that asymmetrical interdependence has most explanatory power. Some Member

States have more at stake than others. They will work harder to influence outcomes. The role of the Commission in this reading of the process is not considered to be very important. According to Moravcsik three factors are likely to determine the outcomes of interstate bargaining:

1   The value of unilateral policy alternatives, relative to the status quo, which underlies credible threats to veto;
2   The value of alternative coalitions, which underlies credible threats to exclude;
3   The opportunities for issue linkage or side-payments, which underlie 'package deals' (Moravcsik 1998: 63).

Summarising, the discussion of the first point Moravcsik says: 'those who more intensely desire the benefits of cooperation will concede more to get them'. With regard to the second point his view is: 'the credible threat of exclusion is likely to generate an even more powerful pressure on recalcitrant states than does the threat of nonagreement'. With respect to linkage strategies Moravcsik observes that the major constraint lies in their domestic distributional implications. Concessions often create domestic losers, which will limit the use of package deals (Moravcsik 1998: 63–67).

The third stage, institutional choice, explores why states choose to delegate or pool decision-making in international institutions. Delegation in the EU case refers to the powers transferred to the Commission and the European Court of Justice (ECJ). Pooling of sovereignty refers to the application of majority decisions in the Council, in practice mostly QMV. To explain institutional choice Moravcsik contrasts three possible explanations: federalist ideology, centralised technocratic management or more credible commitment. The answer he gives is that states delegate and pool sovereignty to get a more credible commitment. Pooling and delegation is a rational strategy adopted by the Member States to pre-commit governments to future decisions, to encourage future cooperation and to improve future implementation of agreements (Moravcsik 1998: 73).

Using theories of decision-making, negotiations and international political economy in general in an elegant combination has allowed Moravcsik to construct a parsimonious framework for the study of international cooperation including international integration.

The question to be asked here is, could we use liberal intergovernmentalism to explain the Nice bargain?[3] To do so we would have first to study the process of preference formation in the Member States, especially the bigger and more influential ones. Next we would have to study the bargaining process during IGC 2000. This should in principle be possible, but without a major research effort we just do not have all the information we need to give a conclusive answer to the question. Based on available information it is possible to say a few things about the process.

Concerning preferences in respect to re-weighting of votes the most important variable was size. These issues were largely pitting the big against the small Member States. The big wanted a re-weighting in their favour. The small resisted this. Many big countries wanted to reduce the size of the Commission. Many small countries wanted to retain 'their' Commissioner. Using Moravcsik's terms this might to a large extent fall more under geopolitics rather than economic interests as such. But even that would not necessarily be the best way to look at it. The questions concerning Council voting and Commission composition were fundamental ones about institutional design or even constitutional choice. What kind of considerations do actors make when they design new institutions? Moravcsik does not include that kind of question in his considerations about 'institutional choice'. Since institutions are about future decisions actors are interested in increasing their influence and control. Voting weights are directly linked to influence. Control is linked the 'blocking minority' that follows from the definition of a QMV. Various institutionalist theories could possibly be applied to structure our analysis of these aspects of the Nice negotiations (e.g. Moe 1990, Pollack 1996, Kerremans 1998, Schneider and Aspinwall 2001). This point needs further consideration. There may also be a dimension of pro- versus anti-integration attitudes here, a less rationalist and more reflectivist dimension. Maybe ideas do play a role in constitutional choice (see Christiansen, Jørgensen and Wiener 2001).

Moravcsik's scheme seems more applicable to the question about increased use of QMV. Here size was probably not an important variable in determining attitudes. Specific national socio-economic interests, such as shipping interests in Greece, film industry interests in France, labour market interests in Denmark, would probably go far in explaining national preferences and positions during the negotiations. Moravcsik's propositions would be applicable to the issue of the pooling of sovereignty.

The end game in Nice became a tough bargaining process with ques- tions of national prestige playing an unusual role. The French wanted to get as many votes as the Germans. The Belgians wanted to get as many votes as the Dutch. The Spanish argued that there was a special Spanish problem. Known as tough bargainers the Spanish were treated generously from the outset by the French Presidency (Ludlow 2001). The Germans in the end were compensated by the rule that a QMV should also represent 62 per cent of the EU population. Since Germany has about half the weight of a blocking minor- ity in terms of population the country can expect to become a very attractive coalition partner in the future. The Belgians, in the end had to accept one vote less than the Dutch, but they were promised that future meetings of the European Council gradually would be shifted to Belgium. Another side- payment to Belgium was increased representation in the European Parliament (Best 2001). Portugal, which resented the generous treatment of its neighbour Spain, was also compensated with extra representation in the European Parliament.

As mentioned earlier Nice was mainly about institutional choice (or design) and not so much about substance. If there was a broader question of substance, it was of course enlargement. Those Member States that favoured speedy enlargement may therefore have been in a weaker bargaining position than those who did not mind the postponement of enlargement. This may have weakened Germany and the Nordic members. It strengthened the cohesion countries, especially Spain, which not only got relatively many votes in the Council but also succeeded in getting QMV for structural funds postponed until 2007 or later.

Despite the rather unique character of Nice it can be argued that liberal intergovernmentalism can capture at least the part concerning QMV extension. A tentative conclusion is that various institutionalist theories will also have contributions to make to our understanding of Nice, including historical institutionalism (Pierson 1996). The equality of votes between France and Germany constituted a kind of 'path dependence' that could not be broken, or which could only be broken in an indirect way through the 'demographic filter' of a minimum of 62 per cent of population, which was introduced. Considerations about 'sunk costs' and 'costs of exit' must have played an important role for those countries that disliked the emerging compromise, such as Belgium and Portugal.

Social constructivists have been interested in the process of collective identity formation in Europe (e.g. Risse-Kappen 1996). They may have a point. But in Nice we saw the Heads of State and Government clearly think in 'we' versus 'they' terms. The battle about votes looked very much like a zero-sum game, suggesting that EU Member States also sometimes think in terms of 'relative gains' as realists and neo-realists would argue. The collective interest of Europe was poorly represented in Nice.

The Nice 'leftovers'

In a Declaration on the Future of the Union the Heads of State and Government meeting in Nice said that important reforms had been decided and that the ratification of the Nice Treaty would have completed the institutional changes necessary for the accession of new Member States.

The European Council in Nice also called for 'a deeper and wider debate about the future development of the European Union'. The Heads of State and Government went on to mention the following points for the agenda of that future debate:

- how to establish and monitor a more precise delimitation of competences between the European Union and the Member States, reflecting the principle of subsidiarity;
- the status of the Charter of Fundamental Rights of the European Union proclaimed in Nice;
- a simplification of the Treaties with a view to making them clearer and better understood without changing their meaning;
- the role of the national parliaments in the European architecture.

The Declaration also talked about 'the need to improve and to monitor the democratic legitimacy and transparency of the Union and its institutions, to bring them closer to the citizens of the Member States'.

Obviously the authors of the Treaty of Nice were not completely satisfied with the results. They decided that a new IGC should be convened in 2004 to discuss the above issues. Candidate states that have concluded accession negotiations by then would participate in this coming IGC. Other candidate states would be invited as observers.

So Nice was clearly not the end of the road. The nature of the EU stayed on the agenda. What kind of Union is it? What kind of Union should it become? The issues suggested such a (re)new(ed) debate of a constitutional nature.

At a meeting of the European Council at Laeken, Belgium, in December 2001, it was decided to prepare the next treaty reform through a Convention, which would also include representatives from the European Parliament and national parliaments. From February 2002 until July 2003 such a convention prepared a draft Constitutional Treaty for the EU. The draft treaty proposed to do away with the cumbersome system of voting weights adopted at Nice and instead have a system of double majority, a majority of Member States representing also at least 60 per cent of the EU population. The proposal for the Commission was a two-tired system with fifteen voting Commissioners that would rotate between the Member States. But the remaining Member States would have non-voting Commissioners. The IGC that followed, starting in October 2003, failed to accept these proposals from the Convention at a summit in Brussels in December 2003. Although the IGC may still produce agreement on a Constitutional Treaty, the situation is rather uncertain at the moment.

Lawyers have been telling us for years that the EU is *sui generis*. It is not an international organisation like the UN, nor is it a federal state like the USA. It is in many ways something in between, sometimes referred to as a polity. But a debate about what the Union should be doing, what the Member States should be doing, and discussing a catalogue of competences reminds students of federalism of similar debates in federal systems.

It can be argued that the central feature of a federal system is a double guarantee; of the efficiency of the Union as well as of the continued existence of the Member States. Both the Union and the Member States should have real autonomy in certain spheres (Riker 1964). This autonomy is what the European debate is now about. Some Europeans fear that the Union will interfere too much in domestic matters. Others fear that it will not be able to make the necessary joint decisions required by modern interdependence, especially after yet another enlargement.

Indeed, the EU is in the middle of a constitutional debate, which was formalised with the Convention producing the proposal for a Constitutional Treaty. Some will regret that 'federalism' has had such a bad press in some European countries. In reality there is already a heavy dose of federalism in the EU, especially in the First Pillar. Alberta Sbragia has used federalism as a reference point in some of her writings about the EU (e.g. Sbragia 1992). Many years ago a great student of 'constitutionalism', Carl Friedrich, talked about a federalising process in Europe (Friedrich 1968, 1969). That process is still going on.

Conclusions

It took two IGCs to prepare the EU for the ongoing enlargement. Nice eventually did agree on changes in the composition of the Commission, the weighting of votes in the Council and extended use of QMV. It further made the use of 'closer cooperation' easier in the future. The process was a difficult one. At the moment the EU is preparing yet another treaty reform. But the future of this effort remains uncertain. The current IGC also turned into a battle between small and large Member States concerning the Commission. On the question of voting system in the Council it was mainly Spain and Poland which opposed the proposed change, since they stood to lose relative influence. So once again there is a battle about influence in the future. In March 2004 it was decided to try to complete these negotiations about a new so-called Constitutional Treaty by June 2004.

How to explain the institutional changes that were agreed in Nice? According to liberal intergovernmentalism we have seen pooling of sovereignty and delegation of competences to supranational bodies in the EU in the past because the Member States want to ensure credible commitments. Both Amsterdam and Nice faced issues of credible commitments, especially in view of further enlargements. How to make sure that an enlarged EU can make decisions? How to make sure those decisions will indeed be implemented in the future? These were important aspects of the *problematique*. Looking at national preferences and interstate bargaining help us understand the difficulties. Producing convergence in national positions depended on other options as well as threats and the process required various linkages and side-payments. But the kind of institutional issues faced by Amsterdam and Nice – and now during the post-Nice process – were, and are, especially about influence and control in the future EU. To understand that aspect it may be helpful to look at theories developed to explain 'constitutional' choices in federal systems.

Notes

1 The main actors in an IGC are the Member States, but the Commission also takes part in the meetings. According to the conclusions from the European Council in Madrid December 1995: 'The European Parliament will be closely associated with the work of the Conference so that it is both briefed regularly and in detail on the progress of the discussions and can give its point of view, where it considers this necessary, on all matters under discussion' (quoted from Laursen 2002a: 6).

2 One has of course to be aware of the limitation of these Belmont data. As pointed out by
   Andrew Moravcsik in a communication to the author: (1) What is reported in [these] data
   are public positions. These may be strategic; (2) 'Don't know' reports that the government
   has not determined preferences. In the latter case it may be that the government has not
   consulted civil society and figured out what the preferences are.

3 Moravcsik and Nicolaïdis (1999) have argued that liberal intergovernmentalism can
   explain Amsterdam and it may indeed be the best framework to explain Amsterdam. But
   even here various authors have found various problems (see Laursen 2002c).

Andreas Maurer

10

Negotiating the Nice Treaty: a joint but failed search for efficiency building

Background of the Nice IGC

This chapter investigates the 2000 intergovernmental conference (IGC) with a specific view on the Council of Ministers and the IGC's dossier on the Council's modes for decision-making. Acknowledging that supranational influence is contingent upon both the context and actual strategies employed by supranational actors in an IGC, (Beach 2004: forthcoming), I focus on issues where the Member States' strategic positions were under review. The analysis will investigate the range of opportunities and constraints upon the proposals put on the IGC's table. I argue that the Nice IGC's outcome (Dinan and Vanhoonacker 2000/2001, Galloway 2001) is the product of a trend of Member States who already during the Maastricht reforms started to base their proposals on institutional reform on a non-agreed type measure. If each national interpretation of the EU's task to enhance its capacity to act is used and – more important – inherently accepted by the negotiating partners, any resulting Treaty will no longer provide a coherent set of target objectives and criteria for evaluating and re-revising the EU legal constitution.

The Treaty of Nice is the result of the fifth Intergovernmental Conference on amending the EC/EU Treaties.[1] After a lengthy ratification process, it entered into force on 1 February 2003.

Unlike the Single European Act (SEA) of 1987, the Treaty of Maastricht of 1993 and the Treaty of Amsterdam of 1999 (Hummer 1998, Laursen 2002, Jopp, Maurer and Schmuck 1998, Monar and Wessels 2001, Moravcsik and Nicolaidis 1999: 59–85, Pollack 1999), the Intergovernmental Conference of 2000 almost exclusively focused on amending the institutional and procedural basics of the European Union in order to prepare it for enlargement by up to twelve new states. Past IGCs had usually dealt with both substantive policy issues and some institutional issues. At the Nice IGC the agenda was much more limited to institutional subjects. With this limiting of the negotiating agenda to a few basic but crucial questions regarding the institutional structure of the European Union it was already clear from the very beginning that it would not be as easily possible to combine the negotiations on the allocation of competences in particular fields of public policy with those on institutional concessions in order to more efficiently 'fulfill' the rules on competences, as in Maastricht and Amsterdam where loss of power was exchanged for reformed policies (Schumann 2001).

The mandate for negotiations in Nice was based on a two-tier cascade that was formulated in Protocol no. 7 to the Amsterdam Treaty.[2] It dealt with three related issues known as the Amsterdam 'leftovers' which the Treaty of Amsterdam in 1997 had failed to solve: the increased use of qualified majority voting (QMV) in the Council, the re-weighting of votes in the Council, and the size and composition of the Commission.

In a declaration attached to this Protocol, the governments of France, Italy and Belgium expressed the opinion that the Treaty does not correspond to the necessity to achieve essential progress in strengthening the organs of the European Communities, which is required by the mandate for negotiations. Those three countries[3] further made clear that a total revision focused on institutional issues would be 'a necessary precondition for the conclusion of the first round of negotiations on enlargement'.[4] Consequently, they expressed the opinion 'that a considerable extension of the principle of qualified majority voting is an essential element to be considered' (Amsterdam Treaty, Protocol No. 7).

To facilitate consensus among the 15 Member States, the European Council of Cologne of June 1999 decided to focus on a 'small solution' for the 'leftovers'[5] of Amsterdam (as outlined in the Protocol and in the related declaration) to be tackled by the Intergovernmental Conference that was to be held by the end of 2000 under a French Council-Presidency. According to the mandate that was finally agreed upon in 1999 in Helsinki, the Intergovernmental Conference 2000 was to review

> the size and composition of the European Commission, the balancing of vote casting in the Council, the question of a possible extension of qualified majority voting in the Council, as well as further necessary amendments to the Treaty, as and when they appeared in the context of the implementation of the Treaty of Amsterdam or derived from the above-mentioned problems.

Acting in an enlarged European Union: shared challenges and opportunities

The objective of the Intergovernmental Conference 2000 thus led to a simple question: should and can the European Union enter the twenty-first century as some kind of an ad hoc coalition of organised particular interests or as a structured organization for the representation and execution of 'European

Community interests'? The respective debate (De Schutter, Lebessis and Paterson 2001) that was initiated to optimise the institutional and procedural design of the 'EU XXL' was not to be understood as an exaggerated exposure addressed to Brussels. In view of a dynamic community, from which the citizens expect to act with state-like instruments in almost all areas of public life, rules must be determined providing a unique identity for the EU and its institutional components within the international system. Joschka Fischer in his Berlin speech emphasised three areas of conflict that were intensively and controversially discussed as central moving targets in the media and political science.[6]

According to Fischer, the question of enlargement was dominated by a concentration on the processes of economic transformation and adjustment, or approximation. Hence, the debate on the needs and options for reform of the distributive policies within the existing framework of the European Communities was closely linked to a hidden debate on the institutional and procedural legal aspects of related reforms where the question of procedural rules in the fields of finance, budget, and cohesion policies of the EU appear. No doubt, it makes a difference whether the basic regulations on financially intensive promotional programmes have to be adopted unanimously, with qualified majority, in 'close cooperation', by co-decision, with assent or consultation of the European Parliament. Closely connected with enlargement questions was the discussion of whether institutional and procedural adjustments are necessary in order to secure or to improve the capacity of the European Union to implement common policies in a more democratic, transparent and efficient way.

Finally, in relation to the surrounding international environment the challenges of the EU did increase, rather than decrease. With the end of the East-West confrontation, one of the 'legitimating side scenes' of the unification of Europe was lost. Scenarios of conflict and threat have replaced that, such as regional crisis and civil or cessation wars on the European continent, as well as in other regions outside Europe, where the EU have contact, at least in terms of trade or development cooperation policy. In addition, the globalisation of the production of goods, services and risks, the oligarchic tendencies in the high technology sector and the worldwide competition of economic areas challenge the capacity of the European Union to act.

Therefore, during its negotiations, the Nice Intergovernmental Conference focused on reforms with regard to social and migration rights of third country citizens as well as on trade policy, common foreign and security policy, judicial cooperation in civil and criminal matters, and international aspects of European environmental policy.

Setting the scenes: institutional needs and options for reform

The existing structures of the EC/EU of 1999 were still based on the logic of the Rome Treaties of 1957 and its six members, which acted in a relatively limited field of competences and with wide common or shared interests towards third countries and organisations. Since the Rome treaties, the total number of Treaty articles dealing with specific competences and decision-making rules - the *enumerative empowerments* - has grown considerably from eighty-six (EEC Treaty 1957) to 222 (Amsterdam Treaty 1999). Also, the increasing number of sectoral formats of the Council of Ministers (from four in 1958 to twenty-three in 1998) (Westlake 1995:164–167) as well as the extension of its administrative substructure, indicates that governmental actors have become more and more involved in using their Brussels networks extensively and intensively (Maurer and Wessels 2003).

As for the provisions governing the legal opportunities for the Council's potential efficiency, figure 10.1 shows the absolute proportion of the Council's internal decision-making modes between 1952 until 2003. It can clearly be seen that the total number of rules providing for both unanimity and QMV has considerably increased over time. If we focus on the relative rates of the Treaty-based provisions in the Council (figure 10.2), we also notice an over-proportional growth in QMV in relation to unanimity up to Amsterdam.

The Council did develop as a multi-faceted, chameleon-like institution, which acts as a forum for interstate deliberation, arguing and bargaining, as an executive body and 'principal', and as a legislative state chamber. To understand the Council's evolution, with regard to its legislative roles one has to address the expansion of the role of the European Parliament. Since 1979 the European Parliament augmented its role as a watchdog by making intensive use of its right to ask questions, by keeping a closer eye on EU expenditure (through the

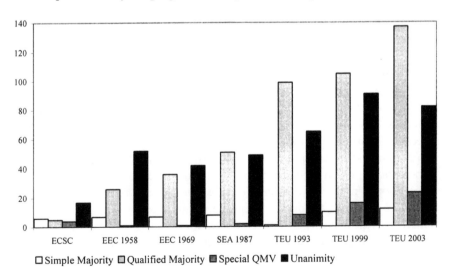

Source: Original ECSC, EEC, EC and EU Treaties (by time of their entry into force).

Figure 10.1   Decision-making modes in the Council of Ministers, 1952–2003 (only EC Treaty area) in absolute numbers

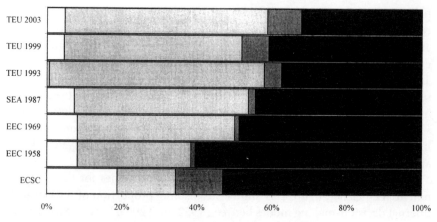

□ Simple Majority ▫ Qualified Majority ▪ Special QMV ■ Unanimity

Source: Original ECSC, EEC, EC and EU Treaties (by time of their entry into force).

Figure 10.2   Decision-making modes in the Council of Ministers, 1952–2003 (only EC Treaty area) in %

Committee on Budgetary Control) and by setting up temporary committees of inquiry. Since 1986/87, EC Treaty amendments did introduce important changes concerning the elective and legislative functions and positions of the European Parliament. On the basis of the positive experiences gained with the cooperation procedure since the entry into force of the SEA (1987), the Maastricht Treaty widened the procedure's scope and created the so-called co-decision procedure. Herewith, the Parliament obtained the right to block a proposed legislative act without the Council having the right to outvote Parliament at the end of the procedure. Co-decision set the Parliament on an equal footing with the Council when the latter performs as a state chamber.

If we focus on the Parliament's legislative evolution since the 1980s, the relative proportion of its 'exclusion' from the EC/EU policy-making process has considerably diminished. However, in view of the absolute increase in Treaty-based decision-making procedures, the numerical growth in consultation, cooperation and co-decision procedures is balanced by a steady augmentation of 'non-participation' in the Council's rule-making process. The main reasons for this development are the dynamics of subsequent Treaty reforms widening the functional scope of European integration and cooperation into new areas. Hence, the vast majority of new competences for the EC/EU did not directly feature the European Parliament as a co-legislative institution. Only after having agreed on a specific competence within a given Treaty 'T−1', the next IGC on 'T−1+n' went on to amend these competences in procedural terms and offered some legislative rights to Parliament. Accordingly, the combination of both the respective powers of the Parliament and Council, does show a remarkable increase in procedural complexity over time. There is no typical procedure which clearly dominates the political system, e.g. QMV and co-decision as the general rule.

But overall, we witness a strong centripetal trend towards 'institutional communitarisation' over time: a push and pull of provisions towards the EC treaties or, within the treaties, towards supranational procedures,[7] or towards EC-like rules within the intergovernmental Pillars of the Union[8] - even if it is with many derogations, such as the case of the area of 'freedom, security and justice' (Title IV ECT) (Monar 1998: 320–35, den Boer and Wallace 2000: 493–519) and even if, in terms of community orthodoxy, 'dirty' communitarisations (Wessels 1997:117–135) and institutional anomalies[9] take place.

This character of Treaty provisions is reinforced by a specific legal feature: if we take a closer look into the treaties, we identify a trend towards procedural ambiguity over time. Whereas the original ECSC and EEC treaties foresaw a restricted (clear) set of rules for each policy field, subsequent Treaty amendments have led to a procedural differentiation with a variety of rule opportunities. As a result, the Treaty provisions do not dictate a clear nomenclature of rules to be applied to specific sectors. Instead, since the SEA, Member States and supranational institutions can, in an increasing number of policy fields, select whether a given piece of secondary legislation - a regulation, a directive or another type of legal act - should be decided by unanimity, simple or qualified majority in the Council; according to the consultation, cooperation or (after Maastricht and Amsterdam) the co-decision procedure; without any participation of the European Parliament or with or without consultation of the Economic and Social Committee, the Committee of the Regions or similar institutions. In other words, different procedural blueprints and inter-institutional codes compete for application and raise the potential for conflict between the actors involved. From a national perspective, this growing variation of institutions and procedures means a mixed set of opportunity structures for access and participation in the EC/EU policy cycle.

Options for actions that are related to specific institutions and policy fields and respective opportunities for an efficient creation of policy within the legal framework of the EC/EU must comply with the specific authorisations to act that are explicitly mentioned in the Treaty. The Treaty of Amsterdam, enacted in May 1999, specifically mentioned a total of 222 authorisations to act with relevant rules for procedures, (i.e. rules for casting votes within the Council, rules for the functions of the Commission, and the participatory rights of the European Parliament, the Economic and Social Committee, the Committee of the Regions and other committees). In 105 cases the Council was allowed to decide with the qualified majority of the weighted votes. However, even following the conclusion of the Treaty of Amsterdam, the Council was still forced to decide on 91 cases unanimously. Not only the cultural policy, the law on migration and the access to independent economic activities were decided unanimously, but also most of the decisions relating to justice and home affairs, common foreign and security policy as well as the trade policy in the fields of services and protection of intellectual properties.

Fifteen times salade Nicoise: main lines of the negotiations on majority voting

In deference to the rules on unanimity, the possibility of majority decisions reflects the awareness and necessity of the Member States to renounce national sovereignty in related policy fields permanently and to implement 'the adopted legal acts also as a defeated minority – possibly against the will of the national parliament's majority – in order to secure the capacity to act and to the efficiency of acting'(Maurer 1996:32). The experience of an effective usage of qualified majority rules in the Council indicates that the extension of the fields of application for majority decisions do not lead to an increase of decisions on the basis of such procedure (Maurer and Wessels 2003). In fact, majority decision-making functions more as a sword of Damocles, which is sweeping above the Council to increase the probability of decision-making in the 'shadow of voting' (Scharpf 1997, Golub 1999: 733–64). The extension of the fields for application of decision-making by a qualified majority was already made in the three Inter-governmental Conferences of 1986/87, 1991/93 and 1996/99, and was declared a goal of the majority of the Member States for the Nice IGC (Dehousse 1999, Duff 1997, MacDonagh 1998, Petite 1998). To emphasise this principle as much as possible would be to secure the capacity to act as an enlarged Union, because it could hardly be imagined how 25 or 27 states could 'only' decide unanimously on distribution and regulation policies, which due to increasing socio-economic differences and resulting differences in interest, would lead to a tendency towards asymmetric distribution of costs and burden.

In order to improve upon the outcome of the Treaty of Amsterdam (Maurer 1998: 49–54) the Commission and the German Federal Government referred to an approach, which basically intended to transpose all the competencies of decision-making defined under the Amsterdam Treaty as unanimous decision-making, into decision-making with qualified majority. Exemptions to this rule were agreed upon according to a concrete catalogue of criteria ('rule-exemption-approach'). Accordingly, the principle of unanimity should have been applied under the following circumstances:

- decisions that are subject to ratification by the Member States;
- decisions with constitutional character that do not require an amendment of the Treaty, for example institutional questions that concern the relative balance of power between the states (e.g. the question of languages, Article 219 EC Treaty), or decisions related to the authorisation of the EU bodies to act in particular areas of policy according to Article 308 EC Treaty;
- decisions in the area of taxation and social security that are not related to the smooth functioning of the internal market;
- decisions related to military policy and defence.

Contrary to this strategy, another approach of organised analysis of particular cases already prevailed under the Finnish Council presidency 1999,[10] according to which any proceedings from the Treaty of Amsterdam must be reviewed for areas of decision-making requiring a qualified majority ('case-by-case-approach'). These cases should coincide with the following criteria:

- cases related to the European Internal Market where procedures for decision-making could be converted into decision-making with qualified majority without a necessity to amend the substantial provisions;
- authorisations for action, which cannot be fully transferred into QMV due to explicit concerns and particular interests of Member States;
- basic principles for actions in the areas of freedom, security and justice that have been incorporated into the EC Treaty;
- rules on assignments and appointments of representatives of particular EU institutions;
- 'institutional anomalies' i.e. rules of the Treaty which are already subject to the procedure of co-decision but still require unanimity, within the Council.

Following the first sessions of the Intergovernmental Conference, which occurred on the level of personal representatives, the idea of subjecting the rules of the Amsterdam Treaty to review in each particular case, according to the above mentioned criteria, led to the identification of 25 areas of policy in which procedures for decision-making should be converted into decision making with a qualified majority. In addition, by the end of April 2000, the Portuguese Presidency was able to address concrete proposals for the re-formulation of Articles 93 (fiscal harmonisation), 42 (social security), 137 and 144 (social policy), 175 (environmental policy) and a new Article 188 bis of the EC Treaty on financial aspects of development and cooperation policy where aspects relevant for unanimous decision-making policy were extracted or at least formulated in a more precise manner and were segregated from the rules of qualified decision-making.[11]

However, the approach for negotiations pursued by the Portuguese Presidency in the Council was also characterised by the fact that the criteria for review were heavily oriented towards a balance of interests between the Member States, rather than towards the abstract criteria seeking to secure the internal and external capacity of the Union to act, which was expected to increase its strategic importance, in view of the envisaged EU enlargement. The multitude of reservations of the Member States to sacrifice 'national sensitivity' options for a veto required the review of the mentioned particular cases.[12] Out of the total seventy-six EC and fifteen EU rules of agreement, which were subject to unanimity under the Amsterdam Treaty, by December 2000, forty-nine were already made subject to negotiations,[13] thirty-one of those made under the French Council presidency.

The negotiations became increasingly tense in November 2000 at the eighteenth meeting of the Representatives.[14] In the area of Freedom, Security and Justice, the delegates did not raise any principal objections against the movement to majority decisions in respect to Article 65 EC Treaty (Judicial Cooperation in Civil Law Matters) and Article 66 EC Treaty (Cooperation between Administrations). The reluctant representatives of Germany and France explicitly approved as well. However, Sweden demanded, with respect to Article 65 of the EC Treaty, to delete the section on Family Law. With respect to both core-articles 62 and 63 of the EC Treaty (policy on visa, external border regulations, internal border regulations, asylum, refugee and immigration policy), France insisted on the principle of unanimity, and the delegates initiated a declaration to the Treaty, which should have expressed that in 2004, under certain circumstances, the Council should move to a decision-making process with qualified majority.

In the field of social policy, during October 2000, a far-reaching approval of the Presidency for Article 137 EC Treaty was recognisable, which aimed at a partial move to majority decision-making. However, it remained under dispute whether or not to shift to majority decision-making legal acts related to the representation and collective negotiation of employers and employees relations, because not only Great Britain but also Spain, Portugal, Ireland and Germany voted in favor of keeping the unanimity rule. Additionally, Great Britain and Denmark rejected the introduction of QMV with respect to Article 42 EC Treaty (Social Security in the context of the freedom of movement). Similar to the case of the room of Freedom, Security and Justice, the chosen strategy for negotiations was orientated on the analysis of a particular case that led to the loss of a coherent approach for reform. By favouring some kind of a 'pick-and-mix' method, each competency for action indicated in the Treaty had been made subject to review from an add-up of fifteen national perspectives.

In the field of tax policy (Article 93 EC Treaty), the British Delegation also declared its principle rejection of every move toward majority decision-making, making it more than clear that attempts of the Presidency to revise positions introducing amendments to the texts would be condemned to fail. Luxembourg and Ireland were hidden behind this British blockade, as well as Spain, Portugal and Sweden, which were considered 'safe' partners of a coalition with Great Britain. In opposition to this Italy, Belgium, France, Finland and Germany, the Commission, as well as the European Parliament (which did not participate in the conference) declared an interest in a more ambitious approach.

Particularly under dispute was the revision of the provisions on decision-making in the area of a common trade policy (Article 133 EC Treaty). In November the Commission distributed a proposal for a compromise, which was based on a complete integration of the areas of services, intellectual property and investments with common trade policy and which was based on a decision-making process with a qualified majority.

In respect to that, limitations were proposed concerning both substance and procedures and it was foreseen that for specific cases the establishment of a 'security net' would have allowed the Council to amend the mandate for negotiations, upon the initiative of the Commission, on the basis of unanimity. The original

proposal of the Commission for a compromise envisioned a complete integration without any exemptions of those three areas into the trade policy, which were
already under dispute in Amsterdam and thus withdrawn from the Commission
itself, so that delegations of the Member States - freed from the conscience of the
'keeper of the Treaty' - were in a position to address proposals for distribution of
institutional and procedural competencies on different levels. One month before
the concluding round on the level of the Head of States and Governments, six
different basic options were lying on the table for negotiations.[15]

The final proposal that was forwarded by the Finnish delegation (see
CONFER 4818/00 from 8 December 2000) took into consideration the French
concerns related to a too-far reaching 'supranationalisation' of trade policy in
the areas under dispute. With that, the Presidency accepted at an advanced stage
of negotiations a number of different options. Thus, France did not respect one
of the essential functions of the Council Presidency; the culmination of negotiations towards a final option. With this 'organised anarchy' of positions, no satisfactory agreement at the final conference was possible. The draft text that was
finally provided by the Finnish delegation included the French concerns toward
a too far-reaching 'supranationalisation' of trade policy in the areas under
dispute. On the positive side, the provisions in Article 133 were extended to 'the
negotiation and conclusion of agreements relating to trade in services and the
commercial aspects of intellectual property'. However, there are a number of
important exceptions, including trade in cultural and audio-visual services,
educational services and social and human health services, and transport.
Moreover, the IGC concluded a blanket restriction on the use of QMV in external negotiations when the latter are concerned with questions for which the EC
has not been given competence internally or with regard to which unanimity is
required internally. Thus overall, trade policy on capital investments remained
excluded from QMV.

Table 10.1   Options for amendment of Art. 133 ECT

	Support from
Original proposal of the Commission European Commission (Option 1)	Italy, Belgium, Luxembourg, Finland, the Netherlands, European Parliament
Proposal of the Commission with a negative list (isolation of areas for unanimity decisions)	European Commission, Italy, the Netherlands, Belgium, Finland, European Parliament
'Option 1 with braces' Compromise forwarded by the Commission	European Commission, Ireland, Portugal, Austria, Great Britain and Denmark
Option 2 of the Presidency (positive list: isolation of areas for qualified majority)	Spain, France
Transition to qualified majority decisions with regard to Art. 133.5 ECT	Germany, Italy, Belgium, Finland
Piris Proposal (Legal Adviser of the Council) for the protocol with procedural rules for WTO	Great Britain

The EU's capacity to act 'in the shadow of uncertainty'

The results of the Nice conference finally led to 31 areas which have been transferred into decision-making by a qualified majority with the enforcement of the Treaty in February 2003. From that, nine provisions concern rules on appointment and approvals of agenda. Additionally, seven authorizations in the Treaty call for the EC/EU to act in respect to decision-making, using a qualified majority under the following conditions. Article 67 EC Treaty on the procedures for asylum policy requires for the introduction of majority decisions and co-decision procedures under framework agreements of the Council which are to be decided earlier with unanimity. In other fields of immigration policy QMV was only introduced from 1 May 2004 onwards. In Articles 161 EC Treaty on structural funds and the Article 279 EC Treaty on the EC's own resources, the transitional period will remain in effect until 1 of January 2007[16] and thus, given the decisions for the period 2007–13 that were already decided upon at the Berlin European Council in 1999, in fact until 2013.

The quality of an enlarged European Union to act in its surrounding international environment (Maull 1997: 81–95, Wessels in Kaiser and Schwarz 2000: 575–590) has been improved upon with the possibility to decide by QMV for the conclusion of agreements concerning trade in services and trade-related aspects of intellectual property (Article 133, par. 5 EC Treaty, Péraldi-Leneuf 2001: 20–1). By contrast, international agreements in the area of trade in cultural and audio-visual services, which fall under the area of education as well as social security and healthcare, remain subject to a mixed competence of the Community and its Member States (Article 133, par. 6, sent. 2 EC Treaty). Consequently, these are further subject to the principle of unanimity. With regard to questions related to the trade in intellectual property (patents, copyrights, trademarks) only an opening clause in favour of majority decisions has been stipulated, which requires a unanimous decision by the Council (Article 133, Par. 7 EC Treaty). These provisions are likely to weaken the central position of the European Commission as an international negotiating partner, if particular EU Member States take advantage of the exemptions from the majority principle as a consequence of national reservations.

The complete overview on the extension of the field of an application for majority decisions clarifies the trend after Nice, at least in terms of quantity, of a continuous reduction of unanimity requirements, notable since 1958 (see Figures 10.1 and 10.2).

At the Amsterdam IGC numerous competences for actions were newly established - first of all in the field of justice and home affairs - where the 'masters of the treaties' established original competencies with decision-making by unanimity. In Nice, a partially successful attempt was made to extend qualified majority decisions step-by-step, against a stronger fragmentation of already existing 'business rules'. Remarkable is the relatively high amount of new majority decisions with regard to appointments. To analyse how much of this is 'empty talk' is irrelevant. The introduction of majority decisions in these areas is to be understood first of all as a door handle for future package deal solutions. Hence the occupation of the post of a General Secretary of the Council, of the head of EUROPOL, or of members of the Court of Auditors, directly concerns the question of the representation of Member States in EU bodies - staff-related questions are not treated 'by the way' in the Council of the European Union.

In the long run, as the Commission will have a larger staff available (Monar 2001), the provisions on appointment procedures and internal working structures will be reformed within the framework of the EC Treaty. These changes will take effect in November 2004.[17] The question of the indirect legitimisation of the Commission by the European Parliament, is closely related to the reform of the future working procedures of the Commission. These issues are dealt with in Article 214 EC Treaty on the relevant appointment procedures, which has been amended in Nice upon an original initiative of Belgium. The new provision allows the Council to nominate the President of the Commission with a qualified majority. The European Parliament is authorised to give its consent. In a second step, the Council, in cooperation with the appointed President, should create a list of candidates for the Commission. For this, again, the consent of the Parliament is necessary, whereby it is likely that the European Parliament will further apply its already twice-conducted procedure of individual candidate hearings. Only after the assent of the European Parliament is granted will the Council appoint the Commission with a qualified majority. These procedural rules constitute a fundamental breach of the institutional balance between Commission, Council and the European Parliament as a consequence of a 'significant reduction of intergovernmental elements' (Krekelberg 2001: 223–229, Ludlow 2001, Pescatore 2001: 265, Van Nuffel 2001: 329–387) in one of the key provisions of the EU's multilevel system.

Bidding for representation: who speaks 'EU'?

The dossier of the re-weighting of the votes, which had been at the basis of the failure of reaching agreement on institutional reform at the Amsterdam IGC, was the second controversial and sensitive question of the Nice IGC agenda. The issue is a clear example and a lesson of zero-sum bidding negotiations: Hence, whenever a Member State is attributed more votes, the relative weight of others automatically declines. Moreover, the issue involved major interests for France, which was at the helm of the final Nice summit. The French Presidency aimed at reinforcing the position of the big Member States, but it also wanted to block any attempt at differentiating the weighted votes of France and Germany.

The reform positions mirrored two opposing views with regard to the re-weighting of the votes: a first group of Germany and primarily small Member States argued in favour of a dual or double majority, a system that had the advantage of reflecting the dual nature of the Union as a Union of states and a Union of peoples. The second group of France, Great Britain and Spain supported the adaptation of the existing system of the weighting of votes. Their main concern was to get a sufficient compensation in the weighting of votes for their loss of their second Commissioner and to make sure that a qualified majority would still represent a minimum population threshold. From the outside 'daily-user-and-voter-perspective' of EC law, the most understandable solution would have been that of a 'simple' dual majority as proposed by the European Commission whereby a proposal would be adopted if agreed by a simple majority of states and a majority of the population.

The negotiations on the re-weighting of votes did not seem to be well prepared by the French Presidency. As Schout and Vanhoonacker rightly point out, 'the complex internal French situation of cohabitation made that there was a plethora of players including President Chirac, Prime Minister Jospin, Foreign Affairs Minister Védrine and European Affairs Minister Moscovici and often the Presidency seemed to be more involved in sorting out its own business than giving priority to the negotiations amongst the Fifteen'.

In the end, alternative options designed to accommodate the variety of different national 'needs' were combined to create three thresholds to get to the necessary quora. Thus, for a decision to be taken in an EU-27, 169 re-weighted votes out of a total of 237 must be secured. In addition, this decision must be supported by a simple majority of Member States. Finally, a demographic filter

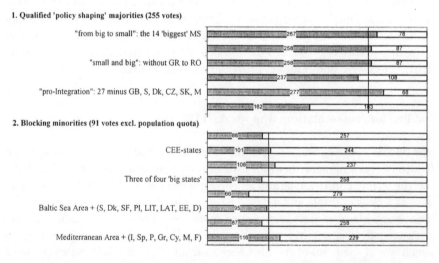

Source: Wessels, Wolfgang, 'Nice Results: The Millennium IGC in the EU's Evolution', *Journal of Common Market Studies,* 39(2)(2001), 197–219, on the basis of Treaty of Nice, provisional text approved by the Intergovernmental Conference on institutional reform, SN 533/1/00 REV 1, Brussels, 22 December 2000 (05 01), Annex I: Protocol on the enlargement of the European Union (p. 71ff); Annex II: Declaration on the enlargement of the European Union to be included in the final act of the conference (p. 78ff).

Figure 10.3   Qualified 'policy-shaping' majorities and blocking minorities in the EU of 27 states

acts as a blocking mechanism, since any 'member of the Council may request verification that the qualified majority comprises at least 62 per cent of the total population of the Union' (Article 205.4 TEC as amended by Article 3 of the Protocol on the Enlargement of the European Union). As figure 10.3 shows, it will become more difficult under the new rules to get to qualified majorities for shaping policies and the power of blocking minorities has been enhanced.

Legal provisions do not determine voting behavior. Thus different expectations arise depending on the new opportunity structures. The quantitative calculation is quite often criticised as an academic ivory tower exercise which does not take into account the limited number of 'real voting' cases and the different overlapping cleavages within the Council. Countries are not always in the same coalition of outvoted minorities. The prospect that these rules might be used is often said to be more important than their day-to-day application: What matters is that they encourage ministers and civil servants to act prudently. We know that about 10 per cent of all Council decisions were taken by qualified majorities in recent years (see table 10.2). However, the risk of a blocked decision machinery is not negligible in a Union with 10 or even more new members. Moreover, it is methodologically unacceptable to extrapolate past-behavioral trends of the present Union into an unknown future with 27 or even more members.

Scenarios of regional or 'socio-economic' coalitions establishing themselves as permanent blocking minorities seem less implausible than a scenario of flexible majorities along sectoral interests. Given a new kind of power game in an enlarged EU some of the present members might also be inclined to establish more permanent coalitions. One issue for debate is the potential repercussions of the traumatic bargaining in the Nice IGC: will the members of the Council build groups according to their size and perhaps create a permanent cleavage in three

Table 10.2   Real voting in the Council, 1985–2000

	1985	1986	1994	1995	1996	1997	1998	1999	2000
Total sum of Council legal acts	615	731	561	458	429	327	438	332	262
Number of cases where 'real voting' occurred	± 70[18]	± 100[19]	64[20]	54[21]	45[22]	31[23]	No figures	31[24]	24
Percentage: number of cases of voting / Council legal acts	± 11.38	± 13.67	11.4	11.84	10.48	9.78	–	9.78	9.16

Source: Maurer, Andreas: Parlamentarische Demokratie in der Europäischen Union. Der Beitrag des Europäischen Parlaments und der nationalen Parlamente, Baden-Baden, Nomos 2002, p. 81. Data are based on: for row one (Total Sum of Council Legal Acts): CELEX database; for rows two and three, see specific endnotes.

groups of small, middle and larger Member States? In this regard, the population clause (Article 205.4 as amended by Article 3 of the Protocol on the Enlargement of the European Union) is also a specific case: will Germany and/or larger countries apply the population criterion extensively? Even if it is not often used such an instrument might create 'anticipatory reactions' as is often assumed with the indirect impact of the Luxembourg compromise. In cases where the potential use of this threshold is mooted informally, the Commission might shape its original proposals to accommodate the interests of an emerging blocking minority.

Clearly, the Nice voting modalities do not point to a trend towards more supranational procedures. Intergovernmental reflexes have dominated at Nice, but not so much as to reverse former trends but rather to limit their further increase. The Treaty architects did not develop enough trust towards the Community institutions and rules to give up a final veto, instead of accepting the 'veil of ignorance' and honouring their own commitments to credible institutions they themselves created. In the shadow of an uncertain future they demonstrated reluctance and a lack of confidence in their own political collectivity.

The EU's Constitutional Convention and the 2004 IGC: the balance between constitutional principles and national preferences

An essential partial result of the Treaty of Nice included the 'Declaration on the future of the European Union', according to which already in December 2001, the European Council of Laeken/Brussels adopted the concrete procedure for the preparation of the Intergovernmental Conference in 2004. Both the Council's voting rights and the European Parliament seats fixed in the Protocol on the Enlargement of the European Union were again proposed as part of the agenda of the post-Nice process, and the results of the Protocol entered into force in June 2004 (European Parliament), November 2004 (Commission) and January 2005 (Council), respectively. As the voting rights and the seats in the European Parliament were closely connected with the readiness of Member States to move to majority decisions it was likely that the revision of the Nice Treaty would again make the application of unanimity requirements a subject of discussion.

In June 2003, the European Constitutional Convention presented the product of its work, the Draft Treaty Establishing a Constitution for Europe (DCT). Among the successful interim results of the Convention was that the number of specific cases for which the authorisation to act must be decided by a unanimous vote had been reduced from 82 to 78. Moreover, the use of QMV was expanded from 137 to 177 policy areas. Issues still requiring unanimity, however, included foreign, security and defence policy, but also the setting of multiannual financial frameworks, tax harmonisation, combating discrimination, decisions regarding structural and cohesion funds, numerous areas of environmental policy, certain aspects of trade policy, cooperation on criminal and family law, and the rules for a European prosecutor.

Like its predecessor the Convention's DCT also mirrored a lack of consensus on the core institutional reforms. Given the residual dissent to the institutional parts of the DCT, there was no getting around the IGC. On 4 October 2003 the Heads of State and government and foreign ministers of all existing and imminently acceding Member States of the European Union, European Commission President Romano Prodi and two representatives of the European Parliament opened the IGC in Rome. Just under nine weeks from that date, by mid-December, after a total of nine meetings, the Constitution was supposed to be adopted. The period elapsing between the official reception of the DCT and the start of the IGC only totalled three-and-a-half months. Bearing in mind the widely differing standpoints, the questions arising with regard to the IGC were as follows: firstly, whether the DCT should undergo any substantial changes, and, secondly, what consequences such changes might have for the EU's further development. All actors involved in the IGC were unhappy with some sections of the DCT. Indeed, in the General Secretariat of the Council more than 1,000 motions for amendments were tabled by October 2003. However, it was also assumed that no government had any serious interest in seeing the IGC fail. The alternative would be the Treaty of Nice, yet it was the style of the Nice IGC and the existence of that Treaty which triggered the Convention's formation in the first place. Finally, it was clear that the Italian EU Presidency was proposing to subject both the institutional and security policy chapters of the Constitution to review by the IGC. However, in addition to this, Italy, France, Germany, the Benelux countries and Denmark had all rejected the call to scale back the DCT considerably, pointing out that any Member State wishing to call into question the Convention's consensus on a particular issue would be responsible for reaching a fresh agreement. Nonetheless, the 2004 IGC had no choice but to word its answers to the questions raised by individual countries that were critical of the DCT in such a way that a consensus of the aforementioned type could be reached.

Those countries which failed to dispatch their foreign ministers to the Convention obviously tended to regard the DCT as a 'basis to work on', in stark contrast to those countries which delegated their foreign ministers to co-write the DCT in the Convention and then duly signed it. The whole post-convention debate was therefore characterised by different conceptions of what the Convention was and the basis for its legitimacy. Indeed, it was viewed either as a kind of 'sherpa' IGC, a constituent power, a parliamentary council or an open forum, and this divergence of views was logically also impacting on the IGC.

The first meetings of the IGC ended in reaching a broad consensus that the following issues should be explored:

- The regular rotation of the EU Presidency (Council of Ministers). The Italian IGC Chair focused on the debate about Group or Team Presidencies alternating every two years. The issues raised here included both the duration of such presidencies and the number of Member States involved in them. Of course, an alternative would have been for every specialist Council of Ministers to elect its own President independently.

- The function and flexibility of the so-called Legislative Council in relation to the other Council formations. On this subject, the IGC delegates (foreign ministers) agreed that no independent Legislative Council should be formed. Instead, the individual Council meetings on specific topics would always serve as 'Virtual Legislative Councils' when they adopt legislative measures and public debates take place in that connection.
- The status and role of the future EU foreign minister. The most controversial issue was the incumbent's position within the Commission, the real questions being these: firstly, whether the minister should also have voting rights in areas that have nothing to do with the CFSP, and ESDP and, secondly, whether a vote of no confidence in the Commission by the European Parliament would also trigger the resignation of the EU foreign minister.

Furthermore, different parties to the IGC negotiations asked questions about the following points:

- the definition of a 'qualified majority' in the Council of Ministers;
- the scope of qualified majority votes in the Council in the areas of foreign and security policy, justice and home affairs policy and the budget;
- the details of structured cooperation in security and defence policy;
- the composition and internal decision-making procedures of the Commission; and
- the minimum share of seats in the European Parliament.

Two main lines of conflict had crystallised by November 2003, though they were nothing new - in principle they have existed ever since the IGC on the Treaty of Amsterdam. Consequently, the only somewhat surprising fact was that the number of protagonists advocating each position was growing. On the one hand, 15 smaller and medium-sized countries found themselves head to head with the six EEC founding members, the United Kingdom and Denmark over the issue of the institutional organisation of the Union. For whilst the 'small countries', which included the accession states, insisted since their meeting in Prague on 1 September 2003 that the rule stipulating that there shall be 'one Commissioner with voting rights per country' should continue to apply in the European Commission, the founding Member States, the United Kingdom and Denmark were backing the Convention's proposal to reduce the number of Commissioners. The line of attack adopted by the 'smaller' countries with respect to retaining the traditional Community method was also reflected in the reservations expressed by Austria, the Czech Republic, Lithuania, Latvia, Finland and Estonia, which opposed the creation of the post of an elected President of the European Council.

A second bone of contention pitted the United Kingdom, Ireland, the Czech

Republic, Slovenia and Malta against the rest. Here, the group headed up by the British government was insisting that unanimous voting should remain the norm in the Council when dealing with issues to do with fiscal and justice policy, social security policy, foreign, security and defence policy, whereas other countries, led by Germany, Belgium and the Netherlands, wanted to see qualified majority voting extended to these areas as well. Latvia, Poland, Sweden, the Czech Republic and Hungary were sceptical about closer or structured cooperation between individual countries on defence policy. Here, in principle, the United Kingdom appeared to be prepared to discuss this matter, though together with Spain it continued to clearly reject a scenario in which the EU would have military structures independent of NATO.

In Germany rumblings in some federal states, the CDU/CSU and some influential ministries started to raise the spectre of broader opposition to EU reform, especially where the Commission's powers in the areas of economic, social, health, criminal justice and immigration policy were concerned.

Finally, there was a massive gulf between Spain and Poland, on the one hand, and the other countries with regard to the planned introduction of the so-called 'double majority' from 1 November 2009 in qualified majority votes taken in the Council (Article I-24 DCT). The principle of the double majority was supposed to make Germany's relative formative force vis-à-vis the other 'big' countries in the Council more visible than in the past, since the size of the population would count as a direct factor alongside the respective country's single vote. Poland and Spain rejected the associated 'downgrading' of the weighted vote they enjoy under the Treaty of Nice. At least Spain was probably less concerned about maintaining its disproportional special status than about retaining its ability to veto structural and cohesion fund policies that are associated with major spending. However, the IGC failed to focus on this very connection.

The December 2003 Brussels summit did succeed in settling some of the Convention's leftovers. But no agreement was found on the possible extension as well as on the definition of qualified majority voting. The weighted-votes system of Nice was still defended vigilantly by Poland while, on the other hand, the double-majority system was still promoted by Germany. The DCT and the question of QMV was therefore carried over to the Irish and the Dutch 2004 presidencies.

By the time of writing the paper, there were two conceivable extreme scenarios for concluding the IGC in 2004:

- The IGC will succeed in subjecting the DCT to some material changes and thereafter adopting it. The risk would then lie with the Member States in the context of the ratification process. Those countries whose parliaments or citizens refused to ratify it would ultimately be forced to leave the EU.
- The IGC will fail, overwhelmed by a flood of proposed amendments. The DCT would then not be adopted and the Treaty of Nice would remain in

force. Those countries prepared to engage in integration according to the DCT's provisions could then enter into a process of closer cooperation outside the EU institutions and European treaties, along the lines established for the Schengen agreements.

There are several arguments in favour of the first option: many countries would emerge as 'winners' if the DCT was adopted in its current form. Undoubtedly not everyone's wishes were fulfilled by the work of the Convention. However, on the other hand, the EU institutions as well as the governments and parliaments of the individual Member States can be said to have emerged as relative winners. For while the national parliaments have been given major supervisory powers vis-à-vis their respective governments and the Commission, the European Parliament's supervisory, legislative and elective powers have been strengthened. Meanwhile, the Commission has gained further rights to take initiatives and also had its role as 'the guardian of Community law' consolidated. At the same time, the respective governments can rejoice at the bolstering of the European Council and the creation of the post of a European Council President, which will clearly boost their influence in Brussels. And yet, this is an extremely unstable situation, for it represents the compromise that can be reached at this point in time, on the basis of which the future development of the EU will have to be reviewed and reformed when the time is right.

If the Irish and the Dutch EU Presidencies for 2004 were to succeed in overcoming the controversial points in orchestrated discourse, the DCT will be able to leave the IGC in its duly modified form.

In the more pessimistic second scenario, the differences of opinion in the points presented could not be overcome. The result would be a fresh but negatively, turned debate on the EU institutions and the distribution of power, which would – in the best-case scenario – end in the kind of horse-trading that went on at the Nice summit, and could end up reaffirming its rules. However, this would raise questions about the institutional balance in the course of the EU's further development and in fact turn that development process upside down. The rules of the Nice Treaty would no doubt then be applied – to the letter – primarily by the larger Member States in an open, confrontational manner, effectively forcing the Commission to coordinate every single legislative proposal in advance with the emerging 'Trilaterale' between Berlin, London and Paris. If even one of these three countries vetoed the proposal in question, the ongoing decision-making process in the Council would not have any prospect of success. Moreover, the Member States would try to impose themselves more directly, forcefully and aggressively on the Commission and Parliament. This would not discredit the method of the Convention as such, but it would mean that the high expectations of the Convention would have to be seriously scaled back. The biggest winners emerging from such a crisis would probably be third countries, whose interest in seeing deeper European integration is minimal and would be all in favour of the creation of distinct, rival groupings within the EU.

A way out of the dilemma? A normative reflection

In the DCT, amendments of the Constitution are made conditional on a unanimous decision by the governments in question and ratification by the respective national parliaments (see Article IV-7 DCT). Bearing in mind the dynamic nature of the process of European integration, this hurdle seems too rigid for a Union of 25 or even more Member States. Consequently, greater flexibility for future adjustments is required. The starting point here would be the Convention's agreed fragmentation of the DCT into four parts and the resulting criticism that even changes made to the operational part III would have to undergo the laborious ratification procedure. The Convention failed to push through proposals concerning the simplification of the procedure for reviewing the Constitution. Many Member States are genuinely fearful of allowing the possibility of all-too-rapid changes being made to the provisions set out in the Constitution, believing it to be a gateway to further attempted infringements on their sovereignty by the EU. In addition, British government representatives will certainly attempt to further erode the transitional clause on the European Council's simple transformation of unanimous into qualified majority votes because the United Kingdom believes this would entail a risk of the Constitution being amended 'via the back door'. Consequently, there will be no choice but to stick to the stringent requirement of unanimous amendments and their confirmation via ratification procedures in all Member States for the first part of the Constitutional Treaty.

Is there a way out of the dilemma? The 2004 IGC reaches its climax in mid-2004, by which time broad agreement should have been attained regarding the various requests for amendments to the DCT. One decisive factor for the success of the endeavour is the agreement of the actors involved on a joint future scenario for the enlarged Union. The familiar trio of more democracy, the ability to take effective action, and transparency is clearly not enough to inject fresh momentum into the EU on the basis of the Constitutional Treaty. Neither can the desired scenario entail an attempt to adopt a Constitution that holds good for the next fifty years. The prospect of such an unchanging Constitution would only be acceptable if the EU was regarded as a Community rooted in shared, firmly established values. But at heart the EU remains an economic and legal community. This state of affairs may gradually be extended to include functions such as a Community sharing the same security and social policy interests if the centripetal forces in foreign and security policy and social and economic policy generate demonstrably higher costs for the Member States than the pooling of such expenditure within a shared EU. In other words, only if the Member States find that going it alone in the aforementioned policy areas costs too much and is not associated with any benefits with a view to their respective national election campaigns will their governments be prepared to engage in closer integration.

If the evolutionary and dynamic nature of the Union is recognised as a functionally determined Community of European citizens and states, this paints a different picture as regards the timeframe for the validity of the DCT and also any resulting objectives with respect to its 'reformability'. This in turn can be reflected in the Constitutional Treaty by having the IGC drawn a clear distinction between the virtually immutable principles of the DCT's first part and the constitutional provisions of its second part, on the one hand, and the institutional provisions and authorisation to take political action of the third part, on the other hand. Consequently, one possible compromise for the IGC would consist of a substantial transfer of content from the first to the third part of the DCT. The shifted content would be the provisions governing the post of the European Council President, the composition of both the European Parliament and the Commission and the various compositions of the Council of Ministers, for these provisions are far too detailed and can, in their present form, only apply to the next phase of the integration process. Such a move would also have to respect the wishes of the smaller and new Member States with regard to the composition of the Commission and the relativisation of the special role played by the President of the European Council. All provisions providing for unanimous decision-making in the Council or European Council should also be transferred to the third part of the DCT. Unanswered questions about the sequence, duration and allocation of Council presidencies should also be set out in the third part of the Constitution as organisational tasks for the European Council. Hence, the conditions determining the environment for such authorisations to take effective action can change rapidly.

At the same time, it would make sense to provide for a super-qualified majority of five-sixths of the Member States and peoples in the IGC for the procedure for amending the third part. Furthermore, a threshold value that was lower than the sum of all Member States would have to be set for the entry into force of any amendments. If this were done, the first part of the Constitutional Treaty would be purged of its technical details, and the third part could be more simply made the object of the verification of the institutional provisions at the heart of the present controversy. In any case, the new Member States and their citizens would then have ample time, until the start of the next term of office of the Parliament and the Commission in 2009, to gather experience with the Union's new contractual basis.

Insight into the dynamic character of the EU can only be gained over time on the basis of the 'application' of the Constitutional Treaty. Mechanisms designed to facilitate the review of the Treaty will clear the road ahead for the Union's dynamic character and therefore constitute a sensible alternative to the laborious scaling back and adoption of the Convention's compromise.

From collective failure to non-pathetic dynamism

Overall, the extension of the field of application of decision-making with qualified majority will lag behind the general targeted objectives of all those who
participated in the IGC negotiations at Nice and in 2004. As for the complaint
that state 'A' or the group of states 'A, B and C' are singly responsible for the poor
outcome of the negotiations is not true. In fact, the IGC is not dominated by
scenarios for conflict in which solid blocks of proponents for integration and
proponents of status quo are acting, but rather by the existence of different
primary interests that are changing due to the specific policy environment. The
concrete experiences and perceptions of policy outcomes in the vast field of the
EU's legal order induce a mix of sectoral demands for more QMV or for less
weighting. In addition, an evident segmentation of procedural authorisations in
the area of trade policy and the area of freedom, security and justice, that
occurred at Nice reflects two newer trends of the development of the European
Union after Maastricht:

- Apparently, the question of more or less 'integration' is no longer on the
  agenda of the participants of the IGCs. Instead, competency norms are
  plucked to pieces so that they can consider developments of policy and particular cases, which were not predictable during the IGC.
- The legitimate actors for decisions assess the evaluation criteria for the
  institutional optimisation of the European Union increasingly as unilateral;
  a superior target perspective for the capacity of the European Union to act
  is increasingly rejected in favor of consciously articulated national socio-
  economic interests.

As a result, all participants can and do assess the results of IGC negotiations as
positive because important partial aspects of their objectives for reforms are
considered and analysed according to a non-agreed type measure. The outcome
of these 'composed puzzle reforms', however, loses credibility in view of the citizens, other states and organizations in the long run, when each national interpretation of the capacity to act on behalf of the Union is used rather than made
subject of dispute and the Treaty itself does no longer provide any coherent
target objectives and criteria for evaluation.

The Treaty of Nice was subject to severe criticism even before it entered into
force. Thus it was placed in line with the list of institutional reforms conducted
since the SEA. These agreements at first were blamed as being setbacks,
minimal results or otherwise not acceptable. Only in the course of their implementation did the opportunities that these agreements provided to those who
participated in the process of decision-making become evident. Consequently,
nothing speaks against the assumption that in the future, the reforms of Nice
or of the DCT will be evaluated in five or ten years as a positive push for further
integration.

Like its predecessor and successors - the SEA, the Amsterdam Treaty and the Nice Treaty - the DCT has to be interpreted as but one 'grand bargain' decision (Moravcsik 1997: 513–553) among Member States along an uncharted path of European integration and cooperation. In this perspective, the Treaty needs to be seen as a peak within an unfixed landscape, moving with regard to time, the functional, institutional and geographical dimensions of supranational integration and interstate cooperation and coordination. Member States – governments, administrations, parliaments, parties and other 'collective actors' (Haftendorn 1990: 401–423) – were and still are important but not exclusive players of the game: their preferences provide an input or a 'voice'[25] on the basis of experience gained while crossing the landscape between the 'peaks' of intergovernmental conferences. We should therefore conceive Treaty revisions and amendments as initial 'offers' to actors working within the EU institutions. Placed within this multi-level and multi-actor framework for governance they create incentives and disincentives to use or to refrain from Treaty articles - legal empowerments only provide the skeleton of a 'living constitution' (Olsen 2000:6, 1996). Institutions and procedures provide arenas and rules for making binding decisions. Therefore, one could argue that Treaty building has a significant effect on the subsequent day-to-day output of the EU and thus on the evolution of the system in general. Consequently one needs to consider the evolution of para-constitutional patterns within the integration process over the whole history of the EU. We should thus expect to identify a post-DCT-implementation phase which will be defined by new decisions either to create, amend or re-design the treaties – the quid pro quo between the 2000–2 European Council's meetings that extensively dealt with the 'internal reform of the Council' and the Convention itself is such a case.

Relations between Treaty reform and Treaty implementation are not unidirectional. Treaty reforms do not emerge from nowhere as a 'deus ex machina'; rather, they represent reactions to prior developments and trends, reflecting both the complex day-to-day machinery at all relevant levels of policy-making as well as the reaction of socio-political actors which do not or only rarely intervene during the 'implementation' of a given set of treaties. Sometimes, Treaty foundations even simply formalise institutional evolutions which have been developed either within existing Treaty provisions, through inter-institutional agreements, institutional rules of procedure and codes of conduct, or outside of the treaties, through bi- or multilateral agreements between EU members (Christiansen 1998: 99–121; Christiansen and Jorgensen 1999). Treaty amendments also attempt to address institutional and procedural weaknesses identified during the implementation of previous adjustments to the rules of the game. Treaty revisions are thus endemic parts of the EU's process. They are not only independent variables affecting the nature and the evolution of the system but also become dependent variables themselves. Institutions and procedures are creations and creators at the same time. In this regard, one specific feature of the EU should be addressed. In negotiating and ratifying Treaty amendments,

Member States challenge their own politico-administrative systems. As long as there is no need for unifying different national constitutions and their related interpretation in daily life, the effect of these challenges will remain to vary according to the nature and the internal dynamics of the political systems in the Member States.

The design of the European Union, which is construed as a polycentric (Schmitter 1996: 132) and polyarchic (Pfetsch 1998: 293–317, 295–301, Milner 1997, Cohen and Sabel 1999) multi-level system, since Nice continues to be confronted with unpredictable needs and latitude for action due to internal and external influences (Maurer 2000: 32). The Treaties constituting the European Union are in this context, indicators for a constitutionally structured community system that - in respect to its authorisations to act that are sanctioned by primary law, its actual application of competencies, its institutions and its policy area related regulations - is not arriving at a *finalité politique* that is agreed upon by all partners. The Treaty of Nice is - and the DCT is likely to be - a further benchmark of an evolutionary and dynamically constituted process of interstate and supranational policy-making,[26] which still has an open end (Petite 2000: 887–903). As a vehicle for further delay or even prevention of the South-East enlargement, it is definitely not suitable.

Notes

1 The Treaty was signed on 26 February 2001.

2 Before admission of the next – 16th - member to the EU, the number of the members of the Commission should have been limited to one person per state, if at the same time the balancing of the casting of votes in the Council of the European Union could have been adjusted (Article 1 of the Protocol). However, a comprehensive revision of the institutional basics of the European Union was only planned for one year before the accession of the 21st Member States through a new Intergovernmental Conference (Article 2 of the Protocol).

3 Originally, the Finnish government intended to support the declaration as well. In its decision about the Treaty of Amsterdam from 19 November 1996 the European Parliament gave its consent to the declaration of the three countries and demanded the adjustment of the balancing of votes and the number of the Commissioners before each enlargement, and the limiting of the fields of application for unanimous decisions to decisions related to the constitutional structure of the EU.

4 See the evaluation of the results of Amsterdam in *Integration*, 4 (1997) and in *Wirtschaftsdienst*, no. 1997/7, 375–385.

5 See Lehne (1999) and Kohler-Koch (2000b).

6 See Fischer (2000b) and Joerges, Mény and Weiler (2000).

7 Qualified majority voting instead of unanimity; co-decision instead of cooperation for the EP.

8 See e.g. article 34 TEU on JHA instruments and procedures as amended by the Treaty of Amsterdam.

9 'Institutional anomaly' was the term used by the Portuguese Council Presidency within the framework of the IGC 2000. See: Conference of the Representatives of the Governments of the Member States, Presidency Note on: IGC 2000: Possible extension of

qualified majority voting – Articles which could move to qualified majority voting as they stand, CONFER 4706/1/00, Brussels, 11 February 2000.

10 See Presidency Paper: Efficient Institutions after Enlargement. Options for the InterIntergovernmental Conference, Helsinki (Dok. No. 13636/99), 7 December 1999, p. 5; as well as in this context the remark of the Portuguese Presidency: question of a possible extension of casting of votes with a qualified majority.

11 See Presidency Note: Possible Extension of QMV, CONFER 4737/00, from 20 April 2000.

12 Concerning the reactions of the delegations of the Member States with regard to the proposals of the Portuguese Presidency: Agence Europe no. 7710 from 5 May 2000. Opposition - for different reasons - by Member States to the Presidency's suggestions for extension of a qualified majority (especially concerning taxation and structural funds).

13 See Presidency Note, Extension of decision-making with a qualified majority, CONFER 4753/00, 3 July 2000: 31 authorisations to this act were identified for a complete move to decision making with a qualified majority as well as 8 provisions with regard to which decision making with a majority should only be applied in regard to a few aspects of the respective provisions that provide authorisations to act. The list was extended in August to 43 (CONFER 4767/00 from 29 August 2000), in September to 46 (CONFER 47790/00 from 14 September 2000 and CONFER 4776/99 from 28 September 2000) provisions of the Treaty. The synthesis of the consultations from 1 December 2000 (CONFER 4815/2000) contains 49 provisions for transfer into decision making with a qualified majority.

14 The following assessments refer to oral statements of three permanent representatives and of one state secretary who participated in the Intergovernmental Conference.

15 See in this respect CONFER 4776/00 from 29 September 2000; CONFER 4800/00 from 16 November 2000; with respect to the WTO expertise and the expertise of the legal advisers: SN 2705/00 from 10 May 2000 and SN 4849/00 from 25 October 2000 as well as CONFER 4753/00 from 3 July 2000.

16 See the Memorandum of the Government of the Federal Republic of Germany to the Treaty of Nice: Memorandum to the Treaty of Nice from 26 February 2001, Berlin, 2001.

17 The President of the Commission can decide on the areas of responsibility of the Commissioners, propose the vice-presidents and their tasks to the assembly and can appoint them. An introduction of different ranking Commissioners could also be envisioned, whereby the Commission, rather than the Member States being responsible for their levels.

18 Source: Answer to Written Question No. 1121/86 by James Elles to the Council of the EC; OJEC, No. C 306/42, 1.12.1986.

19 Source: Answer to Written Question No. 2126/86 by Nicole Fontaine to the Council of the EC; OJEC, No. C 82/43, 30.3.1987.

20 Source: Answer to Written Question No. E-1263/96 by James Moorhouse to the Council of the EU; OJEC, No. C 305/71–75, 15.10.1996, and: Answer to Written Question No. E-858/95 by Ulla Sandbaek to the Council; OJEC, No. C 213/22, 17.8.1995.

21 Source: Commission Européenne (Secrétariat Général): Analyse des décisions adoptées à la majorité qualifiée en 1996, Bruxelles, 14 juillet 1997.

22 Source: *ibid.*

23 Source: Monthly Summaries of Council Acts, January–December 1999, http://ue.eu.int/en/acts. Data for 1997 and 1998: Antwort des Rates auf die schriftliche Anfrage No. E-0917/00 von Christopher Huhne vom 24.3.2000, Abl. der EG, Nr. C 26 E, 26 January 2001, p. 131.

24 Own calculation on the basis of the Monthly Summaries of Council Acts, January–December 1999, http://ue.eu.int/en/acts.

25 See Hirschmann (1970:19) and Weiler (1991).
26 The notion 'European Union as a process' goes back to the activities of a working team in the Centre for interdisciplinary Research Bielefeld, which from 1973 until 1980 under leadership of H. von der Groeben and H. Möller published six studies to the 'opportunities and limits of a European Union', H. von der Groeben, H. Möller (ed.), Die Europäische Union als Prozeß.

11

Towards finality? An assessment of the achievements of the European Convention[1]

Introduction

In his widely received speech on 12 May 2000 at the Humboldt University in Berlin, German Minister of Foreign Affairs Joschka Fischer characterised the debate on the future of the European Union as concerning the 'finality' of European integration. The Convention on the Future of the European Union responded to Fischer's call – in fact, midway through its work, it was even enriched by Fischer's personal participation. Even though the Convention's work is unlikely to determine the structure of the Union once and for all, it at least aspires to put an end to the continuous Treaty-revision process that started with the Treaty of Maastricht in 1992 and then led to Amsterdam and Nice (see chapters 9 and 10 this volume).

The far-reaching aim of the Convention's ambitions is apparent from the name of its end-product and is even underlined by the typesetting adopted on the title page:

'*Draft* TREATY ESTABLISHING A **CONSTITUTION FOR EUROPE**'

(European Convention 850/03 [DTCE][2]: 2). This Constitutional Treaty is to replace the existing treaties as the fundamentals of European cooperation. Thus the Convention has given its own twist to the mandate it received December 2001 from the European Council of Laeken: 'to consider the key issues arising for the Union's future development and try to identify the various possible responses' (European Council 2001). One may want to note however that the concept of a constitution only appeared at the very end of the Laeken Declaration as a possible subject for exploration.

This chapter provides an overview of the main aspects of the Constitutional Treaty proposed by the Convention. It also tries to make a first appraisal of whether the Convention has really provided the final outlines of the European Union or whether it merely constitutes another step along the long and winding road of European political cooperation. The fact that the member governments have adopted the Convention's conclusions as the basis for the Intergovernmental Conference (IGC) that is to finalise the new Constitutional Treaty testifies to the Convention's impact. However, a definite assessment of the Convention's achievements can only be made once its main proposals have successfully passed the IGC and the national ratifications.

Under the guidance of its chair, the former president of France, Valéry Giscard d'Estaing, the Convention has approached its tasks in a rather systematic way. The chair had the Convention first focus on relatively technical issues such as simplification and legal personality. In the second half of 2002 the Convention and a second round of working groups took stock of various fields of Union competences. The most contentious issues involving the institutional order of the Union were purposefully left to last. They only really came onto the Convention's floor with the presentation of the relevant draft articles by the end of April 2003 – less than two months before the Convention was due to present its conclusions. This chapter follows the same logic. First it addresses the overall constitutional structure, then the substantive policies, and finally the institutional framework.[3]

From simplification to constitutionalisation

The single biggest achievement of the first phases of the Convention was the consensus it was able to forge on the need to re-found the Union on the basis of a single comprehensive Constitutional Treaty. Academics have for a long time recognised the Union as having evolved towards a constitutional structure (Mancini 1998, Weiler 1999). Member States have, however, been reluctant to recognise the Union as a political system with some autonomy in allocating power beyond what has emphatically been conferred to it by the Member States. Thus it was quite a bold move for Giscard d'Estaing to assert at the Convention's opening session that the Convention should aim to work towards 'a Constitutional Treaty for Europe' (Giscard d'Estaing 2002: 11). In due course, however, the choice for a Constitutional Treaty in a sense logically emerged from the proceedings of the Convention.

Legal personality and the re-integration of the Treaties
A crucial role in clearing the ground for a Constitutional Treaty was played by the working group on 'legal personality'. This working group was established as part of the first round of working groups in May 2002. Looking beyond the relatively unobtrusive nature of its title, the fact that Convention Vice-Chair Giuliano Amato led this working group might already have been taken as a clue

to its potential importance. Further indications of its prominence were provided by the actual questions included in its mandate (CONV 73/02: 2):

- 'What would be the consequences of explicit recognition of the EU's legal personality?
- And of a merger of the Union's legal personality with that of the European Community?
- Could these contribute to the simplification of the Treaties?'

Indeed the working group quickly agreed on the first two questions. Conferring legal personality on the Union emerged as a rather uncontested issue. For reasons of clarity and simplicity, the working group also concluded that the Union's legal personality should replace the existing legal personality of the Community, rather than having the two exist alongside each other.

Having established the answers to the first two, it was really on the third question that the working group came to the most far-reaching proposals. The working group enthusiastically jumped on the idea that the Union's single legal personality might pave 'the way for a merging of the Treaties and for greater coherence of the Union's constitutional architecture' (CONV 305/02: 4). Notably it was established that 'merger of the two Treaties [TEU and TEC] would be a logical consequence of the merger of the Union's legal personality and that of the Community' (CONV 305/02: 4). The group furthermore suggested that 'the Union should have a single constitutional text' that would replace the existing treaties (CONV 305/02: 2). This text should distinguish two parts, separating the basic constitutional provisions from the more detailed legal bases for the various policy fields as they were already contained in the existing treaties.

The working group proposed a final bold move in advocating the abolition of the Union's Pillar structure that distinguished the old Community Pillar organised around the single market from the Union's Common Foreign and Security Policy (Second Pillar) and from the common policy on Justice and Home Affairs (Third Pillar). Whilst admitting that this step did not follow necessarily from the former steps, it was submitted that retaining the Pillar structure in a future constitutional text 'would seem outdated, not to say obsolete' and, moreover, amount to 'a needless complication' (CONV 305/02: 6).

The full importance of the groundwork done by this working group came into view when late in October 2002, Giscard d'Estaing revealed the 'Preliminary draft Constitutional Treaty' (CONV 369/02). This draft basically presented an outline for the final report of the Convention. Following the suggestions of the legal personality working group, the outline proposed to merge the existing treaties in a single document. It further suggested starting this Constitutional Treaty with a part covering the 'constitutional structure' consisting of about fifty articles. A second part would then set out the legal basis for the various Union policies and a final part was foreseen to deal with (legal) specificities such as revision procedures, entry into force, territorial application, protocols, etc.

Incorporating the Charter of Fundamental Rights

One other constitutional issue that the Convention had to solve was the status of the EU Charter of Fundamental Rights. This Charter had been devised by an earlier Convention over the year 2000, and was 'solemnly proclaimed' by the European Council of Nice. The European Council refrained, however, from incorporating the Charter into the Treaties, leaving its legal status for further consideration. Eventually this task was added to the mandate of the Convention. Among the first wave of working groups, one, led by Commissioner António Vitorino, was to examine the procedures for and consequences of any incorporation of the Charter into the Treaties.

The Charter working group decided that it would not renegotiate the content of the Charter. Still, as the group was aiming for 'an incorporation of the Charter in a form which would make the Charter legally binding and give it constitutional status' (CONV 354/02: 2), some re-negotiation of the so-called horizontal articles defining the scope of the Charter and its position vis-à-vis the national constitutions and traditions turned out to be required. Some passages were added to constrain the scope of the guaranteed rights and to ascertain that the Charter would in no way affect the allocation of competences between the Union and the Member States. There was some debate in the Convention whether or not these amendments did undermine the original character of the Charter. Eventually, however, this is a question of interpretation that will be left to the European judges.

There followed some debate on whether the Charter should be incorporated in full within the Constitutional Treaty or be attached as a protocol. In the end, the Charter was given a prominent place as the second part of the Constitutional Treaty directly following the constitutional part. Those conventioneers who would have preferred a somewhat lower profile for the Charter were placated by the explicit recognition in the Charter preamble of the guiding importance of the 'Charter explanations' originally prepared by the Praesidium of the Charter Convention.

Simplification of legal instruments and procedures

From the beginning of the Convention onwards, the Convention secretariat provided several working documents outlining the formal Treaty situation on specific themes. These papers gave particular attention to the legal instruments available to the Union. As one of the early documents observed: 'Here as elsewhere, the evolution of the Community and of the Union in line with successive Treaties has led to matters being superimposed in a way which ultimately excludes any possibility of systematisation' (CONV 50/02: 4). Over time the Union has come to have at its disposal over thirty different kinds of legal instruments (CONV 2002, WG IX – WD 4). Some of these instruments, whilst bearing different names, have similar effects. What is more, some instruments bearing the same name ('decision') have different effects. Complexity increases even further as we turn to the various procedures in use to adopt Union acts that turned out to amount to more than thirty involving the different EU institutions in different ways (CONV 424/02: 13).

All in all there emerged a clear need for simplification and systematisation. Hence in the second wave of working groups established in July 2002, Convention Vice-President Amato was asked to chair another working group that was to explore the possibilities of reducing the number of legislative procedures as well as the number of legal instruments in the Treaties.

In the little time it had, the working group on simplification succeeded in presenting some far-reaching proposals. The working group singled out the 'co-decision procedure'[4] as the procedure that 'should become the general rule for the adoption of legislative acts' (CONV 424/02: 15). As a consequence this procedure was baptised the Union's 'ordinary legislative procedure' (DTCE Arts. I-33.1 and III-302).

Turning to the number of legal instruments of the Union, the working group proposed to reduce them to no more than six (DTCE Art. I-32). The main Union acts are to be adopted as European laws and European framework laws, the latter leaving Member States free in determining the form and methods by which an agreed objective is to be attained. This choice of words renders the former Eurospeak designations of 'regulations' and 'directives' obsolete. As non-binding instruments 'recommendations' and 'opinions' are maintained.

The remaining two instruments are the most interesting; they are binding but non-legislative in character. First, the concept of (European) 'decision' that over the years has proliferated to be used in all kinds of situation for all kinds of (binding and non-binding) acts, is maintained as a flexible, non-legislative act that can be applied in various situations. In particular, the 'decision' will be the main instrument the Council will use to act in a non-legislative context, above all in the Union's Common Foreign and Security Policy (DTCE Art. I-39.7), where it will thus replace all instruments that the Maastricht Treaty on European Union specifically introduced for this field ('joint action', 'common position' etc.).

Finally, there are 'European regulations', which are acts that serve to implement Union laws or specific Treaty provisions. The working group distinguished two kinds of executive acts. First, the group recognised that the Treaty or the legislator sometimes mandates the Commission to adopt 'implementing acts' to complement Member State implementation of Union law (DTCE Art. I-36).[5] A second kind of executive acts was devised to enable the EU legislator 'to delegate technical aspects or details of legislation whilst retaining control over such delegation' (CONV 424/02: 8). Thus the legislator can empower the Commission to flesh out certain elements of a legislative act by way of a 'delegated regulation' (DTCE Art. I-35). The creation of these delegated regulations should prevent the Union legislature from entering into too much detail. Still the legislator will be able to retain control over the use of delegated regulations by way of ex post mechanisms like call-back or approval rights.

The working group on legal simplification has put its mark on Title V of the Constitutional Treaty that deals with the exercise of Union competences.

However, this title also shows the limits of simplification as it does provide for a number of exceptions for those policy spheres that so far fell outside of the European Community framework: Common Foreign Security Policy (CFSP), defence, and freedom, security and justice. Also whilst the ordinary legislative procedure sets the decision-making norm with qualified majority voting in the Council and co-decision of the European Parliament, in fact there remains a substantial number of competences on which unanimity is required in the Council and/or the involvement of the European Parliament is limited.

Objectives, competences and ability to act

The Laeken Declaration did not ask the Convention to reconsider the objectives of the Union. It did, however, recognise that there is a mismatch between the Union's objectives and citizens' expectations: 'Citizens often hold expectations of the European Union that are not always fulfilled. And vice versa – they sometimes have the impression that the Union takes on too much in areas where its involvement is not always essential' (European Council 2001). Yet, the European Council also recognised a gap between the Union's objectives and its actual performance. This gap is most glaring in the two intergovernmental 'policy Pillars': foreign policy and justice and home affairs. In this regard it is worth noting that citizens rank 'maintaining peace and security in Europe' and 'fighting terrorism' among the top three EU priorities (Eurobarometer, 2002: section 6.1). The terrorist threat and the international engagement in Afghanistan and Iraq that dominated political agendas after September 11th, revealed EU policies in these fields to be lacking still.

The Convention has proceeded on the assumption that 'Union competence corresponded in principle to its tasks, but that there was a need to further clarify the system for delimitation of competence and to strengthen competence in certain areas' (CONV 60/02: 3). Rather than adding new objectives, the Convention has focused on reconsidering the Union's existing objectives: to clarify their focus where needed, to ensure better implementation of the objectives set and, not least, to consider the way competences are divided between the Member States and the Union.

The development of certain competences has been impeded because they still require the Member States to act by unanimity. Obviously, after enlargement the likelihood that agreement can be reached on these matters reduces even further. Hence, the question was whether the Convention could go beyond Amsterdam and Nice in generalising the use of QMV in the Council.

Even if the Council is able to adopt legislation, concrete policy results are often slow to materialise. Beyond Member States' implementation efforts, there emerge ever more demands for effective coordinating and implementing powers at the European level. The Commission does not have powers in such fields as the Common Foreign and Security Policy and police and criminal law, whilst as regards macro-economic policy it has no more than an advisory role. Circumventing the Commission, Member States have delegated certain executive powers to specialised bodies like Europol and Eurojust and turned the Council Secretariat into the European foreign secretariat. Still the question remains whether this executive structure suffices to make the EU deliver on its promises.

Economic and social policy-making beyond the single market

The Convention has had little to add to the Union's powers in the sphere of the internal market. Instead the economic debate was dominated by the question whether, after monetary integration, there is a need to step up European coordination of economic and social policies. In particular, debate focused on the organisation of the macro-economic coordination mechanisms currently in place: the Broad Economic Policy Guidelines and the Stability and Growth Pact. The Convention somewhat strengthens the arbitrating role of the Commission by extending its administrative power to signal warnings. Still, the Member States have retained the final say over the political decision to impose sanctions on a non-complying state.

As after enlargement the Member States that have adopted the Euro will be in a minority in the Union, the recognition of the Euro group in a separate protocol is of particular importance. Whilst this protocol underlines the informal character of the meetings of the ministers of the Euro group, it does enable them to elect their own president for a period of two and half years. The draft Constitutional Treaty provides, moreover, for a separate legal basis allowing the members of the group to deepen the budgetary and macro-economic coordination among themselves (DTCE III-88).

Bordering on the issue of economic governance, there are two policy fields in which Member States fundamentally divide on the desirability of common policies: taxation and social policy. So far the requirement of unanimity prevented any European measures concerning tax. Notwithstanding the vehement opposition from certain countries, the Convention proposes a small opening by introducing qualified majority voting for administrative cooperation and for combating fraud in company taxation where these are necessary for the functioning of the internal market (DTCE Art. III-63).

An intense debate on Social Europe led the Convention to prominently feature the social values of equality, justice, solidarity and non-discrimination (DTCE Art. I-2) as well as social objectives ranging from full employment to solidarity between generations (DTCE Art. I-3.3) in the Constitutional Treaty. However, these general commitments failed to be matched by substantial progress in concrete terms. The Constitutional Treaty includes new legal bases for European laws defining principles and conditions that need to be met by services of general economic interest (DTCE Art. III-6) and for measures to combat major cross-border health scourges (DTCE Art. 179.5). Yet, since the Convention did re-affirm the requirement of unanimity in the Council for key social fields like social security and workers' protection, a genuine social Europe is unlikely to emerge soon.

Towards a European public order

Under the heading of Justice and Home Affairs, the Union has collected a whole range of policies: migration and border policies, civil law, and police and criminal law. Initially, the development of European initiatives in these fields was left to the Council. Over time, and especially with the Treaty of Amsterdam, certain competences have been brought under the Community framework involving the European Parliament as well as the Commission in the legislative and implementation processes. Still, both legislation and, even more so, implementation of common policies have been marked by fragmentation and sluggishness.

To improve the effectiveness and clarity of decision making in this sphere, the Convention has sought to clarify the distinction between legislative and operational tasks. With regard to legislation, the Convention built upon the proposals of the working group on legal simplification in agreeing that European policy-making on Justice and Home Affairs is to be brought under the general legislative procedures of the Union. Thus the specific instruments used so far (e.g. conventions, framework decisions, and common positions) will be abolished.

The Union already enjoys considerable competences in the fields of refugee and migration policies (see chapter 7, this volume). In civil law the Union's competences have so far derived from the requirements of the internal market. The Convention now suggests providing a separate legal basis for Union action in civil law matters, limiting it, however, to matters with cross-border implications (DTCE Art. III-170). Recognising that maintaining the unanimity requirement will prevent much legislative progress, a full-scale transition to qualified majority voting and co-decision is proposed in the fields of refugee and migration policies, and civil law (however, with the exception of family law).

The Convention also makes an important step forward in allowing for European initiatives in the field of criminal law. The Constitutional Treaty identifies a limited number of ('Euro')-crimes with regard to which the Union may adopt legislation defining criminal acts and regulating penalties (DTCE Art. III-172). Unanimity is only maintained for non-Eurocrimes and for various decisions regarding operational powers: the creation of new Union bodies, national police forces and cross-border police activities. Another important proposal is the separate legal basis for European legislation in the field of criminal procedural law, which has great practical value for facilitating closer cooperation in criminal matters (DTCE Art. III-171).

Whilst the Convention recognised that the current organisation of operational tasks lacks efficiency, transparency and accountability (CONV 426/02: 15), it only proposed some relatively minor reforms in this regard. The Convention has shunned away from proposing new authorities such as a common European border guard ('a long-term issue') and has made the establishment of a European Public Prosecutor conditional upon unanimous endorsement by the Member

States (DTCE Art. III-175). With regard to Europol and Eurojust the Convention has sought to clarify their missions and to simplify their legal bases (including the replacement of the Europol Convention by a European law or framework law) whilst ensuring that they remain under proper political control.

A single European voice in the world

The Union's external policy may be considered the ultimate test case of whether member governments not only recognise the merits of cooperation in principle but are actually willing to match their words with the provision of common powers. Acting in unison, the EU could potentially become a global super power. However, in practice governments find it hard to relinquish sovereignty on external affairs. National preferences are at times fundamentally at odds with each other. The deep divisions that emerged in the early months of 2003 between the EU Member States over the intervention in Iraq well underlined this state of affairs and sobered up any far-reaching ambitions the Convention might have had.

Beyond the political differences, effective action of the EU in the world is hampered by the lack of coherence and efficiency in the organisation of the Union's external powers. In particular a fundamental distinction has emerged between the external competences that have been initiated in the context of the European Community (the common commercial policy, community relations with third countries and international organisations and humanitarian aid) and the Common Foreign and Security Policy as developed within the European Union framework. Having already decided upon the integration of the EC and the EU and on the abolition of the Pillars, the Convention has proposed to integrate all external competences in a single title, subject to a single statement of the principles and objectives of EU external action (DTCE Art. III-193).

The Convention also proposes to bring the executive responsibility to represent the Union externally in one hand by creating a Union Minister for Foreign Affairs (DTCE Art. I-27). This function is to merge the present functions of the Commissioner for external affairs and of the High Representative of the CFSP. The Foreign Minister is supposed to become a driving force in forging a common European position in the world. At the same time he or she is to guard the consistency of the policy initiatives. Whilst on the one hand the Minister will be mandated by the Council to carry out the foreign and defence initiatives, he or she will on the other hand operate as a member (in fact even as a Vice-President) of the European Commission with regard to the other external competences. At the operational level a single integrated European External Action Service is to be established to support the Foreign Minister. Whether the Foreign Minister can succeed in the balancing act expected from him or her or whether the Minister is eventually drawn in on either the Council or the Community side, remains to be seen.

Much to the disappointment of part of its membership, the Convention failed to get rid of the unanimity requirement for Council decisions in the Common Foreign and Security Policy. Any use of qualified majority in this field will need to be preceded by a unanimous decision of the Member States to do so (DTCE Art. III-201).

In the specific field of the European Defence and Security Policy the Convention adds a number of tasks – including joint disarmament operations and post-conflict stabilisation – to the so-called Petersburg tasks that have thus far delineated the scope of the Union's activities (DTCE Art. III-210). The Constitutional Treaty explicitly aims for a common European defence adopted by all Member States. Yet it is recognised that both political considerations as well as differences in military capabilities prevent any substantial steps if they require the full commitment of all (DTCE Art. I-40). For that reason the Constitutional Treaty makes various provisions for initiatives to be taken by subgroups of Member States. In line with established practice, the execution of specific international missions need not involve all Member States. At a more structural level the draft Constitutional Treaty suggests the formation of a core-group for defence cooperation of willing and capable Member States. Finally the Convention provides for the possibility of Member States signing up to a mutual defence clause similar to the one underlying NATO and the West European Union (WEU).

Clear resistance against a EU mutual defence clause came from countries that either have a tradition of military non-alignment or fear that such a provision might undermine NATO. Out of the consideration of these objections another proposal emerged that was able to gather broad support in the Convention, a so-called 'Solidarity Clause'. This clause allows each Member State to request the mobilisation of all relevant Union instruments, including the military resources at its disposal, to assist it in handling a terrorist attack or threat, or the consequences of a disaster (DTCE Art. I-42).

Consolidating competences

Thus the Convention has assigned little or no new competences to the Union. Significant extensions of the Council's ability to adopt legislation by qualified majority voting rather than unanimity are only to be found in the field of Justice and Home Affairs. By retaining the unanimity requirement in the Council, Union action in the fields of tax, social policy, foreign policy and defence can be expected to be slow to get off the ground, if at all.

Yet there have been strong reservations about 'a creeping expansion of the competence of the Union', encroaching upon the competences of Member States and regional authorities (European Council 2001). Already in the run-up to the Treaty of Nice, various actors expressed their concern that the Union failed to adhere to the principle of subsidiarity and that a more precise delimitation of the Union's powers was required. German *Länder* even floated the idea of strictly delineating the Union's powers by way of a *Kompetenzkatalog*. From very early onwards a broad majority in the Convention rejected the idea of a *Kompetenzkatalog* preferring a 'flexible system of delimitation of competence allowing for some adaptation of the Union's mission' (CONV 40/02: 6). Still the need for further clarification of the Union's competences was recognised.

Eventually the Convention proposes to distinguish three main categories of Union competences: exclusive competences, shared competences, and areas for supporting action (DTCE I-11). Exclusive competences involve the areas that fall fully under the authority of the Union. In areas of supporting action on the other hand Member States retain their political primacy. In these areas the Union cannot act by laws that entail the harmonisation of Member States policies but only through actions that serve to support, coordinate or supplement the actions of Member States. Whilst the exclusive competences and the areas for supporting action are fully spelled out, the category of shared competences serves as the rest category and encapsulates the great majority of Union powers. The scope of EU competences in these areas is determined only by the precise legal bases provided in part III of the Constitutional Treaty on the policies of the Union. Finally, the Convention has separated out the coordination of economic and employment policies and the CFSP as two specific competences *sui generis.*

Instead of a strict delineation of competences the main guarantee in the Constitutional Treaty against creeping competences probably will come from the reinforcement of the procedural principles of subsidiarity and proportionality (CONV 286/02l; DTCE I-9.3 and I-9.4). The Convention recognises the application of these principles to be essentially a political task, not to be delegated to a (constitutional) court. Besides increasing the sensitivity to these principles among the European institutions (the Commission in particular), the Convention proposes to engage the national parliaments in the monitoring of subsidiarity through the design of an 'early warning system' (see below).

Institutions and democratisation

In the end the institutional organisation of the Union was the focal point of the Convention's work. This is not surprising given the fact that, however you define the constitutional setting and the formal rules of competence, actual decisions eventually emerge from actors interacting with each other through the institutions.

Each of the central Union institutions – Council, Parliament and Commission – faces particular problems of its own. Fundamentally, however, the challenge arises from the institutional framework as a whole lacking in continuity, consistency and effectiveness (cf. Art. 3 TEU). Following further enlargement these deficiencies are bound to worsen. The Treaty of Nice provided some incremental changes in reorganising the composition of the EP, re-weighing the votes in the Council, and re-affirming the principle of equality between Member States in the composition of the Commission. Still these reforms clearly fell short of resolving the fundamental problems that hamper the performance of the institutions.

The Convention faced the puzzle of seeking an optimal allocation of political powers between the various institutions. To appreciate the challenges this puzzle poses, one has to recognise the particularly complex character of the Union as a Union of both citizens and states (cf. DTCE Art. I-1.1). The Union's institutional architecture has to maintain an intricate balance between, on the one hand, its roots in an international agreement among equal Member States and, on the other hand, the equality of all European citizens. This intricate balancing act is reflected in the different roles played by the institutions in the political triangle at the heart of the Union: Parliament, Council and Commission.

The unprecedented political formation of the Union does not allow for the simple superimposition of a separation of powers system as we know it from the national context (Lenaerts 1991). Still, much might be done to clarify the various roles through a more effective bundling as well as a better delineation of responsibilities. Again the adoption of a single legal EU personality and the abolition of the Pillar structure pave the ground for a fundamental reconsideration of the institutional architecture. All Union competences now fall under a single institutional framework (DTCE Art. I-18). At the level of legislation, with the co-decision procedure becoming the Union's standard legislative procedure, the Council and the European Parliament will in principle act as two legislative chambers of equal importance. As has been argued above, the picture of executive powers is far less equivocal (see also Crum 2003). The implementation of Union legislation has always been primarily the responsibility of the Member States, although in many fields there emerges a clear lack of complementary powers to enact, coordinate and monitor implementation on the European level. Indeed the capacities that have emerged at the European level have been dispersed between the Commission, the Council and its secretariat and various independent bodies (ECB, Europol, Eurojust).

Unravelling the Council of Ministers

More than any other institution, the Council has come to reflect the contorted history of European integration. What, on the face of it, appears as a single institution actually hides a conglomerate of different ministerial formations and committees. At its meeting in Seville in June 2002, the European Council already took some first steps towards clarifying the organisation of the Council and improving its effectiveness (European Council 2002). For one thing it reduced the number of Council formations to nine.

The Constitutional Treaty proposed by the Convention stipulates only two specific formations: a separate Foreign Affairs Council and a General Affairs Council. It will be up to the European Council to establish further sectoral formations. Initially the Convention had played with the idea to concentrate all legislative activity of the Council in a single, 'legislative' formation. However, under pressure of the governments this idea was watered down and eventually completely scrapped. Thus legislative activity will remain dispersed across the various Council formations increasing its visibility and accountability only by the requirements that legislative decisions need to be taken in public (DTCE Art. I-49.2) and can involve only representatives at the ministerial level and not (senior) civil servants acting in their stead (DTCE I-23.2).

The Convention left the question who will chair the various Council formations open, with the exception of the Foreign Affairs Council that is to be chaired by the Foreign Minister (DTCE Art. I-23). Still the insertion that chairs should be exercised for at least a year did reveal a concern to increase continuity in leadership. In the course of the Intergovernmental Conference further proposals have been taking shape to have the Council chairs shared among a team of three governments. According to a system of equal rotation, every eighteen months the helm of the Council formations is then to be passed on to another team of three governments.

Finally the Convention has proposed a radical overhaul of the definition of a qualified majority in the Council. Instead of the complicated system of weighted votes and additional requirements designed in Nice, it is proposed to define a qualified majority as a majority of Member States representing at least three-fifths of the population of the Union (DTCE Art. I-24). To allow the Member States to accommodate to this radical reform (cf. Baldwin and Widgren 2003), the Constitutional Treaty provides that this change will not take effect before 1 November 2009. At the moment of writing this proposal turns out to be the main issue of contention in the Intergovernmental Conference. Hence it is far from sure that the Convention's double-majority system will be adopted or that the Member States prefer to stick to the Nice agreement or yet another formula.

Securing focus, continuity and leadership in the European Council

Over the last decades the European Council has emerged at the apex of the institutional architecture, driving the Union forward by opening up new agendas, like the enlargement agenda of Copenhagen 1993, the Justice agenda of Tampere 1999, the defence agenda of Helsinki 1999 and the competitiveness agenda of Lisbon 2000. Still the situation is far from satisfactory. With the notable exception of the enlargement agenda (of which crucial executive tasks have been delegated to the Commission), the actual follow-up to the ambitious statements of the European Council has been rather slow and faltering. Notwithstanding the yearly follow-up on its progress, the boast of the Lisbon European Council that Europe is to be the world's leading economy by 2010 probably best illustrates the gap between European Council rhetoric and the Union's actual implementing capacity.

Whilst the distinctive and powerful role of the European Council cannot be denied, there is a clear need to clarify and focus its role within the institutional framework of the Union as a whole. The Convention has come to recognise the European Council as a separate Union institution, apart also from the Council of Ministers (DTCE Art. I-20). At the same time it underlines that the European Council does not exercise legislative functions, thereby seeking to end the current practice whereby the European Council is regularly called upon to act as a court of appeal when the Council of Ministers fails to reach a decision.

To strengthen the European Council further and to secure continuity in its workings, the Convention has also come to reconsider the system of half-yearly rotating presidencies. Instead, the Convention proposes that the European Council should elect a chairperson for a term of two and a half years, renewable once (DTCE Art. I-21). Initiated by the British, the French and the Spanish governments, this proposal was subject to a very fierce debate within and outside the Convention (Coussens and Crum 2003). Opponents feared that a European Council President might come to develop into a political force of his or her own, invading upon the established competences of other institutions (most notably the Commission) whilst being exempted from any reliable accountability mechanisms. To meet these anxieties, the draft Constitutional Treaty provides a precise list of the tasks of the President, concentrating them around the internal workings of the European Council. As a single exception it is provided that the President shall represent the Union externally in the field of the CFSP at his or her (i.e. 'presidential') level, without, however, prejudicing the responsibilities of the Minister for Foreign Affairs. One final point to note about the European Council President is that the possibility that a national head of state will take up the position besides his or her national responsibilities is explicitly ruled out. The possibility that the Commission President might also serve as President of the European Council is however left open.

Commission: strengthened, but conditionally so

Almost by stealth the Commission may well be the main beneficiary of streamlining of instruments and decision procedures. Whenever the ordinary legislative procedure is applied it enjoys the exclusive right of initiative (cf. DTCE Art. I-25.2). In particular this will mean that the Commission will come to play a crucial agenda-setting role in the field of Justice and Home Affairs. Also, the introduction of delegated regulations and implementing acts considerably clarifies the Commission's remit and may even serve to replace the current surveillance system of comitology by lighter-weight mechanisms such as call-back procedures.

Still, the governmental aspirations of the Commission have been curbed as the Convention has been reluctant to give it any autonomous powers in foreign and defence policy and macro-economic coordination. As indicated above, the Commission may get a much more significant role in the former field if it will be able to fully integrate the Foreign Minister in its organisation. Finally it is important to note that, contrary to the Seville declaration of the European Council, the Commission's initiating role in the annual and multiannual programming of the Union has been affirmed (DTCE Art. I-25.1).

With regard to the Commission's internal organisation the Treaty of Nice left open the question of the sustainability of the principle of one Commissioner for every Member State. The Convention has sought to increase the internal efficiency of the Commission by reducing the size of the College to fifteen (including the Commission President and the double-hatted Minister of Foreign

Affairs who will also act as a Vice-President) (DTCE I-25.3). To meet fears that this reduction would cause a split between insider and outsider states, the Convention insisted on a strict system of rotation and provided that Member States not represented within the College could have a non-voting, 'junior' Commissioner appointed.

Democracy: involving parliaments and citizens

Whilst the issue of democracy featured prominently in the Convention's mandate, the Convention left it as one of the final issues to be addressed. The draft Constitutional Treaty did come to include a separate title on 'the democratic life of the Union'. However, this title remains a rather mixed bag, notwithstanding the valuable provisions on transparency, the consultation of civil societal groups and the provision for a European citizen's initiative (DTCE Art. I-46.4).

The key to the democratic question needs however to be found in the strengthening of the role and the political credibility of parliaments in the Union's decision-making process. The Convention has looked extensively at the position of national parliaments and proposes a combination of measures to increase their involvement in EU affairs. First, national parliaments are now formally guaranteed that they will be equally informed as their governments on all proposals for legislation. Second, all legislative proposals will be subject to a six weeks consideration period before they can be addressed by the Council, thus ensuring that parliaments can express their opinions on them. Having the Council legislate in public will further enable the national parliaments to scrutinise their performance. The Convention has developed the idea of an 'early warning mechanism' that gives national parliaments a formal right to register their objections against any European legislation in progress and requires these objections to be properly addressed, at least when they are shared by one third of all national parliaments.

Where national parliaments' powers find their limits, in principle, the European Parliament should step in to ensure democratic control. The EP gains much from the co-decision procedure becoming the standard EU legislative procedure. The Parliament thus emerges as a full and equal co-legislator beside the Council. Still, some important Union competences remain excluded from its remit, like the CFSP and defence policy, macro-economic policy, the broad economic policy guidelines (BEPGs) and the implementation of the Common Agricultural Policy. Also Parliament's role as a budgetary authority is strengthened as the draft Constitutional Treaty gets rid of the distinction between non-compulsory expenditures (over which the EP did have authority) and compulsory expenditures (over which it did not have authority). Nevertheless, Parliament's final word on the budget is constrained by the fact that it has to comply with the multiannual financial framework which will eventually be decided by the Member States (DTCE Art. I-55 and III-310).

However, earlier substantial extensions of the EP's decision-making powers have failed to be matched by an increase in its electoral appeal. One reform that might boost the Parliament's electoral appeal is to increase its powers over the Union's executive powers, the Commission first of all (cf. Coussens and Crum 2003). Thus the electorate might see a genuine political dynamic unfold between Parliament and Commission. Also the citizens would find the outcome of the EP elections directly reflected in the composition of the Commission.

The draft Constitutional Treaty appears to make a great step in this direction as it affirms that the European Parliament 'shall elect the President of the European Commission' (DTCE Art. I-19.I). However, looking at the details in article I-26, it turns out that this election is predicated on the nomination of a single candidate by the European Council. Still in practice the European Parliament may well be able to put its mark on the procedure as it can vote down the candidate of the European Council and force it to propose a new one. The potential control of Parliament of the election procedure is reinforced by the facts that the European Council is constitutionally bound to take account of the outcome of the EP-elections in its nomination and that it can choose its candidate by a qualified majority of the Member States (and not of all of them as was the case until the Treaty of Amsterdam). Thus these rules seek to secure that the Commission President will enjoy broad support across the various European institutions by subjecting his or her election to a kind of structured conciliation procedure between the European Council and the Parliament.

Before being appointed, all (voting and non-voting) Commissioners including the Minister for Foreign Affairs will be subject to a vote of approval of the European Parliament (DTCE Art. I-26.2). The draft Constitutional Treaty also for the first time explicitly provides that the Commission as a College is responsible to the European Parliament (DTCE Art. I-25.5). The European Parliament retains the power to censure the Commission as a whole (DTCE Art. III-243). Moreover, the Commission President is made to bear a special responsibility to the Parliament for the activities of the Commissioners. In combination with the fact that he or she can now request a Commissioner to resign without needing the approval of the majority of the College, the Parliament also attains considerably more leverage on individual Commissioners.

Conclusion

As it turns out on a number of issues the draft Constitutional Treaty clearly falls short of defining the final, definitive form of the Union. Especially on certain institutional issues, the time, it appears, simply is not ripe. The Convention itself recognises this, since, rather than watering down on the substance of its proposals, it has provided that certain sensitive reforms will not come into effect before 2009 (reduction of the size of the Commission, redefinition of qualified majority voting). In other cases (especially the replacement of unanimity by QMV) the Convention has introduced so-called 'passerelle' clauses that allow the European Council to carry through certain reforms in the future without having to resort to a Treaty revision process.

On other issues a stable solution is only likely to emerge in the long run. One of these is the dispersion of European executive power that has now led to the somewhat ambiguous figure of the so-called double-hatted Foreign Minister. Eventually, both efficacy and democracy are bound to require an integrated EU government, encompassing all executive responsibilities at the European level and subjecting them to proper mechanisms of democratic accountability. Furthermore, in the sphere of policy instruments the distinction between legislative and executive instruments constitutes an important step forward. Still, it is doubtful whether the framework now proposed does justice to the idiosyncrasies of EU policy-making. The Convention eventually shunned away from properly defining soft policy instruments such as the Open Method of Coordination. Finally some policy fields are still in their infancy at the European level. Their ultimate form and content can only be determined in the long run. Foreign and defence policy is the most obvious and dramatic example. The same applies, however, to cooperation in criminal policy.

Yet, the Convention may claim to have laid the groundwork for the form the Union will eventually take. From that perspective its greatest achievement is the transformation of the Union's legal basis from the old Treaties into a new Constitutional Treaty. It provides a much clearer structure for the allocation of competences. It also introduces some important premises for the further development of the institutions.

When and to what extent the Constitutional Treaty drafted by the Convention will actually come into effect remains to be seen. In July 2003 its chairman, Valéry Giscard d'Estaing, handed the Constitutional Treaty over to the European Council that will use it as the basis for the Intergovernmental Conference. At that occasion he underlined that the draft 'is a finished product, with no loose ends to be tied up, no options left open'. Hence he called upon the European Council 'to have the text left as it stands. Reopening it, even in part, would cause it to unravel' (Giscard d'Estaing 2003: 5). As might have been expected, the governments were not to agree on the Constitutional Treaty without further ado. Importantly, however, the Intergovernmental Conference has genuinely taken the Convention's Constitutional Treaty as the basis of its work and focused its attention on specific provisions only. The governments have agreed on a number of amendments, involving, most notably, the organisation of the Council and the Foreign Minister. However, the composition of the Commission and, above all, the definition and scope of qualified majority voting turn out to be more difficult to settle and keep the conclusion of the IGC in suspense at the moment of writing.

Once the governments have agreed on a new Constitutional Treaty, there remains what may well be the most difficult part of the process: ratification. Of the 25 Member States that will make up the Union in 2004, up to 20 are likely to hold a referendum on the Constitutional Treaty. Anticipating that a negative referendum outcome in one or more Member States might create difficulties to having the Constitutional Treaty ratified, the Convention has suggested that in such a case the situation will need to be considered by the European Council.

If the Constitutional Treaty enters into force by 2005 or even later, it will be put to the test right away. The world will not have waited in the meantime. Enlargement will have taken effect, Europe is likely to have lived through another economic slump, new challenges on the international scene will have to be faced, and indeed some European governments that were present during the drafting process will have been replaced. The Constitutional Treaty clarifies considerably the political playing field in which these challenges are faced and makes it easier to navigate. It does not, however, provide a binding roadmap. Whilst the Convention has come a long way in integrating the legal framework, it leaves it up to future generations of politicians to decide upon the further political integration of Europe.

Notes

1 A first version of this paper was circulated in March 2003 as an ARENA working paper (WP 03/4). I thank the members of the ARENA programme for the stimulating and inspiring exchanges we have had. This research has been made possible by the support of a Marie Curie Fellowship of the European Community under contract number HPMF-CT-2002-01706.

2 The abbreviation DTCE is used here to refer the Draft Treaty establishing a Constitution for Europe (CONV 850/03 of 18 July 2003) and to the articles in which the proposals discussed have eventually found their place.

3 The focus of this chapter is on the substance of the Convention's work. It touches only marginally on the procedures followed by the Convention and on the ways in which the debates have developed inside and outside its sessions. The procedural organisation and politics of the Convention have already received considerable attention. See for example Magnette (2002), Closa (2003), Shaw (2003), Norman (2003) and Crum (2004).

4 The 'co-decision procedure' is currently defined by Article 251 TEC (cf. DTCE III-302). Basically, it involves the EP and the Council deciding on an equal standing on a proposal for legislation of the Commission. For this purpose the article provides for two rounds of readings involving both legislative institutions. If this does not suffice to reach an agreed text, the two institutions meet within a so-called 'conciliation procedure'.

5 In fact besides regulations implementing the Constitutional Treaty also provides for the possibility of implementing decisions that instead of being pursuant to a (framework) law follow from a decision.

AMY VERDUN, OSVALDO CROCI AND MELISSA PADFIELD

Conclusion

The 'Eastern' enlargement has catalysed the need for the EU and its Member States to address the issue of institutional and policy-making reform seriously. The issue was repeatedly tackled in the 1990s but with no major results since vested national interests often stood in the way of change. Member States held the belief that some institutional structures and policy outcomes were a 'right' that they did not easily want to give up. However, all Member States did subscribe to the *principle* that reform was necessary. One could examine these reforms with various theoretical lenses. The difficulties in bringing about changes in governance and policies encountered in the 1990s could be seen as the result of national preferences to which some countries tried to hold on (Moravcsik 1998). Yet, this view would find it difficult to explain why later, in the early 2000s during the Convention discussions and in the 2003 IGC, Member States were willing to consider making some of those changes. One could also explain those difficulties from an institutionalist perspective. Such a view would underline how institutions survive over time and how changes are path dependent and hence, very slow (Pierson 1996). It is difficult, however, to use an institutionalist approach to explain exactly why and when changes happen. Such an approach, in fact, is more suited to analyse long-term *change* than short-term *changes.*

This volume set out to explore the institutional and policy-making challenges in light of the fifth enlargement. The main question addressed was: how does the EU need to change in light of the 'Eastern' enlargement? The eleven chapters in this volume have adopted analytical frameworks that are less 'grand' than the two mentioned above. They have focused on short 'moments' of the integration process and have brought out its 'messiness' as well as the gradual and incremental character of changes in the institutions, governance mode, and policies of the EU. To be sure, some of these changes might have been also characterised by Member States fighting for their national interest, or be seen as following logically from previous choices.

Amy Verdun examined the current enlargement in light of previous ones. On the one hand, the 'Eastern' enlargement seems to have raised the same fears and concerns as in the past (mass migration from the accession countries, redistribution of limited funds, ability of the current institutional set-up to function in an enlarged setting, etc.), even if they all turned out, eventually, to be largely unfounded. On the other hand, previous enlargements did not lead to any major institutional change and brought about only minor adjustments to existing policies (e.g. agriculture) and, occasionally, the development of new ones (e.g. regional policy). Verdun is sceptical about the capacity of the EU to muddle through also this time. Institutional and policy changes are long overdue and the EU cannot keep adding countries without making fundamental reforms. Verdun's conclusions are somewhat pessimistic since the challenge the EU faces with its 'Eastern' enlargement is indeed a formidable one: to strike a compromise 'between what is fair and just for newcomers and what is politically feasible in Member States that are net contributors'. Helen Wallace argues that scepticism about the ability of the EU to 'digest' the 'Eastern enlargement' might be justified if one looks at it only through the lenses of what she calls the 'conventional practitioners' narrative'. From this perspective, the deepening of the integration process is seen as being made more difficult by enlargement. Hence, while the EU limits itself to some institutional and policy tinkering, the bulk of the adjustments must rest on the shoulders of the accession countries. The historical record, however, seems to show that further deepening has not been hampered by enlargements. Besides, one should not look at the integration process as being linear. There is not one EU model but several ones operating at the same time. Monnet's 'Community method' coexists with 'regulatory', 'distributional', 'benchmarking' and 'intergovernmental' models. The question therefore is not whether the new members will adjust to the EU modus operandi, but rather how fast will they be able to internalise all methods? Wallace concludes that the answer lies in their ability to 'Europeanise' themselves which means acquiring the capacity to practice what she calls 'constructive multilateralism' and conjugate domestic preferences with the management of transnational independence. 'Europeanisation' is a precondition, but not a synonym, of EU-isation. After all, as Kohler-Koch argues, the future of the EU is not in its acquisition of statehood qualities, nor in the progressive extension of the 'Community method'. According to her, the future is likely to witness the further development of what she calls 'network governance', which does not supersede national governments but links them together. 'Network governance', moreover, is not limited to the EU or to Europe, but is extending beyond it.

Precisely the lack of sufficient 'Europeanisation' (understood also as completion of the reform of the administrative apparatus and upgrading of technical and health standards) in the accession countries gave the EU a convenient reason to phase in the CAP in the new Member States and thus avoid the danger of what was perceived as a potential budgetary crisis. This means that the CAP reform has not really been accelerated by the 'Eastern' enlargement. Worse, the new Member States are more likely to be preoccupied with obtaining their share of the existing funds rather than with reform. Pressure for reform, therefore, is likely to continue to come mainly from outside the EU, in particular from the WTO. For the near future, however, Grant foresees that the EU will, at best, adopt a two-tier CAP system: the most competitive sectors will compete on world markets while more marginal ones will continue to be supported even if the justification for payments might be increasingly phrased in terms of pursuit of social and environmental objectives. New members, for their part, are likely to face many difficult social problems in their rural areas. They might also find it difficult to ensure the proper implementation of the service liberalisation directive, not because of their reluctance but because – as argued by Steen Knudsen – of their insufficient institutional capacity. They will also find it difficult to put into place protective social clauses not only because of their scarcity of government financial resources but also because, unlike the case of Germany, their economic and social actors such as unions and employers associations, which play a key role in securing agreement on social clauses, are still weak. Indeed, such a weakness represents another obstacle to overcome in the process of Europeanisation they face. Steen Knudsen's conclusion is that further service sector liberalisation within the EU might slow down as it becomes more difficult for new member governments to convince their constituents of the benefits of reform.

The conclusions offered by Regelsberger and Wessels concerning the future of the CFSP are more optimistic. They argue that the history of the CFSP shows that a 'dynamic of convergence' has been at work. Such a dynamic has increasingly involved Community institutions in the development of national foreign policies. Although it has not led to the communitarisation of foreign policy, Regelsberger and Wessels think it is logical to conclude that such a dynamic is irreversible, even if it might stagnate at certain levels or plateaux before moving forward again. This does not necessarily imply that the EU will have a common foreign, security, and even defence policy any time soon, but it means that the process of dynamic convergence at work will not be slowed down by enlargement. A policy area in which 'Eastern' enlargement has actually led to some substantial changes even before the accession of new members is that of The Third Pillar of the EU, which used to be called 'Justice and Home Affairs'. As Lavenex has argued, it was precisely the prospect of the enlargement, which contributed to the decision of moving immigration, asylum policies, control over external borders and cooperation in civil law matters to the communitarian Pillar I of the EU and led to the renaming of The Third Pillar 'Police and Judicial Cooperation in Criminal Matters'. Hence, this is a case in which enlargement rather than causing the weakening the Community method actually favoured its extension to policy areas which had until then been characterised exclusively by inter- and trans-governmentalism.

All is not smooth, however. As Guild shows, in fact, a number of contradictions are likely to generate some discontent. Citizens from new Member

States will have to wait some time before enjoying the freedom of movement to the EU-15 as workers (albeit they can move immediately as self-employed persons). At the same time, new Member States' government will be obliged to adopt the EU rules with regard to their Eastern neighbours (Ukraine, Belarus, Moldova etc.). This means that the CEECs governments will be applying EU rules on access for employment to their Eastern neighbours, which are not in the EU, while these same rules are applied by the EU-15 to their nationals even if they are already EU members.

Part III of the book focuses attention on institutional changes from Amsterdam through Nice, to the 'Convention'. Laursen argues that the relative failure of Amsterdam and the relative success of Nice in dealing with institutional changes such as the re-weighting of votes in the Council, the composition of the Commission, and the increased use of Qualified Majority Voting in the Council was primarily the result of the timing of the IGC. More precisely, by the time of the Nice IGC, there was a feeling among Member States that certain institutional changes, which dealt with the key issue of the future efficiency and legitimacy of the Union, could no longer be delayed. It is as if the Member States seemed to be more inclined to find the compromises necessary to fashion creative solutions when they are working under time constraints and a moderate level of stress. Maurer stresses that the Nice treaty (as well as the one that will eventually result from the 'Convention') are not steps towards a predetermined or even identifiable *finalité politique* but only milestones that mark the changing composition of intergovernmental and supranational elements in what is an evolutionary policy-making process.

Such is the conclusion also reached by Crum. The results of the 'Draft treaty establishing a constitution for Europe' might have gone a long way in suggesting ways to simplify the EU mode of governance in order to make it both more efficient and democratic, or at least transparent. In the end, however, the resulting institutional architecture will have to reflect the fact that the EU is both an international agreement among still sovereign Member States as well as an emerging polity.

This book has sought to shed both theoretical and substantive light on some of the institutional and policy reforms undertaken by the EU in preparation for its 'Eastern' enlargement. Neither this volume, nor more unfortunately the EU, has been able to deal with all relevant issues. The EU-25 will have a lot more work to do and it is yet unclear whether the changes wrought so far will provide a more efficient institutional setting for it. It is our hope that the analyses provided in this book will help the reader understand where the EU is, how it got here, and what lies ahead.

BIBLIOGRAPHY

Agence Europe, various issues.

Albert, Mathias and Brock, Lothar (2000) 'Debordering the World of States: New Spaces in International Relations', in Albert, Mathias, Lothar Brock and Wolf Klaus-Dieter (eds), *Civilizing World Politics: Society and Community beyond the State*, Lanham: Rowman & Littlefield, pp. 19–45.

Albrow, Martin (1996) *The Global Age: State and Society Beyond Modernity*, Cambridge: Polity Press.

Algieri, Franco (2001) 'Die europäische Sicherheits- und Verteidigungspolitik – erweiterter Handlungsspielraum für die GASP', in Werner Weidenfeld (ed.), *Nizza in der Analyse*, Gütersloh: Verlag Bertelsmann Stiftung, pp. 161–201.

Alt, James and Gilligan, Michael (1994) 'Survey Article: The Political Economy of Trading States: Factor Specificity, Collective Action Problems, and Domestic Political Institutions', *Journal of Political Philosophy*, 2 (20), 165–92.

Anderson, Malcolm (2000) *Border Regimes and Security in an Enlarged European Community: Implications for the Entry into Force of the Amsterdam Treaty*, RCS Working Paper 2000 (8), Florence: European University Institute.

Anderson, Malcolm, den Boer, M., Cullen, P., Gilmore, W.C., Raab, D.C. and Walker, M. (1995) *Policing the European Union*, Oxford: Clarendon Press.

Annual Report of the Council to the European Parliament (1998) http://ue.eu.int/pesc/.

Annual Report of the Council to the European Parliament (1999) http://ue.eu.int/pesc/.

Annual Report of the Council to the European Parliament (2000) http://ue.eu.int/pesc/.

Antalovsky, D., et al. (1998) *Assozierungsabkomen der EU mit Drittstaaten*, Vienna.

Antola, Esko (1999) 'From the Rim to the Core: The European Policy of Finland in the 1990s', in Finnish Institute of International Affairs (ed.), *Northern Dimensions*, Helsinki, pp. 5–10.

Avery, G. and Cameron, F. (1998) *The Enlargement of the European Union*, Sheffield: Sheffield Academic Press.

Baggehufvudt, Niels von (1993) 'Dienstleistungsmonopole in der Telekommunikation under EG-rechtlichen Aspekten' ('Aspects of EU Legislation Concerning Service Sector Monopoly in Telecommunications'), *Zeitschrift für Rechtsfragen. Archiv für Post und Telekommunikation*, 45 (2), 174–80.

Baldwin, R. and Widgren, M. (2003) 'Power and the Constitutional Treaty', CEPS commentary, Brussels, 19 June.

Baldwin, Robert E. (1970) *Nontariff Distortions of International Trade*, Washington, DC: Brookings Institution.

Beach, Derek (2004) 'Bringing Negotiations Back: Supranational Actors and the Negotiation of Intergovernmental Conferences in the EU', Ph.D. dissertation, to be published by Odense University Press.

Belmont European Policy Centre, *Challenge*, various issues.

Best, Edward (1994) 'The Maastricht Treaty: What Does It Actually Say and Do?', in Finn Laursen and Sophie Vanhoonacker (eds), *The Ratification of the Maastricht Treaty: Issues, Debates and Future Implications*, Dordrecht: Martinus Nijhoff, pp. 17–44.

Best, Edward (2001) 'The Treaty of Nice: Not Beautiful but It'll Do', *Eipascope*, 2001/1, 2–9.

Best, Edward, Gray, Mark and Stubb, Alexander (eds) (2000) *Rethinking the European Union: IGC 2000 and Beyond*, Maastricht: European Institute of Public Administration.

Beuter, Rita (2002) 'Germany: Safeguarding the EMU and the Interests of the *Länder*', in Finn Laursen (ed.), *The Amsterdam Treaty: National Preference Formation, Interstate Bargaining and Outcome*, Odense: Odense University Press, pp. 93–120.

Biagosch, Patrick (1984) 'Dienstleistungsfreiheit in der Versicherungswirtschaft' ('Freedom to Provide Insurance Services'), *Versicherungswirtschaft*, 12, 257–62.

Bieber, Roland and Monar, Joerg (eds) (1995) *Justice and Home Affairs in the European Union: The Development of the Third Pillar*, Brussels: European Interuniversity Press.

Bigo, Didier (1996) *Polices en Réseaux*, Paris: Presses de la Fondation Nationale des Sciences Politiques.

Blair, Tony (2000) *Europe's Political Future*, Speech to the Polish Stock Exchange, 6.10.2000 (www.fco.gov.uk/news/speechtext.asp?4913).

Boer, Monica den (1997) 'Wearing the Inside Out: European Police Cooperation between Internal and External Security', *European Foreign Affairs Review*, 2 (2), 491–508.

Boer, Monica den (1999) 'An Area of Freedom, Security and Justice: Bogged Down by Compromise', in David O'Keeffe and Patrick Twomey (eds), *Legal Issues of the Amsterdam Treaty*, Oxford: Hart Publishing, pp. 303–21.

Boer, Monica den and Wallace, William (2000) 'Justice and Home Affairs: Integration through Incrementalism?', in Helen Wallace and William Wallace (eds), *Policy-making in the European Union*, Oxford: Oxford University Press, pp. 493–519.

Boidevaix, Francine (1997) *Une Diplomatie informelle pour l'Europe. Le Group de Contact Bosnie*, Paris: Foundation pour les Etudes de Défense.

Boissier, Dieter (1986) 'Der deutsche Versicherungsmarkt im Wandel' ('Changes in the German Insurance Market'), *Versicherungswirtschaft* (15), 942–5.

Bond, Martyn and Feus, Kim (eds) (2001) *The Treaty of Nice Explained*, London: Federal Trust.

Bort, Eberhard (2000) *Illegal Migration and Cross-Border Crime: Challenges at the Eastern Frontier of the European Union*, RCS Working Paper 2000 (9), Florence: European University Institute.

Börzel, Tanja and Risse, Thomas (2002) 'Who Is Afraid of European "Federalism"?', paper delivered at the 43rd Annual International Studies Association Convention, New Orleans, 23–27 March.

Bretherton, C. (2001) 'Gender Mainstreaming and EU Enlargement: Swimming against the Tide?', *Journal of European Public Policy*, 8 (1), 60–81.

Bretherton, Charlotte and Vogler, John (1999) *The European Union as a Global Actor*, London and New York: Routledge.

Brinkmann, G. (2001) 'Family Reunion, Third Country Nationals and the Community's New Powers', in E. Guild and C. Harlow (eds), *Implementing Amsterdam: Immigration and Asylum Rights in EC Law*, Oxford: Hart, p. 241.

Bruggeman, Willy (2000) 'Europol: A European FBI in the Making?', Online Lecture of the Cicero Foundation, Paris: www.cicerofoundation.org/p4bruggeman.html.

Bruszt, Laszlo (2002) 'Making Markets and Eastern Enlargement: Diverging Convergence', *West European Politics*, 2 (25), 121–40.

Caporaso, James A. and Keeler, John T.S. (1995) 'The European Community and Regional Integration Theory', in Carolyn Rhodes and Sonia Mazey (eds), *State of the European Union*, Boulder, CO: Lynne Rienner, pp. 29–62.

Castells, Manuel (2000) *The Information Age: Economy, Society and Culture, Volume I. The Rise of the Network Society*, Oxford: Blackwell.

Christiansen, Thomas (1998) 'Bringing Process Back in: The Longue Durée of European Integration', *Journal of European Integration*, 1, 99–121.

Christiansen Thomas and Jørgensen, Knud E. (1999) 'The Amsterdam Process: A Structurationist Perspective on EU Reform', *European Integration Online Papers* 3 (1/1999): www.eiop.or.at/eiop/texte/1999-00la.htm.

Christiansen, Thomas, Jørgensen, Knud E. and Wiener, Antje (eds) (2001) *The Social Construction of Europe*, London: Sage Publications.

Closa, C. (2003) 'Improving EU Constitutional Politics? A Preliminary Assessment of the Convention', Constitutionalism Web-Paper (ConWEB), no. 1, University of Manchester.

Cohen, Joshua and Sabel, Charles (1999) 'Directly Deliberative Polyarchy', unpublished paper, Columbia Law School.

Coleman W.D. and Tangermann, S. (1999) 'The 1992 CAP Reform, the Uruguay Round and the Commission', *Journal of Common Market Studies*, 37 (3), 385–405.

Commission of the European Communities (1994) *Communication to the Council. Follow-up to Commission Communication on 'The Europe Agreements and Beyond: A Strategy to Prepare the Countries of Central and Eastern Europe for Accession*, Brussels: COM (94) 361 final.

Commission of the European Communities (1997) *Agenda 2000: For a Stronger and Wider Union*, Brussels.

Commission of the European Communities (2001a) *Biannual Update of the Scoreboard to Review Progress in the Creation of an 'Area of Freedom, Security and Justice' in the European Union (Second Half of 2001)*, COM (2001) 682, 30.10.2001

Commission (of the European Communities) (2000) *The Commission and Non-governmental Organisations: Building a Stronger Partnership*, Brussels: Commission Discussion Paper, COM (2000) 11 final.

Commission (of the European Communities) (2001a) *European Governance. A White Paper*, Brussels, 25.7.2001, COM (2001) 428 final.

Commission (of the European Communities) (2001b) *Communication from the Commission to the Council and the European Parliament on an Open Method of Coordination for the Community on Immigration Policy*, Brussels, 11.7.2001, COM (2001) 387 final.

Committee for Post and Telecommunications (Auschuss für Post und Telekommunikation) (1997) Deutsche Bundestag, *Beschlussempfehlung und Bericht des Ausschusses für Post und Telekommunikation, Drucksache 13/8702* (final recommendations and report), 7 October.

Conference of the Representatives of the Governments of the Member States (2003): 'Addendum to the Presidency Note', CIG 60/03 ADD1.

Consolidated Treaties (1997) Luxembourg: Office for Official Publications of the European Communties.

Convention (2002, WG IX–WD 4) 'Liste des instruments d'action dont dispose l'Union', Brussels, 11 October.

Convention (286/2002) 'Conclusions of Working Group I on the Principle of Subsidiarity', Brussels, 23 September.

Convention (305/2002) 'Final Report of Working Group III on Legal Personality', Brussels, 1 October.

Convention (354/2002) 'Final Report of Working Group II', Brussels, 22 October.

Convention (369/2002) 'Preliminary Draft Constitutional Treaty', Brussels, 28 October.

Convention (40/2002) 'Note on the Plenary Meeting: Brussels, 15 and 16 April', Brussels, 25 April.

Convention (424/2002) 'Final Report of Working Group on Simplification', Brussels, 29 November.

Convention (426/2002) 'Final Report of Working Group X, "Freedom, Security and Justice"', Brussels, 2 December.

Convention (50/2002) 'The Legal Instruments: Present System', Brussels, 15 May.

Convention (73/2002) 'Mandate of the Working Group on Legal Personality', Brussels, 31 May.

Convention (850/2003) 'Draft Treaty Establishing a Constitution for Europe', Brussels, 18 July.

Council of the European Union (1997) 'Action Plan to Combat Organized Crime', OJC 251, 28/04/1997.

Council of the European Union (1999) 'Report from the Council to the European Parliament on the main aspects and basic choices of CFSP, including the financial implications for the Communities' budget (point L of the Interinstitutional Agreement on the financing of the CFSP) – 1998' (http://ue.eu.int/pesc/).

Council of the European Union (1999a) 'Action Plan of the Council and the Commission on How Best to Implement the Provisions of the Treaty of Amsterdam on an Area of Freedom, Security and Justice', OJ 1999 C19/1, Doc.n.13844/98.

Council of the European Union (1999b) 'Presidency Conclusions' Tampere', European Council, 15–16 October 1999.

Council of the European Union (2001a) 'Annual report from the Council to the European Parliament on the main aspects and basic choices of CFSP, including the financial implications for the general budget of the European Communities (point H, paragraph 40, of the Interinstitutional Agreement of 6 May 1999) – 2000' (http://ue.eu.int/pesc/).

Council of the European Union (2001b) 'Council Decision 2001/78/CFSP of 22 January 2001 setting up the Political and Security Committee', *Official Journal of the EC*, L 27, 30 January.

Council of the European Union (2003) 'Council Press Release No. 321/14500/03'.

Court of Auditors (2001) 'Special Report No. 13/2001 on the Management of the Common Foreign and Security Policy (CFSP), together with the Council's Replies and the Commission's Replies', *Official Journal of the EC*, C338 of 30 November.

Coussens, W. and Crum, B. (2003) *Towards Effective and Accountable Leadership in the Union*, EPIN Working Paper no. 3, Centre for European Policy Studies (CEPS), Brussels.

Cowles, Maria Green (2003) 'Non-State Actors and False Dichotomies: Reviewing IR/IPE Approaches to European Integration', *Journal of European Public Policy*, 10 (1), 102–120.

Crum, B. (2003) 'Legislative-Executive Relations in the European Union', *Journal of Common Market Studies*, 41 (3), 375–395.

Crum, B. (2004) 'Power and Politics in the European Convention', *Politics*, 24 (1), 1–11.

Curtin, Deirdre and Meijers, Herman (1995) 'The Principle of Open Government in Schengen and the European Union: Democratic Retrogression?', *Common Market Law Review*, 32, 391–442.

Hodson, D. and Maher, I. (2001) 'The Open Method as a New Form of Governance', *Journal of Common Market Studies*, 39 (4), 719–46.

Daugbjerg, C. (1999) 'Reforming the CAP', *Journal of Common Market Studies*, 37 (3), 407–428.

Dehousse, Franklin (1999) *Amsterdam: The Making of a Treaty*, London: Kogan Page.

Dehousse, Renaud (1998) *The European Court of Justice: The Politics of Juridical Integration*, London: Macmillan.

Deloche-Gaudez, Florence (2002) 'France: A Member State Losing Influence?', in Finn Laursen (ed.), *The Amsterdam Treaty: National Preference Formation, Interstate Bargaining and Outcome*, Odense: Odense University Press, pp. 139–60.

Den Boer, M. (1997) *The Implementation of Schengen: First the Widening, Now the Deepening*, Maastricht: EIPA.

Deregulation Commission (Deregulierungskommission) (1991) *Marktöffnung und Wettbewerb (Market Opening and Competition)*, Bonn.

De Schutler, Olivier, Lebessis, Nicolas and Paterson, John (eds) (2001), *Governance' in the European Union*, Luxembourg: Office for Official Publications of the European Union.

Devuyst, Yves (1998) 'Treaty Reform in the European Union: The Amsterdam Process', *Journal of European Public Policy*, 5 (4), 615–31.

Dieke, Alex Kalevi and Campbell, James, I. (2003) *Survey on Some Main Aspects of Postal Networks in EU Adhesion Candidate Countries*, Bad Honnef, Germany: WIK Consult, August.

Dinan, D. (2001) 'Governance and Institutions 2000: Edging Towards Enlargement', *Journal of Common Market Studies*, 39 (Supp.), 25–42.

Dinan, Desmond and Vanhoonacker, Sophie (2001) 'IGC 2000 Watch', parts I–II, *ECSA Review*, 13 (2), 19–21; 14 (1), 1, 20–21.

Duff, Andrew (1997) *The Treaty of Amsterdam: Text and Commentary*, London: Federal Trust.

Duke, Simon (2000) *The Elusive Quest for European Security: From EDC to CFSP*, Oxford: Macmillan.

Dumond, Jean-Michel and Setton, Philippe (1999) *La politique étrangère et de sécurité commune (PESC)*, Paris: La Documentation Française.

Durand, Marie-Francoise and de Vasconcelos, Alvaro (1998) *La PESC. Ouvrir l'Europe au monde*, Paris: Presses de Sciences Po.

Dyson, Kenneth (1999) 'Economic and Monetary Union in Europe: A Transformation of Governance', in Beate Kohler-Koch and Rainer Eising (eds), *The Transformation of Governance in the European Union*, New York: Routledge, pp. 98–119.

Dyson, Kenneth and Featherstone, Kevin (1999) *The Road to Maastricht. Negotiating Economic and Monetary Union*, Oxford: Oxford University Press.

Easton, David (1965) *A Systems Analysis of Political Life*, New York: Wiley.

EEA, European Express Association (2002) *Letter to the Hungarian Prime Minister*, 8 January, Brussels.

Eising, Rainer and Kohler-Koch, Beate (1999) 'Introduction: Network Governance in the European Union', in Beate Kohler-Koch and Rainer Eising (eds), *The Transformation of Governance in the European Union*, New York: Routledge, pp. 3–13.

Eising, Rainer and Kohler-Koch, Beate (eds) (2004) *Interessenpolitik in Europa*, Baden-Baden: Nomos.

Eisl, Gerhard (1999) 'EU Enlargement and Co-operation in Justice and Home Affairs', in Karen Henderson (ed.), *Back to Europe: Central and Eastern Europe and the European Union*, London: UCL Press, pp. 169–82.

Eurobarometer (2002) *Standard Eurobarometer*, 57, Brussels: European Commission.

Eurobarometer (2003a) *Standard Eurobarometer* (Fieldwork March–April), July, Brussels: European Commission.

Eurobarometer (2003b) 'Candidate Countries', *Eurobarometer*, 2003.3. Full Report. 'Public Opinion in the Canadiate Countries', September.

European Commission (2001) *The Economic Impact of Enlargement*, Brussels: European Commission.

European Convention (2003) *Draft Treaty Establishing a Constitution for Europe*, CONV850/03.

European Council (1999) *Presidency Conclusions: Cologne European Council 3 and 4 June 1999.*

European Council (2000a): *Declaration 23 on the Future of the Union.* Adopted by the European Council in December 2000 and annexed to the Treaty of Nice (http://europa.eu.int/comm/justice_home/unit/charte/en/declarations-nice.html).

European Council (2000b) *Presidency Conclusions of the Lisbon European Summit*, 23–24 March 2000.

European Council (2001) *The Future of the EU: Declaration of Laeken*, 15 December (SN 273/01).

European Council (2002) *Presidency Conclusions*, Seville European Council, 21 and 22 June (SN 200/02).

European Parlament, Committee on Constitutional Affairs (2001) *Draft Treaty of Nice (Initial Analysis)*, PE 294.737. Bruxelles, 10 January.

Europol (2000) 'Green Light to Europol for Cooperation with Non-EU States and Bodies in Fighting International Organised Crime!', Press Release 02/00, The Hague, 27 April.

Farny, Dieter (1991) 'Die Regulierung der privaten Versicherungswirtschaft: Von einer guten Vergangenheit in eine bessere Zukunft' ('The Regulation of Private Insurance. From a Good Past to a Better Future'), in Franz W. Hopp and Georg Mehl (eds), *Versicherungen in Europa. Heute und Morgen* (*Insurance in Europe. Today and Tomorrow*), Karlsruhe: Verlag Versicherungswirtschaft, pp. 67–93.

Fennelly, Nial (2000) 'The Area of "Freedom, Security and Justice" and the European Court of Justice: A Personal View', *International and Comparative Law Quarterly*, 49 (1), 1–14.

Fijnaut, Christian (1993) 'The "Communitization" of Police Cooperation in Western Europe', in H.G. Schermers, *et al.* (eds), *Free Movement of Persons in Europe*, Dordrecht: Nijhoff, pp. 75–92.

Finance Committee in the German Bundestag (1990) Public hearing concerning the implementation into German legislation of the Second Non-Life Insurance Directive

(Finanzausschuss, *Öffentliche Anhörung zum Zweiten Durchführungsgesetz/EWG zum VAG*), 25 April.

Fischer, J. (2000a), 'From Confederacy to Federation', Speech at the Humboldt University, Berlin, 12 May.

Fischer, J. (2000b), 'Vom Staatenbund zur Föderation: Gedanken über die Finalität der europäischen Integration', *Integration*, 23 (3), 149–56.

Fischler, F. (1998) 'Keynote Address', Agra Europe conference on the Reform of the Common Agricultural Policy, Brussels, 23 April.

Forster, Anthony and Wallace, William (2000) 'Common Foreign and Security Policy', in Helen Wallace and William Wallace (eds), *Policy-making in the European Union*, 4th edn, Oxford: Oxford University Press, pp. 461–92.

Frankfurter Allgemeine Zeitung (1984) 'European News: West Germany Opposes UK Insurance Move', 10 February, 2.

Frankfurter Allgemeine Zeitung (1992) 'Gespräch mit Christian Schwarz-Schilling' ('Talk with Christian Schwarz-Schilling'), 23 March, 7.

Frankfurter Allgemeine Zeitung (1997) 'Der Bundesrat verlangt ein unbefristetes Briefmonopol für die Post' ('The Bundesrat Demands Unlimited Letter Monopoly'), economics section, 17 May, 14.

Frieden, Jeffrey A. (1991) 'Invested Interests: The Politics of National Economic Policies in a World of Global Finance', *International Organisation*, 45 (4), 425–51.

Frieden, Jeffrey A. and Rogowski, Ronald (1996) 'The Impact of the International Economy on National Policies: An Analytical Overview', in Robert Keohane O. and Helen Milner (eds), *Internationalisation and Domestic Politics*, Cambridge, MA: Cambridge University Press, pp. 25–47.

Friedrich, Carl J. (1968) *Constitutional Government and Democracy*, 4th edn, Waltham: Blaidell.

Friedrich, Carl J. (1969) *Europe: An Emergent Nation*, New York: Harper & Row.

Friis, Lykke and Murphy, Anna (2000) 'Enlargement: A Complex Juggling Act', in Maria Green Cowles and Smith Michael (eds), *State of the European Union: Risks, Reform, Resistance, and Revival*, Oxford: Oxford University Press, pp. 186–204.

Frisch, Thomas (2000) *Der Hohe Vertreter für die GASP: Aufgaben und erste Schritte*, Ebenhausen: Stiftung Wissenschaft und Politik.

Galloway, David (2001) *The Treaty of Nice and Beyond: Realities and Illusions of Power in the EU*, Sheffield: Sheffield Academic Press.

GDV, the Gesamtverband der Deutschen Versicherungswirtschaft (German Insurance Association), *Annual Yearbook*, various years.

Genscher, Hans Dietrich and Colombo, Emilio (1981) 'Die Genscher/Colombo-Initiative zur Europäischen Union', in *Amtsblatt der Europäischen Gemeinschaften: Verhandlungen des Europäischen Parlaments. Sitzungsperiode 1981–1982*, 16–20 November, pp. 232–54.

German Constitutional Court 1993 (1995) 'Judgement of October 12, 1993', in Andrew Oppenheimer (ed.), *The Relationship between European Community Law and National Law: The Cases*, Cambridge: Cambridge University Press.

Ginsberg, Roy H. (1999) 'Conceptualizing the European Union as an International Actor: Narrowing the Theoretical Capability-Expectation Gap', *Journal of Common Market Studies*, 37 (3), 429–54.

Ginsberg, Roy H. (2001) *The European Union in International Politics*, Lanham: Rowman and Littlefield.

Giscard d'Estaing, V. (2002) 'Introductory Speech to the Convention on the Future of Europe', SN 1565/02, Brussels, 26 February.

Golub, Jonathan (1999) 'In the Shadow of the Vote? Decision-making Efficiency in the European Community 1974–1995', *International Organization*, 53 (4), 733–64.

Gormley, Laurence W. (1999) 'Reflections on the Architecture of the European Union after the Treaty of Amsterdam', in David O'Keeffe and Patrick Twomey (eds), *Legal Issues of the Amsterdam Treaty*, Oxford: Hart Publishing, pp. 57–70.

Government Commission for Telecommunications ('Witte Commission') (1988) *Restructuring of the Telecommunications System*, Heidelberg, Germany: R.v. Decker's Verlag.

Grabbe, Heather (2001) 'How Does Europeanization Affect CCE Governance? Conditionality, Diffusion and Diversity', *Journal of European Public Policy*, 8 (6), 1013–11031.

Grabbe, Heather (2002) 'Stabilizing the East while Keeping Out the Easterners: Internal and External Security Logics in Conflict', in Sandra Lavenex and Emek Uçarer (eds), *Migration and the Externalities of European Integration*, Lanham: Lexington Books.

Grabitz, Eberhard, Schmuck, Otto, Steppat, Sabine and Wessels, Wolfgang (1988) *Direktwahl und Demokratisierung. Eine Funktionsbilanz des EP nach der ersten Wahlperiode*, Bonn: Europa Union Verlag.

Grande, Edgar (1989) *Vom Monopol zum Wettbewerb? Die neokonservative Reform der Telekommunikation in Grossbritannien und der Bundesrepublik Deutschland*, Wiesbaden, Germany: Deutscher Universitätsverlag.

Grant, Charles (1998) *Can Britain Lead in Europe?*, London: Centre of European Reform.

Grant, W. (1987) 'Introduction', in W. Grant (ed.), *Business Interests, Organizational Development and Private Interest Government: An International Comparative Study of the Food Processing Industry*, Berlin and New York: Walter de Coruyter.

Green Cowles, Maria and Smith, Michael (eds) (2000) *State of the European Union: Risks, Reform, Resistance, and Revival*, Oxford: Oxford University Press.

Green Cowles, Maria, Caporaso, James A. and Risse, Thomas (eds) (2001) *Transforming Europe: Europeanization and Domestic Change*, Ithaca, NY: Cornell University Press.

Greenwood, Justin and Ronit, Karston (1994) 'Interest Groups in the EC: Newly Emerging Dynamics and Forms', *West European politics*, 17 (1), 31–52.

Griller, Stefan, Droutsas, Dimitri P., Falkner, Gerda, Forgo, Katrin and Nentwich, Michael, (2000) *The Treaty of Amsterdam. Facts, Analysis, Prospects*, Vienna and New York: Springer.

Groenendijk, K. (1998) 'Long-term Immigrants and the Council of Europe', *European Journal of Migration and Law*, 1 (3), 275–92.

Groenendijk, K. Guild, E. and Dogan, H. (1998) *Security of Residence of Long-term Migrants: A Comparative Study of Law and Practice in European Countries*, Strasbourg: Council of Europe.

Guild, E. (1996) *A Guide to the Right of Establishment in the Europe Agreements*, London: ILPA/BS&G.

Guild, E. (2001) 'Primary Immigration: The Great Myths', in E. Guild and C. Harlow, *Implementing Amsterdam: Immigration and Asylum Rights in EC Law Hart*, Oxford: Hart, p 65.

Guild, E. (2001) *Immigration Law in the European Community*, The Hague: Kluwer Law International.

Guild, E. (2001) *Moving the Borders of Europe*, Nijmegen University, inaugural lecture.

Guild, E. and Niessen, J. (1990) *The Developing Immigration and Asylum Policies of the European Union*, The Hague: Kluwer Law International.

Guiraudon, Virginie (2000) 'European Integration and Migration Policy: Vertical Policy-Making as Venue Shopping', *Journal of Common Market Studies*, 38 (2), 251–71.

Gutmann, R. (1995) *Die Assoziationsfreizügigkeit türkisher Staatsangehöriger*, 2 auflage, Baden-Baden: Nomos Verlag.

Haas, Ernst B. (1958) *The Uniting of Europe*, Stanford: Stanford University Press.

Haftendorn, Helga (1990) 'Zur Theorie außenpolitischer Entscheidungsprozesse' in Volker Rittberger (ed.), *Theorien der Internationalen Beziehungen. Bestandsaufnahme und Forschungsperspektiven*, Opladen: Westdeutscher Verlag, pp. 401–23.

Hailbronner, Kay (1989) *Möglichkeiten und Grenzen einer europäischen Koordinierung des Einreise-und Asylrechts: ihre Auswirkungen auf das Asylrecht der Bundesrepublik Deutschland*, Baden-Baden: Nomos.

Hailbronner, Kay (2000) *Immigration and Asylum Law and Policy in the European Union*, The Hague: Kluwer.

Hall, Peter (1986) *Governing the Economy: The Politics of State Intervention in Britain and France*, Cambridge: Polity Press.

Hall, Peter and Soskice, David (2001) 'An Introduction to Varieties of Capitalism', in *Varieties of Capitalism: The Institutional Foundations of Comparative Advantage*, Oxford: Oxford University Press.

Hallstein, Walter (1972) *Europe in the Making*, London: Allen and Unwin.

Hargreaves, Deborah (2000) 'Brussels Advances on Postal Reform', 10 May 2000: 3.

Hedemann-Robinson, M. (1996) 'Third Country Nationals, European Union Citizenship and Free Movement of Persons', *Yearbook of European Law*, 16, 321.

Héritier, Adrienne (2002) 'New Modes of Governance in Europe: Policy-Making without Legislating?', in Adrienne Héritier (ed.), *Common Goods: Reinventing European Integration Governance*, Lanham: Rowman & Littlefield, pp. 185–206.

Herolf, Gunilla (2000) 'Inside and Outside Nordic Cooperation', in Alfred Pijpers (ed.), *On Cores and Coalitions in the European Union: The Position of Some Smaller Member States*, The Hague: Clingendael, pp. 131–51.

Hirschmann, Albert O. (1970) *Exit, Voice and Loyalty: Response to Decline in Firms, Organizations and States*, Cambridge.

Hix, Simon (1999) *The Political System of the European Union*, New York: St Martin's Press.

Hodson, Dermot and Maher, Imelda (2001) 'The Open Method as a New Mode of Governance: The Case of Soft Economic Policy Co-ordination', *Journal of Common Market Studies*, 39 (4), 719–46.

Hoffmann, Stanley (1966) 'Obstinate or Obsolete? The Fate of the Nation State and the Case of Western Europe', *Daedalus*, 95, 892–908.

Holland, Martin (1997) *Common Foreign and Security Policy: The Record and Reforms*, London and Washington: Pinter.

Hooghe, Liesbet and Marks, Gary (2001) *Multi-level Governance and European Integration*, Lanham: Rowman & Littlefield.

Howorth, Jolyon (2000) *European Integration and Defence: The Ultimate Challenge?* Chaillot Papers 43, Paris: Insitute for Security Studies, November 2000: www.europa.eu.int/comm/dgs/justice_home/pdf/scoreboard_30oct01_en.pdf.

Hueglin, Thomas O. (1999) *Early Modern Concepts for a Late Modern World. Althusius on Community and Federalism*, Waterloo: Wilfried Laurier University Press.

Hummer, Waldemar (ed.) (1998) *Die Europäische Union nach deth Vertrag von Amsterdam*, Vienna.

Imig, Doug and Tarrow, Sidney (2001) *Contentious Europeans: Protest and Politics in an Integrating Europe*, Boulder, CO: Rowman & Littlefield.

Ingebritsen, Christine (1998) *The Nordic States and European Unity*, Ithaca: Cornell University Press.

International Labour Organization (1998) *Structural and Regulatory Changes and Globalization in Postal and Telecommunications Services: The Human Resources Dimension*, Geneva.

International Monetary Fund (1995) *International Financial Statistics Yearbook*, Washington DC.

Isaksen, Susanne, Toft, Ole and Bødtcher-Hansen, Jens (1998) *En traktat bliver til. Amsterdam-traktaten. Forberedelse, forhandling og resultat*, Copenhagen: J.H. Schultz Information A/S.

Iversen, Torben and Wren, Anne (1998) 'Equality, Employment and Budgetary Restraint: The Trilemma of the Service Economy', *World Politics*, 50 (July), 5–46.

Jachtenfuchs, Markus (2001) 'The Governance Approach to European Integration', *Journal of Common Market Studies*, 39 (2) 245–64.

Joerges, Christian, Mény, Yves and Weiler, Joseph (eds) (2000) 'What Kind of Constitution for What Kind of Polity? Responses to Joschka Fischer', Florence, EUI.

Jopp, Mathias (1997) 'The Defence Dimension of the European Union: The Role and Performance of the WEU', in Elfriede Regelsberger/Philippe de Schoutheete de Tervarent and Wolfgang Wessels (eds), *Foreign Policy of the European Union: From EPC to CFSP and Beyond*, Boulder, CO and London: Lynne Rienner Publishers, pp. 153–69.

Jopp, Mathias (2000) 'Gemeinsame europäische Sicherheits- und Verteidigungspolitik', in Werner Weidenfeld and Wolfgang Wessels (eds), *Jahrbuch der europäischen Integration 1999/2000*, Bonn: Europa Union Verlag, pp. 243–50.

Jopp, Mathias and Regelsberger, Elfriede (2003) 'GASP und ESVP im Verfassungsvertrag – eine neue Angebotsvielfalt mit Chancen und Mängeln', *Integration*, 26 (3), 550–63.

Jopp, Mathias, Maurer, Andreas and Schmuck, Otto (eds) (1998) *Die Europaische Union nach Amsterdam: Analysen und Stellungnahmen Zum neuen EU-Vertrag*, Bonn: Europa Union Verlag.

Josling, T. and Tangermann, S. (1999) 'The WTO Agreement on Agriculture and the Next Negotiating Round', *European Review of Agricultural Economics*, 26 (3), 371–88.

Journal of Common Market Studies (2001) Special issue on 'The Changing Politics of the European Union', November, 39 (4).

Kadunce, Wedell H. (1995) *Baltic–Nordic Relations*, in Bericht des Bundesinstituts für ost-wissenschaftliche und internationale Studien 9, Cologne.

Keohane, Robert O. and Nye, John S. (1974) 'Transgovernmental Relations and International Organizations', *World Politics*, 27 (October), 39–62.

Kerremans, Bart (1998) 'The Problem of Capacity and Control in an Enlarged EU Council', in Pierre-Henri Laurant and Marc Maresceau (eds), *The State of the European Union*, Vol. 4: *Deepening and Widening*, Boulder, CO: Lynne Rienner, pp. 87–109.

Kerremans, Bart (2002) 'Belgium: From Orthodoxy to Pragmatism', in Finn Laursen (ed.), *The Amsterdam Treaty: National Preference Formation, Interstate Bargaining and Outcome*, Odense: Odense University Press, pp. 43–70.

Knudsen, Jette S. (2001), 'Breaking with Tradition: Liberalisation of Services Trade in the European Union', unpublished Ph.D. dissertation, MIT, Cambridge, MA.

Kohler, Beate (1982) *Political Forces in Spain, Greece and Portugal*, London: Butterworth Scientific.

Kohler-Koch, Beate (1996) 'Catching up with Change: The Transformation of Governance in the European Union', *Journal of European Public Policy*, 3 (3), 359–80.

Kohler-Koch, Beate (1998) 'Europe and the Regions: The Issue of Multi-Level Governance and Sovereignty', paper presented at the conference on Democracy in Europe, University of Twente, 12–14 February.

Kohler-Koch, Beate (1999) 'The Evolution and Transformation of European Governance', in Beate Kohler-Koch and Rainer Eising (eds), *The Transformation of Governance in the European Union*, New York: Routledge, pp. 14–35.

Kohler-Koch, Beate (2000a) 'Europäisierung: Plädoyer für eine Horizonterweiterung', in Michèle Knodt and Beate Kohler-Koch (eds), *Deutschland zwischen europäisierung und Selbstbehauptung*, Bd. 5, Campus: Frankfurt a.M., pp. 11–31.

Kohler-Koch, Beate (2000b) 'Regieren in der Europäischen Union. Auf der Suche nach demokratischer Legitimität', *Aus Politik und Zeitgeschichte*, B 6/2000, 30–8.

Kohler-Koch, Beate (2002) 'On Networks, Travelling Ideas, and Behavioural Inertia', in Thomas Conzelmann and Michèle Knodt (eds), *Regionales Europa – europäisierte Regionen*. Frankfurt/New York: Campus, pp. 87–103.

Kohler-Koch, Beate and Eising, R. (eds) (1999) *The Transformation of Governance in the European Union*, London: Routledge.

Krasner, Stephen D. (1993) 'Westphalia And All That', in Judith Goldstein and Robert O. Keohane (eds), *Ideas and Foreign Policy*, Ithaca: Cornell University Press, pp. 235–264.

Krekelberg, Astrid (2001) 'Der Vertrag von Nizza: Grundlage fur Mehr Handlungsfanigkeit und Legitimat', *Integration*, 2, 223–29.

Krenzler, Horst Günter (1998) *The Geostrategic and International Political Implications of EU Enlargement*, European University Institute, RSC Policy Paper, April 1998, No. 98/2.

Kuijper, P.J. (2000) 'Some Legal Problems Associated with the Communitarisation of Policy on Visas, Asylum and Immigration Under the Amsterdam Treaty and Incorporation of the Schengen Acquis', *Common Market Law Review*, 37, 345–66.

Laffan, B. and Shackleton, M. (2000) 'The Budget', in H. Wallace and W. Wallace (eds), *Policy-Making in the European Union*, 4th edn, Oxford: Oxford University Press, pp. 211–41.

Lambsdorf, Otto G. (1991) 'Wettbewerb in der Versicherungswirtschaft: Fluch oder Segen?' ('Competition in Insurance Services: Curse or Blessing'), in Franz W. Hopp and Georg Mehl (eds), *Versicherungen in Europa: Heute und Morgen (Insurance in Europe: Today and Tomorrow)*, Karlsruhe: Verlag Versicherungswirtschaft.

Landau, A. (2001) 'The Agricultural Negotiations in the WTO', *Journal of Common Market Studies*, 39, 913–25.

Langdon, Anthony J. (1995) *Justice and Home Affairs Cooperation with Associated Countries*, Report to the European Commission, Brussels.

Lankowski, Carl (ed.) (1999) *Governing Beyond the Nation-State: Global Public Policy, Regionalism or Going Local?*, AICGS Research Report, no. 11, Washington.

Laursen, Finn (1995) 'On Studying European Integration: Integration Theory and Political Economy', in Finn Laursen (ed.), *The Political Economy of European Integration*, The Hague: Kluwer, pp. 3–29.

Laursen, Finn (2001a) 'EU Enlargement: Interests, Issues and the Need for Institutional Reform', in Svein S. Andersen and Kjell A. Eliassen (eds), *Making Policy In Europe*, 2nd edn, London: Sage, pp. 206–228.

Laursen, Finn (2001b) 'Nice and Post-Nice: Explaining Current and Predicting Future

Developments in the EU', paper prepared for delivery at conference on 'New Trends and Perspectives in European Studies' organized by the EU-China Higher Education Co-operation Programme in Beijing, 10–13 July.

Laursen, Finn (ed.) (2002) *The Amsterdam Treaty: National Preference Formation, Interstate Bargaining and Outcome*, Odense: Odense University Press.

Laursen, Finn (2002a) 'Introduction: Overview of the 1996–97 Intergovernmental Conference (IGC) and the Treaty of Amsterdam', in Finn Laursen (ed.), *The Amsterdam Treaty: National Preference Formation, Interstate Bargaining and Outcome*, Odense: Odense University Press, p. 19.

Laursen, Finn (2002b) 'Institutions and Procedures: The Limited Reforms', in Finn Laursen (ed.), *The Amsterdam Treaty: National Preference Formation, Interstate Bargaining and Outcome*, Odense: Odense University Press, pp. 565–90.

Laursen, Finn (2002c) 'Explaining and Evaluating the Amsterdam Treaty: Some Concluding Remarks', in Finn Laursen (ed.), *The Amsterdam Treaty: National Preference Formation, Interstate Bargaining and Outcome*, Odense: Odense University Press, pp. 639–655.

Lavenex, Sandra (1999) *Safe Third Countries: Extending the EU Asylum and Immigration Policies to Central and Eastern Europe*, Budapest and New York: Central European University Press.

Lavenex, Sandra (2001a) *The Europeanisation of Refugee Policies: Between Human Rights and Internal Security*, Aldershot: Ashgate.

Lavenex, Sandra (2001b) 'Migration and the EU's New Eastern Border: Between Realism and Liberalism', *Journal of European Public Policy*, 8 (1), 24–42.

Lavenex, Sandra (2001c) 'The Europeanization of Refugee Policies: Normative Challenges and Institutional Legacies', *Journal of Common Market Studies*, 39 (5), 851–74.

Lavenex, Sandra (2002) 'EU Trade Policy and Migration Control', in Lavenex, Sandra and Uçarer, Emek (eds), *Migration and the Externalities of European Integration*, Lanham: Lexington Books.

Lavigne, Marie (1998) 'Conditions for Accession to the EU', *Comparative Economic Studies*, 30 (3), 38–57.

Lehne, S. (1999) 'Institutionenreform 2000', *Integration*, 4, 221–30.

Lenaerts, K. (1991) 'Some Reflections on the Separation of Powers in the European Community', *Common Market Law Review*, 28, 11–35.

Lindberg, Leon N. and Scheingold, Stuart A. (1970) *Europe's Would-be Polity: Patterns of Change in the European Community*, Englewood Cliffs: Prentice Hall.

Lindenberg, Donna (2001) 'The Battle of Nice: Expanding the EU', *Mondial*, April.

Link, Werner (2001) *Die Neuordnung der Weltpolitik. Grundprobleme globaler Politik an der Schwelle zum 21: Jahrhundert*, 3rd edn, Frankfurt: Beck.

Linklater, Andrew and MacMillan, John (1995) *Boundaries in Question: New Directions in International Relations*, London, New York: Pinter.

Lippert, Barbara (2000) 'Die Erweiterungspolitik der Europäischen Union – Stabilitätsexport mit Risiken', in Barbara Lippert (ed.), *Osterweiterung der Europäischen Union – die doppelte Reifeprüfung*, Bonn: Europa Union Verlag, pp. 105–64.

Lloyds List (1988) 'West Germany: Monopoly Commission Recommends More Freedom for Insurers', 27 August: 8 (no author).

Loewenhardt, John, Hill, J. Ronald and Light, Margot (2001) 'A Wider Europe: The View From Minsk and Chisinau', *International Affairs*, 77, 3.

Ludlow, Peter (2001) 'The Treaty of Nice: Neither Triumph nor Disaster', *ECSA Review*, 14 (2), 1, 3–4.

Magnette, P. (2002) 'Deliberation vs. Negotiation: A First Analysis of the Convention on the Future of the Union', paper presented at the first Pan-European Conference on European Union Politics, Bordeaux, 26–28 September.

Mancini, F. (1998) 'The Case for Statehood', *European Law Journal*, 4 (1), 29–42.

March, James G. and Olsen, Johan P. (1989) *Rediscovering Institutions: The Organisational Basis of Politics*, New York: Free Press.

Marks, Gary, Hooghe, Liesbet and Blank, Kermit (1996) 'European Integration from the 1980s: State-Centric v. Multi-level Governance', *Journal of Common Market Studies*, 34 (3), 341–78.

Maull, Hanns W. (1997) 'Europa als Weltmacht? Perspektiven für die gemeinsame Außen- und Sicherheitspolitik', in Thomas Jäger and Melanie Piepenschneider (eds.), *Europa 2020: Szenarien politischer Entwicklung*, Opladen: Leske und Budrich, pp. 81–95.

Maurer, Andreas (1996) 'Reformziel Effizienzsteigerung und Demokratisierung: Die Weiterentwicklung der Entscheidungsmechanismen', in Mathias Jopp and Otto Schmuck (eds), *Die Reform der Europäischen Union*, Bonn: Europa Union Verlag, pp. 23–40.

Maurer, Andreas (1998) 'Die Institutionellen Reformen: Entscheidungseffizienz und Demokratie', in Jopp *et al.*, pp. 41–82.

Maurer, Andreas 'Die institutionelle Ordnung einer größeren Europäischen Union – Optionen zur Wahrung der Handlungsfähigkeit', in Barbara Lippert (ed.), Osterweiterung der Europäischen Union – die doppelte Reifeprüfung, Bonn, Europa Union Verlag, pp. 27–52.

Maurer, Andreas and Grunert, Thomas (1998) 'Der Wandel in der Europapolitik der Mitgliedstaaten', in Mathias Jopp, Andreas Maurer and Heinrich Schüneider (eds), *Europapolitische Grundverständnisse im Wandel. Analysen und Konsequenzen für die politische Bildung*, Bonn: IEP, pp. 213–300.

Maurer, Andreas and Wessels, Wolfgang (eds) (2001) *National Parliaments on their Way to Europe. Losers or Latecomers?*, Baden-Baden: Nomos Publishers.

Maurer, Andreas and Wessels, Wolfgang (2002) 'The EU Matters: Structuring Self-made Offers and Demands', in Wolfgang Wessels, Andreas Maurer and Jürgen Mittag (eds), *Fifteen into One? The European Union and Member States*, Manchester: Manchester University Press.

Maurer, Andreas, Mittag, Jürgen and Wessels, Wolfgang (2002) 'Preface and Major Findings: The Anatomy, the Analysis and the Assessment of the "Beast" ', in Wolfgang Wessels, Andreas Maurer and Jürgen Mittag(eds), *Fifteen into One? The European Union and Member States*, Manchester: Manchester University Press, pp. 1–5.

Mazey, Sonia and Richardson, Jeremy (eds) (1993) *Lobbying in the European Community*, Oxford: Oxford University Press.

McDonagh, Bobby (1998) *Original Sin in a Brave New World: An Account of the Negotiation of the Treaty of Amsterdam*, Dublin: Institute of European Affairs.

McKeown, Timothy (1984) 'Firms and Tariff Regime Change: Explaining the Demand for Protection', *World Politics*, summer, 214–33.

Michalski, A. and Wallace, H. (eds) (1992) *The European Community: The Challenge of Enlargement*, 4th edn, London: Royal Institute of International Affairs.

Migration Statistics, Eurostat, Luxembourg, 1994, 1995 and 1996.

Milner, Helen (1997) *Interests, Institutions and Information: Domestic Politics and International Relations*, Princeton.

Milward, Alan (1992), *The European Rescue of the Nation-State*, Berkeley, CA: University of California Press.

Milward, A. with assistance of Brennan, George and Romero, Frederico (2000) *The European Rescue of the Nation-State*, 2nd edn, London: Routledge.

Ministers Responsible for Immigration (1991) 'Report to the European Council', WGI 930 SN 4038/91 of 3.12.

Moe, Terry (1990) 'Towards a Theory of Public Bureaucracy', in Oliver E. Williamson (ed.), *Organization Theory*, Oxford: Oxford University Press, pp. 116–53.

Monar, Jörg (1995) 'Democratic Control of Justice and Home Affairs: The European Parliament and the National Parliaments', in Roland Bieber and Jörg Monar (eds), *Justice and Home Affairs in the European Union: The Development of the Third Pillar*, Brussels: European Interuniversity Press, pp. 243–58.

Monar, Jörg (1997a) 'The European Union's Foreign Affairs System after the Treaty of Amsterdam: A Strengthened Capacity for External Action?', *European Foreign Affairs Review*, 2, 413–436.

Monar, Jörg (1997b) 'The Finances of the Union's Intergovernmental Pillars: Tortuous Experiments with the Community Budget', *Journal of Common Market Studies*, 1, 57–78.

Monar, Jörg (1998) 'Ein Raum der Freiheit, der Sicherheit und des Rechts: Die Innen-und Justizpolitik nach Amsterdam', in Matthias Jopp, Andreas Maurer and Otto Schmuck (eds), *Die Europäische Union nach Amsterdam: Analysen und Stellungnahmen zum neuen EU-Vertrag*, Bonn: Europa Union Verlag, pp. 127–54.

Monar, Jörg (2001a) 'Justice and Home Affairs After Amsterdam: The Treaty Reforms and the Challenge of Their Implementation', in Jörg Monar and Wolfgang Wessels (eds), *The European Union after the Treaty of Amsterdam*, London and New York: Continuum, pp. 267–95.

Monar, Jörg (2001b) 'The Dynamics of Justice and Home Affairs: Laboratories, Driving Factors and Costs', *Journal of Common Market Studies*, 39 (4), 747–64.

Monar, Jörg and Wessels, Wolfgang (eds) (2001) *The European Union after the Treaty of Amsterdam*, London and New York: Continuum.

Monnet, Jean (1976) *Mémoires*, Paris: Fayard.

Monopoly Commission (1988) *Unterrichtung durch die Bundesregierung, Siebentes Hauptgutachten der Monopol Kommission* (*Study for the Federal Government: The Seventh Report of the Monopoly Commission*), 1986/87, 19 July, Cologne: Germany.

Moravcsik, Andrew (1993) 'Preferences and Power in the European Community: A Liberal Intergovernmentalist Approach', *Journal of Common Market Studies*, 31 (4), 473–524.

Moravcsik, Andrew (1997) 'Taking Preferences Seriously: A Liberal Theory of International Politics', *International Organisation*, 4, 513–55.

Moravcsik, Andrew (1998) *The Choice for Europe: Social Purpose and State Power from Messina to Maastricht*, Ithaca, NY: Cornell University Press.

Moravcsik, Andrew (1999a) 'The Choice for Europe: Current Commentary and Future Research: A Response to James Caporaso, Fritz Scharpf and Helen Wallace', *Journal of European Public Policy*, 6 (1), 168–79.

Moravcsik, Andrew (1999b) *The Choice for Europe: Social Purpose and State Power from Messina to Maastricht*, London: UCL Press.

Moravcsik, Andrew and Kalypso, Nicolaïdis (1999) 'Explaining the Treaty of Amsterdam: Interests, Influence, Institutions', *Journal of Common Market Studies*, 37 (1), 59–85.

Morgan, Kevin and Webber, Douglas (1986) 'Divergent Paths: Political Strategies for Telecommunications in Britain, France and West Germany', *West European Politics*, 9 (4), 56–79.

Noam, Eli (1992) *Telecommunications in Europe*, New York: Oxford University Press.

North, Douglass C. (1990) *Institutions, Institutional Change and Economic Performance*, Cambridge: Cambridge University Press.

Norman, P. (2003) *The Accidental Constitution*, Brussels: EuroComment.

Nuttall, Simon (1992) *European Political Cooperation*, Oxford: Oxford University Press.

Nyiri P., Toth, J. and Fullerton, M. (2001) *Diasporas and Politics*, Budapest: Centre for Migration and Refugee Studies.

OECD (2000) *OECD Agricultural Outlook 2000–2005*, Paris: Organization for Economic Cooperation and Development.

O'Keeffe, David (1995) 'Recasting the Third Pillar', *Common Market Law Review*, 32, 893–920.

Olsen, Johan P. (2000) *Organizing European Institutions of Governance. A Prelude to an Institutional Account of Political Integration*, ARENA Working Papers WP 00/2.

Olsen, Johan P. (2002) *The Many Faces of Europeanization*, ARENA Working Papers WP 01/2.

Olson, Mancur (1965) *The Logic of Collective Action: Public Goods and the Theory of Groups*, Cambridge, MA: Harvard University Press.

Orden, D., Paarlberg, R. and Roe, T. (1999) *Policy Reform in American Agriculture*, Chicago: University of Chicago Press.

Paemen, Hugo and Bensch, Alexandra (1995) *From the GATT to the WTO: The European Community in the Uruguay Round*, Leuven: Leuven University Press.

Papademetriou, D. (1996) *Coming Together or Pulling Apart? The European Union's Struggle with Immigration and Asylum*, New York: Carnegie Endowment for International Peace.

Peers, S. (1999) 'Who's Watching the Watchmen', *International Yearbook of European Law*.

Pelkmans, Jacques (2001) *European Integration Methods and Economic Analysis*, 2nd edn, London: Prentice Hall.

Peraldi-Lenenf, Francois (2001) 'La réforme de la politique commerciale par le Traité de Nice (article 133): un difficile regoce', *La Gazette du Palais*, No. 171–173, pp. 20–1.

Pescatore, Pierre (2001) 'Nice: Aftermath', *Common Market Law Review*, 2 (April), 265–271.

Peters, Guy (1999) *Institutional Theory in Political Science: The 'New Institutionalism'*, London and New York: Cassell Academic.

Peterson, John (1995) 'Decision-making in the European Union: Towards a Framework for Analysis', *Journal of European Public Policy*, 2 (1), 69–93.

Peterson, John (2001) 'The Choice for EU Theories: Establishing a Common Framework for Analysis', *European Journal of Political Research*, 39, 289–318.

Petite, Michel (1998) *The Treaty of Amsterdam*, Jean-Monnet Chair Working Paper Series, no. 2/98, Harvard: www.law.Harvard.edu/Programs/Jean-Monnet/Papers/98&/98-2.html.

Petite, Michel (2000) 'Nice, traité existential, non essential', Revue du dvoit de l'Union europeenne, 4, 887–903.

Pfetsch, Frank (1998) 'Negotiating the European Union: A Negotiation – network Approach', *International Negotiation*, 3, 293–317.

Pierson, Paul (1996) 'The Path to European Integration: A Historical Institutionalist Analysis', *Comparative Political Studies*, 29 (2), 123–63.

Pijpers, Alfred (2000) 'Afterthought and Perspective', in Alfred Pijpers (ed.), *On Cores and Coalitions in the European Union: The Position of Some Smaller Member States*, The Hague: Clingendael, pp. 185–94.

Pijpers, Alfred, Regelsberger, Elfriede and Wessels, Wolfgang (eds) (1988) *A common Foreign Policy for Western Europe? European Political Cooperation in the 1980s*, Dordrecht: Nijhoff.

Pinder, John (2001a) 'Nice: Towards a Federal or an Intergovernmental Europe?', in Jopp, *et al.* (eds), *Das Vertragswerk von Nizza und die Zukunft der Europäischen Union*, Bonn: Europa Union Verlag, pp. 50–7.

Pinder, John (2001b) *The European Union: A Very Short Introduction*, Oxford: Oxford University Press.

Pollack, Mark A. (1996) 'The New Institutionalism and EC Governance: The Promise and Limits of Institutional Analysis', *Governance*, 9 (4), 429–58.

Pollack, Mark, A. (1999) 'Delegation, Agency and Agenda Setting in the Treaty of Amsterdam', European Integration online Papers (EIoP), 3 (6): http://eiop.or.at/eiop/texte/1999-006a.htm.

Pollack, Mark A. (2000) 'The End of Creeping Competence? EU Policy-Making since Maastricht', *Journal of Common Market Studies*, 3, 519–38.

Pollack, Mark A. (2001) 'International Relations Theory and European Integration', *Journal of Common Market Studies*, 39 (2), 221–44.

Pool, Bill (1990) *The Creation of the Internal Market in Insurance*, Luxembourg: Office for Official Publications of the European Communities.

Pouliquen, A. (2001) *Competitiveness and Farm Incomes in the CEEC Agri-food Sectors: Implications before and after Accession for EU markets and Policies*, Brussels: European Commission.

Presidency Conclusions (2003) Brussels European Council 12 December.

Press and Information Office of the Federal Government (ed.) (1982a) 'First Report of the Foreign Ministers to the Heads of State and Government of the European Community of 27 October 1970 (Luxembourg Report)', *European Political Cooperation (EPC)*, Wiesbaden, p. 30.

Press and Information Office of the Federal Government (ed.) (1982b) 'Report on European Political Cooperation Issued by the Foreign Ministers of the Ten on 13 October 1981 (London Report). Part I', *European Political Cooperation (EPC)*, Wiesbaden, p. 272.

Press and Information Office of the Federal Government (ed.) (1982) 'Second Report of the Foreign Ministers to the Heads of State and Government of the Member states of European Community of 23 July 1973 (Copenhagen Report)', *European Political Cooperation (EPC)*, Wiesbaden, p. 43.

Preston, C. (1997) *Enlargement and Integration in the European Union*, London: Routledge.

Price Waterhouse (1997) *Employment Trends in the European Postal Sector*, Study Prepared for the European Commission, May.

Prodi, Romano (2000) *Shaping the New Europe*, Strasbourg: European Parliament, 15.2.

Reflection Group (1995a) 'Reflection Group's Report. Messina 2nd June 1995. Brussels

5th December 1995.' Downloaded from http://europa.eu.int/en/agenda/igc-home/eudoc/reflect/final.html.

Reflection Group (1995b) 'A Strategy for Europe'. Final Report from the Chairman of the Reflection Group on the 1996 Intergovernmental Conference, Brussels: SN 519/95, Reflex 20.

Reflection Group (1999) 'The Long-term Implications of EU Enlargement: The Nature of the New Border', Florence: European University Institute.

Regelsberger, Elfriede (2000) 'Gemeinsame Außen- und Sicherheitspolitik', in Werner Weidenfeld and Wolfgang Wessels (eds), *Jahrbuch der europäischen Integration 1999/2000*, Bonn: Europa Union Verlag, pp. 233–42.

Regelsberger, Elfriede (2001a) 'Gemeinsame Außen- und Sicherheitspolitik', in Werner Weidenfeld and Wolfgang Wessels (eds), *Jahrbuch der europäischen Integration 2000/2001*, Bonn: Europa Union Verlag.

Regelsberger, Elfriede (2001b) 'Die Gemeinsame Außen- und Sicherheitspolitik nach Nizza' – begrenzter Reformeifer und außervertragliche Dynamik in der ESVP', *Integration*, 2/01, 156–66.

Regelsberger, Elfriede and Schmalz, Uwe (2001) 'The Common Foreign and Security Policy of the Amsterdam Treaty: Towards an Improved EU Identity on the International Scene', in Jörg Monar and Wolfgang Wessels (eds), *The European Union after the Treaty of Amsterdam*, London and New York: Continuum, pp. 249–266.

Regelsberger, Elfriede, de Schoutheete de Tervarent, Philippe and Wessels, Wolfgang (eds) (1997) *Foreign Policy of the European Union: From EPC to CFSP and Beyond*, Boulder and London: Lynne Rienner Publishers.

Richardson, Jeremy J. (1996) *European Union: Power and Policy-making*, London: Routledge.

Riker, William H. (1964) *Federalism: Origin, Operation, Significance*, Boston: Little, Brown & Company.

Risse-Kappen, Thomas (1996) 'Collective Identity in a Democratic Community: The Case of NATO', in Peter J. Katzenstein (ed.), *The Culture of National Security: Norms and Identity in World Politics*, New York: Columbia University Press, pp. 357–99.

Robertson, Roland (1995) 'Globalization: Time-space and Homogeneity-heterogeneity', in Mike Featherstone, Scott Lash and Roland Robertson (eds), *Global Modernities*, London: Sage, pp. 25–44.

Rogers, N.A. (2000) *Practitioners' Guide to the EC–Turkey Association Agreement*, The Hague: Kluwer Law International.

Rosamond, Ben (2000) *Theories of European Integration*, Houndmills: Palgrave.

Ruggie, John Gerard (1993) *Territoriality and Beyond, International Organization*, 47 (1), 139–74.

Rummel, Reinhardt and Wessels, Wolfgang (eds) (1978) *Die europäische politische Zusammenarbeit*, Bonn: Europa Union Verlag.

Sandholtz, Wayne (1993) 'Institutions and Collective Action: The New Telecommunications in Western Europe', *World Politics*, 45 (2), 242–70.

Sbragia, Alberta M. (1992) 'Thinking about the European Future: The Uses of Camparison', in Alberta M. Sbragia (ed.), *Euro-Politics: Institutions and Policymaning in the 'New' European Community*, Washington, DC: The Brookings Institution, pp. 257–91.

Scharpf, Fritz, W. (1975) *Demokratietheorie zwischen Utopie und Aupassung*, Kronberg/Ts.

Scharpf, Fritz W. (1997a) *Balancing Positive and Negative Integration: The Regulatory Options for Europe*, Cologne: Max Planck Institute for the Study of Societies, no. 97/8.

Scharpf, Fritz W. (1997b) *Games Real Actors Play: Actor-Centered Institutionalism in Policy Research*, Boulder, CO: Oxford.

Scharpf, Fritz W. (ed.) (2000) *Democratic Legitimacy under Conditions of Regulatory Competition: Why Europe Differs from the United States*, Madrid: Centro de Estudios Avanzados en Ciencias Sociales.

Schimmelfennig, Frank (2001) 'The Community Trap: Liberal Norms, Rhetorical Action, and the Eastern Enlargement of the EU', *International Organization*, 55 (1), 47–80.

Schmalz, Uwe (1998) 'The Amsterdam Provisions on External Coherence: Bridging the Union's Foreign Policy Dualism?', *European Foreign Affairs Review*, 3, 421–42.

Schmidt, Susanne K. (1991) 'Taking the Long Road to Liberalisation: Telecommunications Reform in the Federal Republic of Germany', *Telecommunications Policy*, June, 209–22.

Schmidt, Susanne K. (1998) *Liberalisierung in Europa: Die Rolle der Europäischen Kommission*. Frankfurt a.M.: Campus. Schriften des Max-Planck-Instituts für Gesellschaftsforschung.

Schmidt, Susanne K. (2001) 'The Impact of Mutual Recognition: Inbuilt Limits and Domestic Responses to the Single Market', paper presented to workshop 20: National Regulatory Reform in an Internationalised Environment, ECPR joint sessions of workshops, Grenoble, 6–11 April.

Schmitter, Philip (1996) 'Imaging the Future of the Euro-Polity with the Help of New Concepts', in Gary Marks, Fritz W. Scharpf, Philip Schmitter and Wolfgarg Streek (eds), *Governance in the European Union*, London: Sage, pp. 1–14.

Schneider, Gerald and Mark Aspinwall (eds) (2001) *The Rules of Integration: Institutionalist Approaches to the Study of Europe*, Manchester: Manchester University Press.

Schoutheete, Philippe de (1986) *La coopération politique européenne*, Brussels: Labor.

Schumann, Dieter (2001) *Die Bedeutung politikfeldübergreifender Koppelgeschäfte für die europäische Energiewirtschaft: Das Beispiel der Liberalisierung des Elektrizitätsbinnenmarktes*, Diskussionspapiere, Ruhr-Universität Bochum, no. 01-2, Bochum.

Schwegmann, Christoph (2003) Die Jugoslawien-Kontaktgruppe in den internationalen Beziehungen. Baden-Baden: Nomos.

Sedelmeier, U. (2000a) 'Eastern Enlargement; Risk, Rationality, and Role-compliance', in Maria Green Cowles and Smith Michael (eds), *State of the European Union: Risks, Reform, Resistance, and Revival*, Oxford: Oxford University Press, pp. 164–85.

Sedelmeier, U. (2000b) 'East of Amsterdam: The Implication of the Amsterdam Treaty for Eastern Enlargement', in Karlheinz Neunreither and Antje Wiener (eds), *European Integration After Amsterdam: Institutional Dynamics and Prospects for Democracy*, Oxford: Oxford University Press, pp. 218–37.

Sedelmeier, U. (2001) 'EU Eastern Enlargement in Comparative Perspective', *Journal of European Public Policy*, 8 (4), 662–70.

Selm, Joanne van (2002) 'Immigration and Asylum or Foreign Policy: The EU's Approach to Migrants and their Countries of Origin', in Sandra Lavenex and Emek Uçarer (eds), *Migration and the Externalities of European Integration*, Lanham: Lexington Books.

Shaw, J. (2003) 'Process, Responsibility and Inclusion in EU Constitutionalism', *European Law Journal*, 9 (1), 45–68.

Sidenius, Niels Christian (1999) 'Business, Governance Structures and the EU: The Case of Denmark', in Beate Kohler-Koch and Rainer Eising (eds), *The Transformation of Governance in the European Union*, New York: Routledge, pp. 173–88.

Singh Grewal, Shivdeep (2001) 'The Paradox of Integration: Habermas and the Unfinished Project of European Union', Politics, 21 (2), 114–123.

Smith, Julie (2000) 'Introduction and Overview', *International Affairs*, 76 (3), 437–42.

Smith, Michael E. (2001) 'Diplomacy by Decree: The Legalisation of EU Foreign Policy', *Journal of Common Market Studies*, 1, 79–104.

Social Democratic Party (2001) 'Responsibility for Europe, Germany in Europe', Resolution of the National Conference of the Social Democratic Party of Germany, Nuremberg, 19–22 November: www.spd.de/english/politics/Beschluss_Europa%20EN_101201.pdf.

Solana, Javier (2001) 'Common Strategies Report', *Europe Documents*, no. 2228, 31 January.

Stability Pact Organisation (2000) 'Strategic Paper on Justice and Home Affairs', www.stabilitypact.org/stabilitypactcgi/catalog/view_file.cgi?prod_id=3497&prop_ty pe=en.

Stadler, Klaus-Dieter (1993) *Die Europäische Gemeinschaft in den Vereinten Nationen: die Rolle der EG im Entscheidungsprozeß der UN-Hauptorgane am Beispiel der Generalversammlung*, Baden-Baden: Nomos.

Staples, H. (1999) *The Legal Status of Third Country Nationals Resident in the European Union*, The Hague: Kluwer Law International.

Starke, Ernst (1988) 'Europas Zukunft: Vollendung des Binnenmarktes' ('Europe's Future: Implementing the Single Market Program'), *Versicherungswirtschaft*, 7, 510–11.

Stone Sweet, Alec and Sandholtz, Wayne (eds) (1998) *European Integration and Supranational Governance*, Oxford: Oxford University Press.

Stubb, Alexander C.-G. (2000) 'Negotiating: Flexible Integration in the Amsterdam Treaty', in Karlheinz Neunreither and Antje Wiener (eds), *European Integration After Amsterdam. Institutional Dynamics and Prospects for Democracy*, Oxford: Oxford University Press, pp. 153–74.

Sucharipa, Ernst (1999) 'Nationale Belange spielen weiter mit: Die Europäische Union auf dem Weg zu einer gemeinsamen UN-Politik', in *Der Überblick. Quartalsschrift der Arbeitsgemeinschaft Kirchlicher Entwicklungsdienst*, No. 4, pp. 79–82.

Sucharipa, Ernst (2003) 'Die Gemeinsame Außen- und Sicherheitspolitik (GASP) der Europäischen Union im Rahmen der Vereinten Nationen', in Frowein *et al.* (eds), *Liber amicorum Tono Eitel*, Heidelberg: Max Planck Institut, pp. 773–97.

Süddeutsche Zeitung.

Svensson, Anna-Carin (2000) *In the Service of the European Union: The Role of the Presidency in Negotiating the Amsterdam Treaty 1995–97*, Acta Universitatis Upsaliensis, Uppsala: Statsvetenskapliga föreningen.

Swann, Dennis (1999) *The Economics of the Common Market: Integration in the European Union*, 8th edn, London: Penguin.

Tampere European Council (1999) *Presidency Conclusions*, Brussels: Council of the European Union.

Tangermann, S. (2000) 'Agenda 2000: Tactics, Diversion and Frustration', *Agra Europe*, 28 May 1999, pp. A/1–A/4.

Thurner, Paul W., Stoiber, Michael and Pappi, Franz Urban (2002) *National Interministerial Coordination and International Negotiations: The IGC 1996. A Data Handbook*, Ms. MZES.

Twomey, Patrick (1999) 'Constructing a Secure Space: The Area of Freedom, Security and Justice', in David O'Keeffe and Patrick Twomey (eds), *Legal Issues of the Amsterdam Treaty*, Oxford: Hart Publishing, pp. 351–74.

van Brabant, Jozef M. (1998) 'Transformation, EU Integration, and Regional Cooperation in Eastern Europe', *Comparative Economic Studies*, 40 (4), 33–59.

Van Nuffel, Pieter (2001) 'Le traité de Nice: Un Commentaire', Revue du Droit de l'Union européene, 2, 329–87.

Verderame, Gianfranco (1999) 'Le traité d'Amsterdam et ses suites: instruments de réalisation d'une identité européenne dans le domaine de la politique extérieure', *Revue du Marché Unique*, 15–29.

Verdun, Amy (2000) *European Responses to Globalization and Financial Market Integration: Perceptions of Economic and Monetary Union in Britain, France and Germany*, Houndmills: Palgrave-Macmillan / New York: St Martin's Press.

Verdun, Amy and Osvaldo Croci (eds) (2003) *Institutional and Policy-making Challenges to the European Union in the Wake of Eastern Enlargement*, Manchester: Manchester University Press.

Verheugen, Guenter (2001) 'Le Processus d'Elargissement Communiautaire au Lendemain du Sommet de Nice', *Politique Etrangere*, 2, 301–10.

Vested-Hansen, J. (1999) 'Non-admission Policies and the Right to Protection: Refugees' Choice versus States' Exclusion?', in F. Nicholson and P. Twomey (eds), *Refugee Rights and Realities*, Cambridge: Cambridge University Press, p. 269.

Vibert, Frank (2001) *Europe Simple, Europe Strong: The Future of European Governance*, Cambridge: Blackwell.

Vogel, Steven K. (1996) *Freer Markets, More Rules: Regulatory Reform in Advanced Industrialized Countries*, Ithaca, NY: Cornell University Press.

Walker, Robert B.J. (1993) *Inside/Outside: International Relations as Political Theory*, Cambridge: Cambridge University Press.

Wallace, Claire and Stola, Dariusz (eds) (2001) *Patterns of Migration in Central Europe*, London: Palgrave.

Wallace, H. (1999) 'Whose Europe is it Anyway?', *European Journal of Political Research*, 35 (3), 287–306.

Wallace, H. (2000) 'EU Enlargement; A Neglected Subject', in Maria Green Cowles and Michael Smith (eds), *State of the European Union: Risks, Reform, Resistance, and Revival*, Oxford: Oxford University Press, pp. 149–63.

Wallace, H. (2000a) 'The Institutional Setting', in Helen Wallace and William Wallace (eds), *Policy-making in the European Union*, 4th edn, Oxford: Oxford University Press, pp. 3–37.

Wallace, H. (2000b) 'The Policy Process', in Helen Wallace and William Wallace (eds), *Policy-making in the European Union*, Oxford: Oxford University Press, pp. 39–64.

Wallace, H. (2000c) 'Der Wandel britischer Europapolitik: Ein neuer Partner für Deutschland?', in Michèle Knodt and Beate Kohler-Koch (eds), *Deutschland zwischen Europäisierung und Selbstbehauptung*, Jahrbuch des Mannheimer Zentrums für Europäische Sozialforschung, Bd. 5, Frankfurt: Campus, pp. 225–34.

Wallace, H. (2000d) 'Flexibility: A Tool of Integration or a Restraint on Desintegration?', in Karlheinz Neunreither and Antje Wiener (eds), *European Integration After Amsterdam: Institutional Dynamics and Prospects for Democracy*, Oxford: Oxford University Press, pp. 175–91.

Wallace, W. (1983) 'Less Than a Federation. More Than a Regime: The Community as a Political System', in Helen Wallace and William Wallace (eds), *Policy-making in the European Community*, 2nd edn, Chicester: John Wiley & Sons, pp. 403–36.

Wallace, W. (1990) 'Less Than a Federation, More Than a Regime: The Community as a

Political System', in H. Wallace, W. Wallace and C. Webb (eds), *Policy-making in the European Community*, Chichester: Wiley.

Wallace, W. (2000) 'From the Atlantic to the Bug, from the Arctic to the Tigris? The Transformation of the EU and NATO', *International Affairs*, 76 (3), 475–94.

Wallace, H. and Wallace W. (eds) (2000), *Policy-making in the European Union, 4th edn*, Oxford: Oxford University Press.

Weiler, Joseph H.H. (1991) 'The Transformation of Europe', *The Yale Law Journal*, No. 8/1991, 2403–83.

Weiler, J.H.H. (1999) *The Constitution of Europe*, Cambridge: Cambridge University Press.

Weiler, Joseph and Wessels, Wolfgang (1988) 'EPC and the Challenge of Theory', in Alfred Pijpers, Elfriede Regelsberger and Wolfgang Wessels (eds), *A Common Foreign Policy for Western Europe? European Political Cooperation in the 1980s*, Dordrecht: Nijhoff, pp. 229–58.

Werle, Raymund (1999) 'Liberalisation of Telecommunications in Germany', in Kjell A. Eliassen and Marit Sjoevaag (eds), *European Telecommunications Liberalisation*, New York: Routledge.

Wessel, Ramses A. (1999) *The European Union's Foreign and Security Policy: A Legal Institutional Perspective*, The Hague/Boston/London: Kluwer Law International.

Wessels, Wolfgang (1992) 'Staat und (westeuropäische) Integration: Die Fusionthese', in Michael Kreile (ed.), *Die Integration Europas, Politische Vierteljahresschrift*, Sonderheft No. 23, pp. 36–61.

Wessels, Wolfgang (1997) 'An Ever Closer Fusion? A Dynamic Macropolitical View on Integration Processes', *Journal of Common Market Studies*, 35 (2) 267–99.

Wessels, Wolfgang (2000a) 'Die Europäische Union als Ordnungsfaktor', in Karl Kaiser and Honspeter Schwarz (eds), *Weltpolitik im neuen Jahrhundert*, Bonn: Verlag fur Internationale Politik, pp. 575–590.

Wessels, Wolfgang (2000b) *Die Öffnung des Staates. Modelle und Wirklichkeit grenzüberschreitender Verwaltungspraxis 1960–1995*, Opladen: Leske und Budrich.

Wessels, Wolfgang (2001a) 'Nice Results: The Millennium IGC in the EU's Evolution', *Journal of Common Market Studies*, 39 (2), 197–220.

Wessels, Wolfgang (2001b) 'The Evolution of the EU System: Amsterdam and Nice "Ratchet" Fusion in the Making', contribution to the 7th ECSA Biennial International Conference, Workshop: From Amsterdam to Nice: Comparing European Integration's Major Theoretical Contenders, Cologne.

Wessels, Wolfgang and Linsenmann, Ingo (2002) 'EMU's Impact on National Institutions: Fusion towards a "Gouvernance économique" or Fragmentation?', in Kenneth Dyson (ed.), *European States and the Euro: Playing the Semi-Sovereignty Game*, Oxford: Oxford University Press, pp. 53–77.

Wessels, Wolfgang, Maurer, Andreas and Mittag, Jürgen (2002) 'The European Union and Member States: Analysing Two Arenas Over Time', in Wolfgang Wessels, Andreas Maurer and Jürgen Mittag (eds), *Fifteen into One? The European Union and Member States*, Manchester: Manchester University Press, pp. 11–37.

Westlake, Martin (1995) *The Council of the European Union*, London: Cartermill.

Westle, Bettina (1989) *Politische Legitimät: Theorinen, Konzepte, empirische Befund*, Baden-Baden: Nomos Verlag.